IN THE CITY
THAT BLOWS YOUR MIND

HERE AT LAST IS THE GUIDE
THAT WILL BLOW YOUR MIND

Know the city as you have never known it before, whether you explore it on foot, by San Francisco's celebrated transportation, or as an armchair tourist.

Revel in a book you will read and re-read, before your arrival, during your stay, and after your departure, for information and for sheer enjoyment.

In a city so old that every nook and cranny holds a colorful story—and so young that the shadows of the founding fathers still fall on its cosmopolitan streets—you want to get beyond the standard guide to a splendor that is totally unique. AN OPINIONATED GUIDE TO SAN FRANCISCO gets you there, and leaves you breathless.

**AN OPINIONATED GUIDE
TO SAN FRANCISCO**

No visit is complete without it

AN OPINIONATED GUIDE TO SAN FRANCISCO

Franz Hansell

Photos by
Chazz Sutphen

BALLANTINE BOOKS • NEW YORK

Some of this material previously appeared in
California Living Magazine

Copyright © 1973 by Franz Hansell

SBN 345-03274-8-195

First Printing: May, 1973

Printed in the United States of America

Cover photo by Tim Lewis

BALLANTINE BOOKS, INC.
101 Fifth Avenue, New York, N.Y. 10003

Contents

An Opinionated
Guide to
San Francisco

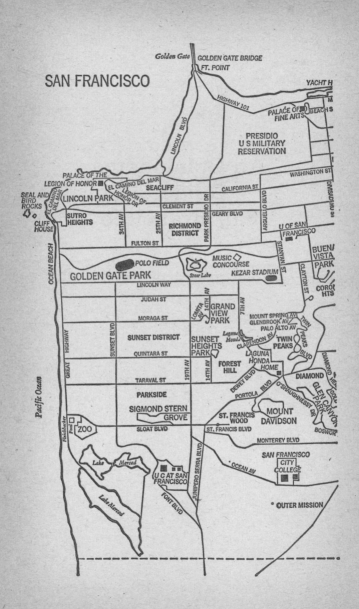

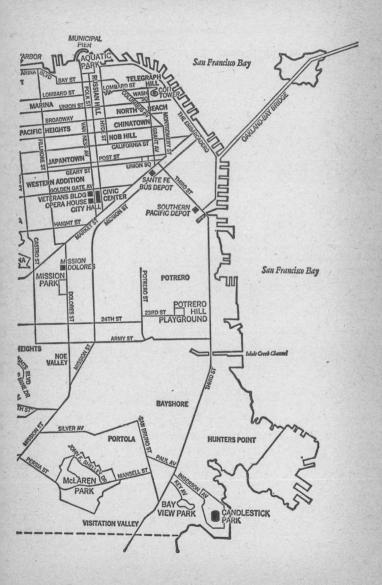

Preface

Yet another book about San Francisco might seem superfluous. Is there any more to say about this city? Has any aspect not been commented upon, analyzed, rhapsodized about—and especially written down in a book? From the sheer poundage of print about San Francisco, it is hard to imagine that not all bases have been touched. But there is still something to say about the city that is new, original, and interesting. That is why I have written this book.

My San Francisco has always been unique. For one thing, I was plunged here in my maturity without any previous thoughts about the town whatsoever. I was in the army and sent to Monterey to study Russian at the language school, when my uncle Paul, a San Franciscan, guided me to some interesting bars such as Shields and the Black Cat, when it was still Bohemian. It wasn't until I left the army, went back to school, and got a part-time job at Tro Harper's bookstore on Market Street that the glories and joys of the city began to unfold. At that time, it had to be the goddamnedest bookstore in town, with the possible exception of City Lights on Broadway. Curt Gentry (author of *Last Days of the Late Great State of California*, *Killer Mountains*, and *Madams of San Francisco*) was day manager and John Murtaugh was there at night. It was at Tro's that I first realized the magic, the traditions and the mystique of San Francisco. Tro's Market Street store is right on the fringe of the Tenderloin, and bookstores, more than any other mercantile establishment except

1

bars, seem to be magnets for the out-of-the-ordinary citizen, the crazy, and the sublime. The store was always full of tourists, transvestites from the Sixth Street bars, literate shoplifters, lonely retired folks from the cheap hotels, drunks looking for a place out of the wind, religious and political cranks looking for people to argue with, male and female prostitutes, professional beggars of all persuasions. Added to these were Curt's and John's interesting and lively friends who passed through. Alfred Knopf, Evan Connell, and others would suddenly appear in the store to see Curt, along with the leaders and members of many metaphysical cults, and notables like Herb Caen, Clancy Sigal, Dr. Tom Dooley, and Sal Mineo. John Murtaugh's friends were equally fascinating, and two of them at least, were celebrated persons. His closest friends were Benny Bufano, one of the greatest sculptors in America, and Al, who owns the sidewalk flower stand on the corner of Stockton and Geary and has appeared in at least a hundred movies and TV programs as the weasely hoodlum's weasely hoodlum. Al is also the unofficial mayor of the Armenian community and hid Saroyan from his creditors whenever Saroyan came back to town for a visit. John's other friends were just as interesting because as a book finder he met those who worked on the fringe of a fringe, connoisseurs of buttons, patterns of silverware, lace, pewter, medals, glassware—the numberless small items that people will pay money for. There is a small army of these searchers in San Francisco, not getting rich at it, but earning enough to stay afloat.

At Tro's I realized that San Francisco was unlike any other city in the world. It wasn't a case of love at first sight. But then again, falling in love with a city is not unlike falling in love with a woman. It's not usually the sheer beauty of a city or a woman that finally grabs you, because beauty is not that rare. (I had been to Copenhagen, Amsterdam, London— beautiful towns all.) No, true love usually starts with infatuation with a detail—a dimple, the curve of the breasts or bottom, shade of hair or softness of gesture—then spreads to include the whole person. It was the San Franciscans in the bookstore on Market Street that first made me take real joy in San Francisco.

The budding infatuation at Tro's blossomed to full-blown romance when I was manager of a small apartment house on Fulton and 32nd Avenue, right across from Spreckel's Lake in Golden Gate Park. Living so close let me explore the wonders of the park in depth. Then, finally, I got perhaps the most glorious job a person in love with the city could hope to find. I became a meter reader for the San Francisco Water Department. In this job, I was able to examine the city intimately from sea to shining bay. My foot has trod literally every street and dusty byway in town. I have scaled the heights of San Francisco (all forty-two) and sunk to the very depths, in that I have read meters in the basements of nearly every major building in the city. Who can write knowingly about San Francisco when they have never wandered, as have I, among the myriad hanging sausages in the Gallo salami factory, or wet their boots in the irrigation waters of the bean sprout farms off Grant Avenue? I have seen the collection of leg art from turn-of-the-century cigarette cards hidden in the bowels of the Society of California Pioneers museum, and the research kennels hidden on the very top of Mount Sutro. Few writers about San Francisco have been set upon by dogs on Bernal Heights and faggots in the cellars of Tenderloin bars.

With the super-anonymity of the meter reader, you can see more than either the average citizen or the deliberate researcher. During the Hunter's Point riots fifteen of us were scattered through the district, vulnerable as hell on the streets, lifting meter covers. Nothing happened to any of us. Another time Rup Sutton, a fellow meter reader, let himself into a Chinatown basement and suddenly found himself in the middle of a high-powered gambling set-up. (Two months previously, the basement had been a storage room for a herb shop.) Tables were piled high with fifty- and one-hundred-dollar bills. He stood there for a minute and three very bad-looking Chinese Mafia types came at him, reaching in their pockets. He said that he blurted, "Water department. I only want to read the meters," and they sort of shrugged and turned their backs on him. You don't get that kind of entree in every job.

Being on foot lets you look at things more closely. The high points of this town have been touched upon so often they are almost worn away. Every writer in the world has tried to tell about the cable cars, Nob, Russian, and Telegraph Hills, Chinatown, and North Beach in language increasingly highflown until the very city floats three feet above the earth. Well, it does to those who love it, but there's so much more to San Francisco than that. What about the wonder of those Mexican grocery stores on Mission Street that stock yucca root as a staple? What about the Columbus Founders Savings & Loan on San Bruno Avenue, whose door announces that its tellers speak French, Spanish, Italian, Portuguese, and *Maltese!* No one has written about that neighborhood. What about Mr. Bond's Peace Garden, or the San Francisco Memorial Columbarium, or the Fireman's Pioneer Museum, or the fine cactus garden right off Randolph Street in the Ingleside. Tourists have never read about them and the only natives that know about them live around the corner. Much has been written about our elegant restaurants, but few know that the Star Cafeteria on Kearny, next to Cookie Pucelli's still sells two eggs, potatoes, toast, and coffee for 63 cents. And look at our bars—a subject that could fill volumes but gets short shrift in the standard guides. And look at our monuments and our good streets and our fascinating neighborhoods and . . . well . . . look at this book.

F.T.H.

1
A Long Look at San Francisco—What Makes a City Great

> The city is built to music, therefore
> never built at all, and therefore
> built forever
> —Tennyson, Idylls of the King

It is a very complicated business to try to understand just why San Francisco is not only an important American city but a world city whose very name is touched with magic. Historically it is young, in terms of area, it is tiny; San Francisco lags behind even Milwaukee in population. Granted, there is great beauty in its setting—the hills and sweeping views of the city, Bay, and ocean—but other large cities in beautiful settings (say, Seattle, Denver, Louisville) do not have the special appeal of San Francisco. San Francisco is a rich town, full of money and the power and accouterments that devolve from money; fine buildings and residences, fine restaurants, deluxe hotels, culture with a capital "C"—opera, symphony orchestra, ballet—but then again, other cities (Houston, Pittsburgh, Dallas, Detroit) are as rich and powerful and these cities do not have the same magic. San Francisco is a major port and therefore has a built-in whiff of adventure and excitement, strange lands and exotic peoples. But other major ports in America and abroad lack the magic. No one sings, I Left My Heart in Newark, New Jersey, for example. Other contributing factors might be mentioned—our climate, which year-round seems to be at the very spiciest, most invigorating moment of early autumn; the fact that this is the only American city upon which the Orient has made a major impact; our cosmopolitan population (one out of seven citizens here was born in a foreign country or has foreign-born parents); but even all these things together do not explain it. I believe that to understand the peculiar essence and magic of San Francisco we must go back to the beginning.

And the beginning is best seen at the James Lick Memorial at the corner of Hyde and Market streets near the Civic Center. James Lick bequeathed $100,000 1870 dollars to capture in stone and bronze *The Spirit of California* (which in those days was Northern California and specifically San Francisco). The result sculptured by Frank Happersberger in the 1880s, was a magnificent and peculiar statuary complex. On a two-tiered central column stands California herself, with shield, spear, and bear. Surrounding her are four projecting piers—two allegories, two tableaux—and medallions, plaques, low reliefs, high reliefs, inscriptions, ornamental fences, etcetera, all in all a grand work. Three miners panning for gold constitute the frontispiece of the Memorial. Here are three slightly larger-than-life miners looking at a handful of gold-bearing gravel. Their boots are cracked, their clothes wrinkled and mud stained. They are unshaven, in great need of baths. These three miners are one of the few nonmilitary statuary tableaux in the world deliberately made to look thoroughly dirty —probably in need of fumigation.

The three miners are gazing into that handful of gravel with all the intensity, solemnity, and rapture of Charlton Heston meeting God face to face upon the mountain. They are heroically portrayed because one had to be a hero merely to have survived the journey to California to pan for gold. Whether they came by a two-thousand-mile cross-country trek or an equally dangerous six-thousand-mile sail around the Horn, the statement, "The weak never made it to California, the timid never started out," applied to each in a very real way and each knew it. Every early San Franciscan was a hero and carried with him the huge self-esteem and self-assurance of a hero. They were so immensely proud of themselves that the second thing they did after arriving (the first was to look for gold) was to set up pioneer societies celebrating themselves and their survival.

Unlike any other founder's memorial in existence, notice that this monument does not epitomize the spirit of California by piously portraying three heroic founders gazing with heartfelt gratitude at a sheaf of new-harvested wheat (and bearing a title something like "A Beneficent God and Bountiful Nature Reward Immense Expense of Physical Labor, Perseverance, and Patient Endurance"). No, these founders are looking with such huge reverence at *money,* or the possibility of it, acquired as the Result of Immense Expense of Physical Labor, Perseverance, Patient Endurance . . . and Pure, Blind Ass Luck. Luck always played an important role in the life of San Franciscans and they never forgot. Neither did they ever confuse the lucky with the worthy, or confer upon the lucky the older notion that because a man is rich, that means that God loves him and he is righteous.

By premiering the three gold-seekers, the monument makes an explicit statement about our founders. San Francisco's founders were not colonists. They were not motivated to emigrate because of population pressures or worn-out farms, business depression, or religious persecution: they didn't come to seek free land or to make a new start on a new frontier (the primary reasons for the westward expansion from the beginning of our history). Not these founders. Nearly to a man, our founders left home with a whoop and a holler, hell-bent to make a million dollars and devil take the hindmost. This means that, in the main, they were strong-willed, rambunctious, against-the-grain, adventurous, out-for-the-main-chance, nonconforming, energetic, optimistic, and greedy dreamers.

This heady combination of personality traits describes the archetypal American. Part of the uniqueness of San Francisco lies in the fact that San Francisco is the most American of American cities. Though founded in 1776, to all intents and purposes, San Francisco did not exist until the discovery of gold. Then it became an instant city—no, instant metropolis, built from scratch by hand by the most daring of the young men of America and their counterparts from France, Germany, England, Chile, Mexico, Hawaii—the whole world. Except for the Chinese, who were imported like cattle and discriminated against from the first, all these young men started on exactly the same footing as far as chances for success were concerned. What happened was a unique, large-scale exercise in what the whole idea of the promise of America meant. All was brand-new here. There was no establishment to fight, work around, or overcome. There was little obligation to eastern or foreign capital, which, in other surviving boom towns like Dallas and Denver, could name the game. In the beginning, one did not need financing for oil rigs or metal processing plants. A man's capital was in his own muscle, initiative, quickness of wit, and hardiness. They were their own men and the city they created was a reflection of themselves on one hand and on the other an amalgamation of back-home American political institutions lengthened and broadened to lean toward the superdemocratic, superegalitarian ideal of Jefferson or the mining camps. Nobody owed anybody: nobody inherited anything.

The result was a remarkable, dynamic urban democracy not before seen in the world, closely resembling the fire and bustling energy of modern Israel—Israel without the Arabs, and the quest not a homeland but *money*. That statement might seem to denigrate the memory of our founders because of their sheer crassness, but when you examine it, it explains much of the uniqueness, the mysterious essence that lingers yet in San Francisco, indeed becomes perhaps their most important legacy.

The founders of San Francisco had a singular and acknowledged lack of piety in their intentions for coming here. If civilizing the West or building America came as a natural result of their energies, it had nothing to do with their primary intentions.

The magic of San Francisco lies mainly in this. San Francisco is the only major city in America that has ever, *ever* openly admitted to flaws of character in its founders. It's unusual enough when one man fully acknowledges that he is venal; that he is a proud man, occasionally full of lust or anger; that he covets the wealth of the earth and the respect of his fellow man—and is envious of those who have gained it; that he hugely prefers steak, oysters, and good wine to the equally nutritious vegetable soup and tap water. If a person admits to himself that he is chock-full of six of the seven deadly sins (the only one missed was the sin of sloth, which has only recently become practicable in San Francisco), he is apt to look with a good deal of tolerance upon his fellow citizens' idiosyncracies, character flaws, failings of the flesh and outrageous behavior. When a new city of a hundred thousand founders admitted to (or had no inclination or justification to deny) precisely these spiritual errors, it generated an aura of personal freedom that has endured for one hundred years and is still so real that it can almost be breathed in the very air.

San Francisco's freedom from pious intentions on the part of its founders nurtured an atmosphere of tolerance, an attitude of live-and-let-live not seen in any other city in America. It's probably the first predominantly Christian city in the world where the citizens fully realize that sin and sinning, morality or the lack of it is strictly an individual matter: where the majority of citizens do not waste huge amounts of time fretting about their neighbors' odds in the Resurrection.

This legacy is seen not only in the obvious and gross examples, such as San Francisco's toleration of the beatniks, the hippies, the radicals and militants and homosexuals and topless joints; but, more pertinent, in small, often hilarious and mind-boggling exercises in tolerance that leave the stranger to the city gasping. Consider America's first Satanist church newly founded plunk in the heart of a middle-class neighborhood, a San Francisco neighborhood. The neighbors complained to the police about it finally, but not for the well-publicized unholy goings on that took place there—black masses performed upon the supine bodies of naked virgins—but because the roaring of the minister's pet lion kept them awake at night. Toleration in things like San Francisco's most powerful labor leader perversely registering Republican year after year for the hell of it. Or the newly elected Mayor Alioto turning down "National Decency Week." That was something! National Decency Week was a Southern California proposition to have everybody think decently about smut and sin for a week. Alioto didn't explain why he refused to sign the proclamation, but it was, to my knowledge, the first time in the history of politics that a mayor of any major city rejected a free, no-expense, no-effort, no-commitment opportunity to put himself on the side of rampant decency.

This tolerance extends to religion and San Francisco is probably the only city in America where one is regularly proselyted not only by Mormons and Jehovah's Witnesses, but also by two different denominations of Buddhist doorbell ringers; where one is not only preached at on downtown street corners by the garden variety Christian shouters, but finger-cymbaled at and chanted at by yellow-robed shaved-headed Hindus. Personal freedom, like Victorian guilt, is self-perpetuating. When either one flourishes, it's almost impossible to stamp it out. Of course, it takes a tougher-minded attitude to exercise personal freedom than it does to stay on the tracks of what you've been taught. Alternatives to your original faith are all around you here. Not one-tenth of the Christians in the world have been missionaried at as though they were heathens. Hearing the arguments of the proselyting Buddhists, who claim that Christ was merely an episode in an ongoing metaphysical process (and gaining points by arguing that the numerical superiority of Buddhists indicates God's greater approval), forces one to determine just what it is that he does believe. Not many cities force this decision by constant reminders. San Francisco also, like no other city, illustrates the universality of man in that a man crazy about God (a "religious nut" in the vernacular) differs not from land to land but only in the brand of religion he's pushing.

Tolerance and huge personal fredom also account for much of San Francisco's unique flavor in the areas of sex and politics. From the beginning, San Francisco has enjoyed the reputation of being a happy, wicked, racy, high-life, exciting resort; of having memorable places to feast, convivial places to drink, music, theater, and entertainments to enjoy, and never lacking women, or men for that matter, who would be libidinous on the stage or in your bed for money. It's one of the few towns in the country where wickedness and fun are more or less synonymous, where one can roister and carouse without guilt, where it's almost impossible to disgrace oneself. Only a handful of other cities have this touch of spice to their very names: It's probably no coincidence that these towns are also music towns—American music: jazz, swing, rock, country-Western.

Every large city has strip joints, and always had, but San Francisco was the first place where they attained titular supremacy as an attraction. It is my firm conviction that the whole topless thing was initiated and financed by the Chamber of Commerce.

Every other large town has homosexuals and gay bars. In other towns, they are snickered at, repressed, and generally treated as moral lepers. San Francisco has homosexuals, gay bars, homosexual newspapers, militant homosexual organizations, even homosexual entertainments (the Halloween dragqueen ball is covered by all media). It is obvious, to San Franciscans at least, that the mere presence of homosexuals does not contaminate—otherwise the tens of thousands of tourists who have gone by the busloads to see the performing transvestites at Finocchio's (the most durable nightclub on Broadway) over the years would have already ruined the world.

Every other town in America, large and small, has sources for dirty books, photos and movies. The difference in San Francisco is that it is not underground, limited to the members of the Elks, the Moose, American Legion, and college fraternities, but available to anybody who wants to pay money for it. Personal freedom in San Francisco is so strong that it is hard for the D.A. to find a jury willing to convict *anyone* of obscenity. This is because San Francisco is a literate town and knows that pornography, written or pictorial, is an extremely relative thing: one man's pant is another man's yawn. Historically, those interior decorating shops on Jackson and

Pacific streets, right off Broadway, are housed in the restored buildings of the old Barbary Coast. The same theater, the Bella Union, that recently closed its years-long run of *You're a Good Man, Charlie Brown,* was notorious throughout the world as a gambling hell–groggery, with naked "waiter ladies," obscene performances on the stage, and a whorehouse upstairs. Maiden Lane, the two-block alley off Union Square, is full of equally elegant establishments transformed from even more degraded "cribs and cow yards." A full night, in those days of Christian rectitude and poignant memory, included not only gambling, drunkenness, and lechery, but a trip to Chinatown for a pipeful at one of the many opium dens.

San Francisco's approach to politics shows tolerance, as well as the same incongruities that make this city fascinating. Here we have a strong union, pro-labor town, with a solid Democratic majority, that regularly elects Republican mayors, makes Hayakawa a political force, and is notorious as a hotbed of radicalism. I am sure that the rampant radicalism is more unnerving to visitors than is the sin. It must shock those who have never seen a Communist in the flesh to be confronted not only by garden variety Moscow Communists, but also by Mao Communists, Castro-Che Communists, Trotskyite Communists, Anarchists, and militant Socialists (in their infinite variety), all selling their newspapers openly on the downtown street corners. And competing with these are the black militants (Muslims, Panthers, US, etcetera), a whole host of young destroy-the-system revolutionaries and special pleaders for their various tangent philosophies such as sexual freedom and macrobiotics—all against the American grain to a man.

Like everything else, this attitude has its roots in the past. The capital-labor situation in San Francisco has always been unique. All who came here started on nearly the same footing. Fortunes were gained immediately and often in absurd ways. Hard work, sacrifice, and pluck often went hungry while sheer luck found the gold mine. Everything happened so quickly that capital and great wealth never had a chance to acquire the moral shine it had in the East. It takes some time to establish an establishment.

Labor always commanded prime wages here. Businessmen in early San Francisco had to pay top dollar to make it more attractive for the new arrival to stay in town than to go to the hills to seek his fortune; mine owners in the hills had to do the same to tempt miners from their own speculations. The nearest sources of labor were across the continent or the oceans. Very early, the workers learned the value of organization and assessed their political muscle correctly. In the late 1870s the Workingman's party elected a mayor and made a major impact on state politics. The Union Labor party did the same at the turn of the century and the lesson was never lost. Nearly every worker belonged to a union (and does to this day, there being over three hundred unions in San Francisco as of 1970). This resulted in a curious combination of attitudes. Powerful labor compelled respect from capital and politics; money and capital was still venerated by the laboring classes (with a little bit of luck . . .) but capitalists were never overrespected or kowtowed to—they were merely looked upon as lucky devils who had made it. It might be mentioned that since San Francisco was never dominated by a single industry (or even a group of related industries), capital was never as monolithic and never had as much leverage as in less diversified towns.

But to get back, this combination produced part of the magic of San Francisco. With all these unions pressuring for premium pay, and getting it, a type of classless society came about that is found in no other town our size for such a length of time. Blue-collar workers have always had as much to spend for housing, for example, as the white-collar worker (often more—the printer and carpenter earning more than a department store buyer, the master plumber taking home more than the average bank branch manager). The dollar value of some labor is such that in '68, when things were still booming, nearly four thousand men applied to fill the vacancies of three hundred longshoremen's jobs. The neighborhoods in SF had no chance to become as rigidly stratified as those in other cities. Comfortable, even lavish, homes dating from the turn of the century are found in every neighborhood in the city. Money and address didn't get the chance to close the doors to social mobility, as they did in other cities. The only working classes really exploited or sweated here (excepting the Chinese again) were the secretaries and retail clerks—lower-echelon white-collar workers. The money value of labor accounts for the paucity of slums in San Francisco. It also accounts for the lack of the employment snobbishness found elsewhere—the "he's only a . . ." syndrome. The situation is so unique in San Francisco that the very peak of the blue-collar pyramid is not occupied by the most skilled of the men with trades, but by our garbagemen, who call themselves *scavengers!* The garbage industry in SF is a worker-owned monopoly, a multimillion-dollar operation, the communist Utopia come down to earth, which makes every scavenger a capitalist. One has to wait in line to buy his way into the business ($7,000 was the going rate, at this writing, when an old scavenger retired) and everyone from the president down has to work on the trucks pushing garbage. The salaries are uniform and high, the fringe benefits are fantastic, and at the end of the year, huge profits are divided among the worker-owners. Not every working class of every city envies its garbage men.

Even more important, though, is the political sophistication that comes from universal unionism and union politics—the diversified unionism of three hundred separate entities. Anyone who has gone through long years of union politics here, even without the uproar of the early battles, becomes politically sophisticated. In the first place, it's forced participation because you have a deeper-than-average interest. Every election is on bread-and-butter issues, money, power, or working conditions, which is what politics is all about in the first place.

But we must not forget the uproar of the early days, because that is part of it, and it's not that far back. So many living San Franciscans witnessed the Mooney-Billings debacle (the most outrageous frame-up of labor radicals since Sacco-Vanzetti) and worked for their pardons; so many were among those fifty thousand who followed the biers of the two workers killed in the waterfront strike of 1934—and participated in the subsequent general strike; so many remember the antilabor madness of the '30s (the American Legion seriously proposed that all Americans be compelled to carry identification cards with photos, race, religion, birthplace, and occupation listed); so many were members of the Communist party or Socialist parties at one time or another (the ranks steadily diminishing as the realities of life in the Soviet Union—the workers' paradise—were disclosed) that it is still fresh in the minds and lore of workers here. And this is part of the political sophistication of San Francisco. The recent bomb-throwing by the New Left is old hat to the older workers. They can never forget that more men were killed in the battles for labor than have yet been killed in all the battles for civil rights.

So it is no wonder that the new revolutionaries are looked upon here with great tolerance. They're not saying anything more disturbing or outrageous than has already been said in this town—and the walls didn't come tumbling down. As they well know, revolution is nine-tenths rhetoric. (The old Communist-party headquarters on Mission Street, vandalized by vigilantes in 1933, had Ping-pong tables and signs on the wall announced a forthcoming pot-luck picnic, according to press reports of that time.) Until the revolutionaries elect a Supervisor, even a member of the Board of Education, they're just newspaper sellers.

Probably because of these things, of all these things, San Francisco is one city in America that has never had a silent majority, always a vocal and outspoken one (with shrill minorities always in the background). It was this outspokenness that for all intents and purposes finished the House Un-American Activities Committee's reign of terror. Although there was scattered opposition across the country to the excesses of the Committee, it was only in San Francisco that they ran head-on into public resistance—crowds of ordinary citizens shouting at them that they were foolish and criminal; two of the three daily newspapers roasting them. They had never met that before and never recovered from it. The same is true of the great freeway revolt. People in other cities saw their towns being torn up by the freeway planners and highway builders but felt powerless to buck the huge financial and political power of the highway-auto-oil-industry combination. After the blight of the Embarcadero Freeway, though, San Francisco called a halt to all further building. And it wasn't the Mayor and Supervisors who stopped it either—they were all for more and bigger freeways—it was the vocal majority who did it by putting *so* much pressure on them and everyone in sight that not only their political lives were in jeopardy but possibly they would be lynched. The people's success in San Francisco was an inspiration to citizens in the same situation all across the country. It astonished builders and planners that any city would reject many millions of dollars just because taking them would have made the city ugly—change its nature.

Again, San Francisco was the city which permitted its students to voice their frustrations about the theory and practice of higher education. It was the focus of the great student revolt—the effects of which are still reverberating across the country. The tolerance in this city toward just complaints provided the atmosphere that permitted these long-overdue criticisms to be heard. I could only compare this to my undergraduate days at Ohio State University in 1951 when McCarthyism was rampant. Faculty and students who protested the administration's actions in politically "screening" visiting speakers were expelled or fired out of hand.

Besides their outspokenness, the citizens of San Francisco share two other attributes that add to much of the magic of the city. The first is their utter complexity and unalikeness. One out of seven of its citizens are first- or second-generation Americans. Every major religion in the world (including Zoroastrianism) is practiced here by significant numbers of people (the banning of prayer in public schools had no opposition whatsoever in San Francisco). And the race problem in San Francisco is extremely complicated, for which we can be extremely grateful. We have large communities of four different races—white, black, yellow (with large communities of two yellow minorities, the Chinese and the Japanese), and brown (represented by a surprisingly large population of Indians, Hawaiians, Samoans, and others from the Far Pacific—together with an increasing number of

American Indians to add salt to the soup). We have both Mexican-Americans and Puerto Ricans among our Spanish-speaking citizens, but they are outnumbered by Spanish-speaking Philippinos (not to mention those speaking Tagalog, and Central and South American immigrants). We are the only city on the North American continent with both a Peruvian restaurant and one featuring dishes from Santo Domingo. Daily or weekly newspapers are published here in German (two), Spanish (three, including the *El Salvador News*), Chinese (four), Danish-Norwegian, Yiddish, French, Japanese (three), Hungarian, Italian, Greek (two), Russian, and Swedish. On the block where I live, there are black, white, Chinese, Japanese families and a Philippino family. The corner grocery store is owned by a Christian Arab family deposed from their home outside Jerusalem by the Israelis. (Since there are several Jewish families in the neighborhood, there are some lively political arguments in Jerry's Market).

No city is without racial, religious, and ethnic prejudice and San Francisco is no exception. It is in the nature of man to gossip about, backbite, and blame the problems of the world on any neighbors who look different from him, worship other than he does, come from different backgrounds, or seem to be trying to take his job. Prejudice is an us-against-them proposition. With so *many* different *them's* and *us's* in San Francisco, though, bitter prejudice lacks the cohesiveness it has in other cities and tends to be a personal thing, varying from individual to individual.

The second thing that San Franciscans have in common, other than their unlikeness, is their nearly universal affection for San Francisco. It is one of the few cities in the world where most of the citizens are citizens without regret. It is still a city of immigrants who take delight in being San Franciscans; people who have searched for and have finally found a home. You won't find here the huge numbers of transplanted citizens so often found in the other large cities of the West, weepy and nostalgic, who immediately join Sons of New Jersey clubs and God How I Wish I Were Back in Good Old Minnesota organizations. Hometowns are seldom mentioned here and when they are it is more in the vein of accident of birth than "Lord, how good it was." This accounts for the pride that borders on narcissism of San Franciscans, commented upon so much.

Such is the magic of San Francisco that affection for it is not limited just to those who choose to live here but touches nearly everyone who even visits here. The sheer beauty of San Francisco, its freedom, tolerance, excitement, exoticness, and the strange gentleness of the city arouse a curious proprietary interest in the place that makes people very protective toward it and want to preserve it from harm. Much has been written about San Francisco as the last chance, the end of the continent, the magnet for those lost—the drunks and suicidal, the misfits and malcontents. There is truth in this; both our alcoholic and suicide rates are way out of proportion to our size. But this is only one small aspect of our city, dramatic and sad, but small. The greater truth is the opposite side of the same coin. The city offers hope at the end of the continent for those misfits and malcontents, those who have the strength to cut old, unsatisfactory ties and come here. Once here, Americans seem to find their voice again and get up on their hind legs and do something about controlling their own fate. America has taken new direction from San Francisco from the beginning to the present decade. San Francisco is a city of luck and hope, and, perhaps, therein lies its greatest magic. Even the climate shouts hope. No matter what the season, there is the feeling in the air that the stifling heat of summer is past, the bitter cold of winter is in the future. Today the blood courses in the veins, fresh, unused air, imported directly from the far Pacific, blows all the cobwebs away and anything can be accomplished.

Such are the greater elements of the magic of San Francisco, although it only begins to touch the whole truth. This book is devoted to a closer examination of the city and I hope to guide you to some of the more interesting and out-of-the-way attractions to help natives, tourists, and friends enjoy the city more fully. This is not a standard guidebook. You won't find restaurants and hotels (and their prices) listed here. The Chamber of Commerce and the Sunday newspaper has up-to-the-minute listings on that score. In the back of the book is a short list and description of the standard tourist attractions of San Francisco (Twin Peaks, Coit Tower, Fisherman's Wharf, cable cars, etcetera), but the Bank of California offers a free map which lists these better, and more concisely than is possible in a book without a complete city map. No, I hope this book will indicate an approach, lead you off the well-trod paths and into the city, this magnificent city, San Francisco.

2
An Over-all View of Views

The magic of San Francisco is so inextricably bound with its views that before we start, it might be well to examine for a moment the phenomenon of views itself. Indeed, of all visual experiences (except traumatic ones) the view is perhaps the most universally grabbing upon the human psyche. There are very few people indeed who are not moved by, do not respond or react to, a view—any view, whether it be of San Francisco Bay or the Chicago stockyards. Views evoke an almost animal response, which means that the chords they touch are deep and visceral.

Part of it, of course, is tied up in our hunting-warring evolution. If you're high up, you can settle into a comfortable feeling of security that no enemy is sneaking up behind you —also, you can get a wide look at what meat is available below. That we're still touched by this can be seen when you look at people looking at views. Most people seem exhilarated by a view; seem to sniff the view with their eyes before they settle down to enjoy it. Notice that people make animal noises when they look at a view—grunts and murmurs. With the feeling of security is also a feeling of the heights and the danger of falling that adds its own tingle. Derived from these two responses, or from something even deeper, is the peculiar importance humankind places upon physical position. With nearly all peoples in the world, a greater height means greater superiority. Kings sit on their thrones above

21

the common folk and gods rule from mountaintops. I believe that part of the lift people get from views is from a hint of this superiority momentarily enjoyed by view watchers.

All this at least partially explains why humans go to such extraordinary trouble, expense, and effort to look at views; why they journey miles to enjoy a view, risk their necks in climbing mountains to see the view. Why, if there are no hills around to give them a view naturally, they will build their own, such as the high-rises in Houston, Dallas, and the Great Plains cities.

These thoughts on views and how views affect people are especially pertinent to San Francisco, for this city undoubtedly has more views per acre than any other city in the nation. We have ocean views, Bay views, and city views. We have a plethora of panoramas; a wealth of magnificent vistas, uncountable dynamic and serene prospects. We have mansions with views and slummy housing projects with views; parks with views and factories with views; hotels with views and dog kennels with views; indeed, two of the finest views in the city are enjoyed by the ill—a magnificent Bay view by those at St. Joseph's Hospital, and an equally magnificent Golden Gate view by the sick at the University of California Hospital. Moving anywhere within the city, whether on foot or in a car, bus, or streetcar, one is constantly treated to the sudden flash of a view down a city street, from the crest of a hill, between buildings. And when one stops, there are the unexpected views from the windows of the homes or office buildings. One gets more accidental lifts in spirit per day in San Francisco just by being here than citizens in other cities get in a month of Fourth of July parades.

There is a problem, though, with so many views. With the choice of views from forty-two separate hills, peaks, ridges, and crests—not to speak of the views from buildings—one becomes educated and perhaps a little jaded. The reasons why one particular vantage point provides a very enjoyable experience while another point a few feet away, overlooking almost exactly the same area, does not move one, are as complex as describing why one painting is a masterpiece and another merely very fine. San Francisco hosts are especially hard on their guests on this point. They will tear a visitor away from what the guest thinks is one hell of a view to take him to a point two blocks away to a view made better because the wall of the condominium doesn't cut off the end of Angel Island. The Japanese are one of the few nations of people who have closely examined views and become view connoisseurs. The stock in trade of the Edo period artists, such as Hiroshige and Utamaro, were their portfolios of views— fourteen views of Fuji, twenty-six views of Fuji, etcetera. (The art of the bonsai culture and Japanese garden also show the Japanese preoccupation with views—views made small and brought into the house or back yard.) The many block prints showing Fuji viewed from the porch or garden of an inn shows that how the view is seen is as important as what is seen. The most magnificent view in the world can be spoiled if one is rushed, uncomfortable, or uneasy in mind, or if it is too hard to get to.

Unfortunately, some of the most popular vantage points in San Francisco fall into these categories. One must be dressed like an Arctic explorer to survive the cold winds of Twin Peaks most days. At the Top of the Mark, the Crown Room of the Fairmont, and the new bar on top of the Bank of America Building, the presence of those hovering outside waiting for your table pressures so you can't really relax. And although the view from Coit Tower is magnificent, the difficulty in getting there on a busy day, the slow grind up the hill breathing the exhaust of the overheated cars above you, is something like waiting in line at a soldier's brothel—the frustration and tedium taking much of the joy from the anticipated pleasure.

This chapter on views is specifically designed for the natives, tourists, and friends of San Francisco who might have skimmed the major views, the advertised views, but have missed much. For the tens of thousands who have shivered while viewing the panorama on Twin Peaks, only a handful have marveled at the beautifully framed Bay Bridge–city view from the fire department reservoir down the hill a piece. While the ocean view has been admired from the Cliff House or Sutro Park, only a very few souls have climbed the sandy steps to the top of Grand View Park for the most glorious ocean view in the city. The vista from Buena Vista Park is touted as being superb, but the better view from Corona Heights just beneath it is unknown. Even the mapmakers don't seem to know how to get to Bay View Park—perhaps the best Bay view in the most exquisite setting in San Francisco.

The only way to enjoy a view is to be forearmed with enough advice, information, and experience so that a multi-directional approach to any given view is possible. Keep the pores open, so to speak. If one goes to meet a lady known far and wide for her charm and beauty, he is prepared to be dazzled by her only on one or two levels. If he is secretly told that she is not only lovely, gracious, and cultured but also that she subsists solely on raw meat and owns the world's largest collection of unicycle memorabilia, new dimensions of appreciation are added. In these peripheral points, this book will be of inestimable help to the seekers of views in San Francisco.

Twin Peaks

Although the view from TWIN PEAKS is not the highest in the city (Mt. Davidson is a few feet higher), it is the most panoramic. It's an excellent place to start, for there, spread beneath your feet is the city, the ocean, the Bay, and the Bay counties in all their various glories. It's amazing the view you get at these 900-odd feet above sea level, for when you think of it, at 900 feet, you aren't exactly sitting on an alp. But then again, there is some interest in the fact that Twin Peaks is the same altitude above sea level as Mecca and when you are standing here, you are almost exactly twice as high above sea level as Chicago is. The view is fascinating but a little too all-encompassing, too broad to get a grip on. It's an extremely interesting view, though, because, like a map, it permits you to see at a glance the landmarks, configurations, and geographical features that contribute to the magic of San Francisco; the physical uniqueness of this city.

The major feature of this view must be the magnificence of San Francisco Bay. It's overwhelming and constantly fascinating. One of the largest landlocked harbors in the world (originally some 700 square miles of open water, now reduced by Bay fill to 400 square miles), it stretches over 30 miles southward and another 50 miles to the north and east. One of the most mind-boggling facts about San Francisco Bay—especially when you are looking at it from Twin Peaks—is that it is so new to Western history; not discovered until the latter part of the eighteenth century. It seems amazing that in all the years of the great navigator-trader-pirate-explorers, since Magellan's time, this huge body of water went undiscovered, but it is true. The Golden Gate, the mile-wide entrance to the Bay, is so often hidden by fog, especially in the summer months, that everybody missed it. Sir Francis Drake, for example, missed it by about 30 miles in 1579 and landed up the coast in what is now the Pt. Reyes National Seashore. San Francisco Bay was finally discovered in 1769 by the explorer Gaspar de Portola. He didn't discover this huge bay by ship, of course. He and his party were on horseback. They were searching for Monterey Bay—some 60 miles south—when they stumbled on it. This bizarre beginning set the pattern for the anomalous development (in the fullest dictionary sense—deviation from the normal rule or variation) that has characterized the history of San Francisco and its Bay since. One would think, for example, that the discovery of this deep-water entry into the heart of an extremely wealthy country, rich in furs, fish, mineral, and agricultural potential would have brought a flood of exploiters. It didn't. Imperial Spain established a *presidio* (fort) and mission here in San Francisco in 1776 and divided the land into huge land grants, which were given to the gentry. This effectively stifled growth and San Francisco–Yerba Buena and the Bay area drowsed for nearly a hundred years till the Gold Rush. Again, it's hard to believe that in such a dramatic setting so little that was historically dramatic touched the place for such a long time. There were no great Indian wars, no intense diplomatic manipulations by great powers, no Alamos, no struggle to survive. And in the frenzy of the Gold Rush, all the old was swept away as if it had never existed—drowned, leaving not even nostalgia for those who were here before. Lord knows there has been drama here since.

Which brings our eyes from a broad sweep of the Bay to a closer look at some of the elements that has made San Francisco such a lovely city. If you examine early lithographs and scenic photographs of San Francisco of the 1840s, '50s, and '60s, you're struck by the fact that except for its position on the Bay, San Francisco was not originally a very pretty place. To see the original topography and vegetation, look behind you, southward to the San Bruno Mountains, or across to the Marin headlands, or east to McLaren Park. San Francisco was the way they are now, rather bare grass-covered hills with fingers of manzanita and live oak snaking up the canyon valleys. San Francisco is one of the few cities in the world, outside of desert towns, made lusher and greener by the hand of man than it was in its natural state. And green on a grand scale. Through the luck of the hills, the luck of San Francisco's position of military importance, and the desire of our founders to build a city that reflected their own grand self-esteem, San Francisco is perhaps the greenest of all the major cities in America.

Louis Mumford in his treatise on cities said that for a city not to drown in its own people, 10 percent of the area of a city should be set aside for park land. San Francisco exceeds that by quite a bit. Of the 44.5 square miles of total land area, the city maintains almost exactly 5.5 square miles of municipal park land. Added to this is the lushly landscaped or wild greenery of the Presidio, Ft. Mason, and Ft. Miley—about 4 square miles all told; plus the .5 square mile of eucalyptus jungle smack in the middle of the city owned by the University of California. Counted all together, about 20 percent of San Francisco is park land or is otherwise governmentally green.

The thing that tilts you off balance about this relatively vast acreage of greenery is that of all cities, San Francisco is the most improbable place where you should find it—it should simply not be able to afford the space. The population of San Francisco is inordinately large for the area. Some 750,000 people (the 1970 census figures notwithstanding) are packed into this town at some 22,000 people per square mile of residential-commercial area available. Although San Francisco ranks thirteenth in population, it is the second most densely populated city in America (even if Newark and Jersey City might have grounds for disputing it).

This accounts partly for the European aspect of the city. It is more vertical than horizontal. There are few rambling homes situated on spacious lawns. San Francisco is a city of apartment houses, blocks of flats, and homes that adjoin wall to wall. The houses take up most of the space on their standard 25- by 100-foot lots with little postage-stamp-sized gardens in back (they can't be called back yards in the American sense). Garages are tucked under the living rooms and cars are kept in the house, like cows in Swiss chalets— indeed, there are probably more people worth a million dollars in San Francisco than there are detached garages. Indeed, such is the value of land in some places that some very expensive homes on Pacific Heights, and Russian and Telegraph hills have *no* garages at all and their owners must leave their Bentleys parked on the street. But again, such is the Alice in Wonderland division of land in the city that immediately to the west, just down the hill from the TV tower on Mt. Sutro, is a *golf driving range!* To my mind, an in-town golf driving range is the greatest imaginable indication of a land-rich city (until 1970, there were *two* golf driving ranges).

But back to the view. The view to the north and northwest is particularly pleasing. Because of the need to defend the approach to the Golden Gate, the headlands of both the San Francisco and Marin peninsulas were set aside as military reservations almost from the beginning and thus kept from private development. The difference in view textures could not have been made more aesthetically perfect if it had been planned. The deep green lushness of the Presidio is a perfect counterfoil to the stark golden hills and craggy outcroppings of Ft. Baker, Ft. Barry, and Ft. Cronkhite across the Bay. It wasn't planned, of course. The Presidio is green largely because of many Arbor Days a generation or two ago. Schoolkids put out thousands of eucalyptus, monterey pine, and cypress trees. When you go down Arguello Boulevard into the

Presidio from Lake Street, you can see how they started out with random, inspired planting, then the novelty wore off (Arbor Day being a parent-inspired celebration) and the kids put in the trees in the quickest way they could—straight rows of eucalyptus like a tree plantation. Arbor Days forested the Presidio as well as Yerba Buena Island. This last was paid for by Adolph Sutro, who provided the seedlings from his nurseries and chartered the ferry boat to take the children to the island. Adolph Sutro was perhaps the champion tree planter in the history of the city. It was he who forested the slopes of Mt. Sutro behind us and Mt. Davidson. It's a pity that Arbor Day, which at one time was an important event, has fallen into neglect. It's one of the few national holidays that embraced the whole of the citizenry in unselfish working together for the good of the community and country—with no gimmicks. Times are ripe for a resurgence of Arbor Day.

San Francisco's strategic military position at the entrance to the Bay, which guaranteed lovely views in that the headlands of both Marin and San Francisco, as well as Angel Island and Alcatraz, were withdrawn from private or civic development and left largely wild (with the exception of Alcatraz). The debt we owe to this lucky fluke of strategic position cannot ever be truly evaluated because it gave us not only beautiful scenery—views from the center of this crowded city onto the contours and textures of landscape largely unchanged from the beginning of time, virgin land, unique of all major cities in America—but it's certainly shaped the thinking of San Franciscans about conservation and the beauty of land left as it was. Because of these headlands, conservation here has never been left to become a remote, do-gooder, abstract kind of saving forests, lakes, or whatever out in the country. Conservation has always been of immediate concern because the scars and blight of unconservation are impossible to hide in this vertical city.

A good example of this conservative conservationism is ALCATRAZ ISLAND. Of all the Bay ornaments that make our views so delightful, Alcatraz is the least pleasing. There is probably no more graceful monumental structure made by

men than the suspension bridge and we have two—the Golden
Gate and the Bay bridges. The other two islands, Angel
Island and Yerba Buena, are green jewels—both the result
of military and/or governmental removal from private development. Angel Island in its rich history has been the site
of military camps as early as 1870; as a quarantine station,
it was the Ellis Island of the West, holding the immigrants
from the Orient till they proved themselves disease free;
prisoner of war camps in both World War I and World War
II; coast guard station, and missile site. Now it's a state park
and soon to be included in the Bay Area Regional National
Park. Yerba Buena is now the anchorage for the two ends
of the Bay Bridge and the site of homes for Navy admirals
and captains, who have their mansions on the heights of
Yerba Buena (as do the generals and colonels in the Presidio
—the higher the rank, the better the view). These islands,
the bridges, the headlands and peninsulas, Belvedere and
Tiburon directly north, are lovely furniture in the Bay. Only
Alcatraz is dramatically ugly, not only because of its history
and connotations, but naturally so. Alcatraz is a bleak, low,
rocky island entirely lacking in water and subjected to the
full brunt of swirling fog and treacherous tidal currents. It
was named originally for the pelicans that nested there in
Spanish days, but as soon as enough people came West to
create a criminal class, it was quickly utilized as a maximum
security prison by the military and later by civilian police,
who saw how they could economize in fences and guards by
sticking miscreants out there.

Now, we have three other rocky, waterless islands immediately off San Francisco—Seal and Bird Rocks near the Cliff
House. These, unlike Alcatraz, are exciting places white-
capped with guano, wheeling birds at the heights, barking
sea lions and the crashing sea at their base . . . endlessly
fascinating. Not so Alcatraz. It hulks off shore full of sadness
and lugubrious vibrations. The only fascination it offers is
morbid. That is, it was that way until recently. In 1963, the
federal penitentiary system gave up on it as an ideal prison.
Not only was it expensive but the heavy salt air had de-
teriorated the facilities so badly that the last two prisoners to

escape dug their way through the walls with kitchen spoons. A sad commentary on building procedures and perhaps a whiff of corruption in high places. Alcatraz was taken over by the Federal Bureau of Prisons in 1933 to house all the vicious criminals generated by the constitutional amendment that told people that they couldn't drink. It lasted a bare forty years. Ft. Point, on the other hand, at the entrance to the Bay and even more exposed to the weather, was built in the 1860s to protect San Francisco from the invading Confederacy and it stands today.

When the federal prison system gave up the island in 1963, the property hung in limbo for several years. Everybody, the city of San Francisco, entrepreneurs, and, as it turned out, Indians, were keeping their eye on it. The intensity of watching is shown in the hilarious events that occurred immediately after the federal government, in all its bureaucratic wisdom declared the island surplus government land! Alcatraz was invaded by a whole passel of land grabbers. There were the people who sneaked ashore and staked out a mining claim (saying that they were going to operate *stone* mines or some damned thing), reserving a section of the island and duly filing the claims with the Bureau of Mines.

Then there were the Indians who claimed that under federal law they have first crack at surplus government lands. Their claims were blithely ignored so finally, they just moved in and occupied the place physically. When the Indians claimed Alcatraz for their own, there was much wringing of hands by the Feds as how to get them off without appearing to be the oppressive, anti-Indian, greedy, land-grabbing souls we have been since 1620. The Coast Guard put up a sort of blockade around the island, forbidding any supplying of food and water to the island defenders, but they didn't cut off supplies. Indeed, a trip to Alcatraz came to be the thing to do for any visiting celebrity. Jane Fonda, Joan Baez, Truman Capote, Marlon Brando—anyone who passed through, sneaked out on one of the regular runs and toured the joint.

In the meantime, there was San Francisco's claim to the island because it falls within the city limits of San Francisco. San Francisco is land poor but controls a vast watery empire.

Its city limits stretch halfway out in the Bay on our South-eastern line and around nearly to the shoreline of Contra Costa County (Yerba Buena and Treasure islands are within San Francisco); over nearly to the Marin tower of the Golden Gate Bridge, which tucks in Alcatraz handily, and out to sea for 30 miles to the Farallones. With Alcatraz in its imminent grasp, San Francisco sent out bids, with hopes of making it less of an eyesore and of generating some revenue. And the bids came rushing in. Every sculptor in the world saw in Alcatraz the perfect pedestal for his statue, which would be, every one of them, the hugest monument since the Lighthouse of Alexandria and the Colossus of Rhodes, with, of course, attendant resort and convention facilities. Then the developers came forward with their schemes. Lamar Hunt of the oil billions wanted to put up a huge Torch of Freedom, hotels, convention halls, with, as a special drawing card, the re-creation of an early San Francisco section—a kind of Disney-land North with all the bawdy charms and excitement of that era to remind us of the elements of American heritage alas eroded by modern times and a socialistic government.

The coalition of Indian groups manning Alcatraz had grand plans for it, but as the months dragged on, the pressure couldn't be maintained and the organization became dis-organized. There were a series of bad incidents on the island —the death of a child and arson of some of the buildings— and a bad element of freeloaders moved in and terrorized the original stalwarts. The Coast Guard finally led the rem-nants without fuss back to the mainland. Alcatraz is once more deserted.

The final utilization of Alcatraz will be the most hotly argued local issue for a long time because San Franciscans realize that whatever is decided will have to be lived with for a long time, inescapable, in constant view. We may hope that it will go back to the pelicans.

But back to the view. Let us start at the main observation area, then circle the figure-eight road around the north and south peaks. I'll describe the gross geographical features and prominent structures and sections of town, so that, when we visit them later, you'll have some idea of where they are in relation to the others. The broad avenue leading northeast in the general direction of the Bay Bridge is Market Street. The bridges are easy to keep separate. The Bay Bridge is the silver one with four towers with the X-shaped trussing; the Golden Gate is orange, two towers with square supports. The suspension sections of the Bay Bridge tie together in mid-Bay at the solid tower that contains more concrete than was poured for the Empire State Building (a piece of obscure, and useless, information always nice to spring on the unsuspecting).

The suspension and cantilever sections of the Bay Bridge anchor at Yerba Buena Island. The long finger of land stretching to the left of the island is Treasure Island. It's fill land from the dredging for the Bay Bridge (on the shallows at the west end of Yerba Buena) and was the site of the 1939 Golden Gate International Exposition, a World's Fair designed to celebrate the completion of the two bridges and generate tourist dollars in the depressed time. Highlights from the Fair were Sally Rand's Nude Ranch and an exhibition of the "Iron Lung," a modern scientific marvel according to the official guide (it's hard to remember that the iron lung was so recent a development). Treasure Island was to be used as an airport after the Fair (the China Clipper already took off from the Bay), but the war came and it was developed as a naval base, which it remains until today.

Market Street is a major division in San Francisco, economically, ethnically, and culturally. North of Market is the financial district, Chinese, Italian, Downtown, nightclubs, and generally white collar. South of Market—South of the Slot, Butchertown—is largely older residential, light and heavy industry, Irish, Spanish, black, and generally blue collar. These are broad generalizations, but the separation is there. There are long-time residents of both areas who have never seen the other side of Market Street outside the tourist attractions—North Beach and Chinatown on the west, Mission Dolores on the east—which is amazing in a town half the size of Columbus, Ohio.

Moving to the north and west, the bare hill immediately below is Corona Heights and the wooded hill immediately to the left of it is Buena Vista Park—both municipal park land. The red-tile-roofed complex between them is St. Joseph's Hospital and Nursing School. In the Bay, along this line, Alcatraz is in the foreground and Angel Island lies beyond. From this view, the tall white building with red roof sticking up between the edges of the islands is an apartment house on the corner of Broadway and Fillmore Street and marks the crest of Pacific Heights that stretches left to the green of the Presidio and right where it blends into Russian, Nob, and Telegraph hills, indistinguishable from here. Pacific Heights and the Marina district down on the other side are rich. The Presidio is that large triangle of green to which, from this view, the Golden Gate Bridge seems to anchor. The broad (half-mile-wide) stretch of greenery that comes from the sea to the middle view is Golden Gate Park. The narrow strip of greenery that goes from the Park to Buena Vista is called the Panhandle. On this side is the Haight-Ashbury district. The twin towers of the impressive Romanesque church is St. Ignatius. Circling around St. Ignatius are the buildings of the University of San Francisco, a Jesuit college that boasts the highest percentage of foreign students of any college in America, as well as having produced more San Franciscan and Californian politicians than any other. The square tower seen beyond it is the San Francisco College for Women, a college for rich Catholic girls which is appropriately sited on a rise named Lone Mountain. Sighting along the edge of Golden Gate Park, the dome you see beyond is the beautiful Jewish Temple Emanu-El. That area between Golden Gate Park and the Presidio from the Temple to the ocean is the Richmond district, a delightfully rich mixture of peoples, largely middle-class but spilling over on either side of the middle, running heavily to White Russian emigrés, Orthodox Jews, and generally cultured folk—there are probably more bookstores along Geary and Clement streets than along any other neighborhood street in town.

Leaving the observation area, we'll circle to the left, west and south, around North Peak. Immediately beneath you is the flat roof of Summit Reservoir and to the right is the bisected oval of the fire department reservoir. That hill behind

Summit Reservoir is Mt. Sutro (with the huge TV transmitting tower).

The University of California Medical School complex lies just over the hill. Beneath us, as we continue are the roofs of the Laguna Honda Hospital and Rehabilitation Center (old folks' home). The two steep, wooded hills in the foreground are interesting examples of antiestablishment neighborhoods established by the establishment. Forest Hill on the left and Edgehill Way on the right were created and are maintained by rich property owners who refused to let the city impose the usual grid plan of streets upon their hills and went it alone. The streets follow the contours of the hills, unlike the earlier, downtown streets that go smack over Russian, Nob, and Telegraph Hills in the true frontier spirit: "Nature ain't going to tell *me* where to build my streets, and so what if it's a 30-degree grade!" Mt. Davidson, the peak with the cross, hides a third such private complex, St. Francis Wood. Mt. Sutro and Sunset Heights effectively block the view of the Sunset District from here. Between Mt. Davidson, the half-wooded hill with the cross (the highest hill in the city) and Sunset Heights, one catches a glimpse of Lake Merced and the Pacific. Lake Merced used to be a part of the sea, but geological movement (the San Andreas fault cuts into the sea just south of here) sealed the exit and now it is fresh water and chock-full of trout. This has to be the only city in the world where one can catch a three-pound rainbow trout, walk a couple of hundred yards to the ocean, and catch three-foot sea bass. On a clear day the Farallon Islands can be seen 27 miles outside the gate.

At the southernmost curve of South Peak, one can see how clearly San Francisco is delineated. In most other cities, the dynamic inner city gives way to residential areas which peter out into city-limits sleaze. In San Francisco these stretches of neon blight are prevented wholly on three sides by the ocean and the Bay. On the south, it is largely prevented by the Crocker family, who own the San Bruno Mountains that stretch across about half the peninsula; and they seem to be sitting on it, not developing to any great extent. Except for the extreme east and west, San Francisco ends abruptly at its city limits, which is unusual in American towns, except for Manhattan Island. Swinging east from south, we sight over the new housing at Diamond Heights to the rather phallic water tower on McLaren Park, the second largest of our city parks. McLaren Park is just now being developed and in a few years, it will be one of the most beautiful parks in the city. Candlestick Park is just below the wooded hill with the radio transmitting tower (Bay View Park) and to the left of that at the Bay you see the Hunter's Point shipyards. That huge ship's crane was received by San Francisco from Germany as part of war reparations. This view from McLaren Park eastward sweeps through the Outer Mission and across neighborhoods as fascinating as any in the city—Portola (accent on the *Port*), Bayview, Hunter's Point, Excelsior—tight-knit little communities, each with its own special character and charm.

The bald hill with the microwave station atop is Bernal Heights. On the slopes of Bernal Heights, one still finds dirt roads and wooden sidewalks. Almost directly èast, located by the gas tanks and the large red brick complex of San Francisco General Hospital, is Potrero Hill, still the home of a large number of Russians of the Molokai Protestant Christian sect, but acquiring a population of refugees from the Haight-Ashbury that has given the area the nickname "Pot Hill." That stretch along the eastern Bay shore from Hunter's Point to the Bay Bridge is the most industrialized section of town, grown up largely because the luck of our hills diverted the railroads from overwhelming the center of town. This has not only visually saved a large part of town from being factoried, but it has kept the air pollution away from the residential areas—the prevailing westerlies blow the pollution over to Oakland, leaving the city unbegrimed, with air as fresh as in the suburbs.

But we are back at the starting point. Taken as a whole, the city is extravagantly beautiful. Even when looked at from less overwhelming views, you'll find that it is beautiful in cameo. While we are in this area, we will first go down to take a look at the view from the Fire Department Reservoir, then go farther down to Corona Heights. The greatest thing

Twin Peaks has to offer is that it is positively the finest kite-flying site in the city. The string jumps in your hands here and the kite tears from you as if frantic to get away. You can sail a kite up a thousand feet quicker here than anywhere else in town.

Fire Department Reservoir

The slopes of Twin Peaks offer several fine views, but my favorite is on Palo Alto at the FIRE DEPARTMENT RESERVOIR. It's a little tricky to reach and for this reason it's not too populated. Coming down from Twin Peaks, slow down when you reach the first street on the right, Burnett Avenue, and look for the first street to the left, Mountain Spring Avenue. There is a small square sign on one of the corners that says, Palo Alto, St. Germain, Glenbrook. Head up it (and I do mean up, it's first gear all the way to the top) and turn to the left up Glenbrook to Palo Alto. As you drive up the hill, you're passing architect-award homes that have appeared in beautiful-house magazines. Turn to the left on Palo Alto and park anywhere. The view lies at the end of the street toward the Bay. Walk past the oval fire department reservoir on your right. This reservoir is one of a system of reservoirs and cisterns built after the earthquake-fire of 1906. The words are always coupled because the greatest loss of life and property didn't happen during the earthquake itself but were caused by the fire. The quake severed the water mains and most of the town was left without means of fighting fires that broke out—exploding gas mains, tipped-over coal and wood stoves, etcetera. Four-fifths of the city burned. The fire was stopped only by dynamiting blocks of buildings as fire-breaks. This reservoir and other tanks and the cisterns in the intersections of many streets (identified by the large circles of cobble-stones with a manhole in the middle), were built as insurance against that ever happening again. And when you think about it, it's amazing that the city hasn't burned down twenty times since. It's a vulnerable city. Because of the earthquake threat, residential building is largely limited to frame construction (wooden buildings give and sway with a quake, unlike plain brick or masonry structures that collapse). Reinforced brick and masonry residences are simply too expensive. These wooden houses are built cheek to jowl; few are detached. And San Francisco has to be one of the windiest cities in America, with 15- to 25-mile-an-hour winds sweeping in from the ocean most months of the year, every hour of the day. The only thing that protects the city is the gallant fire department and their philosophy of overkill. Where a residential fire in another city would bring out one truck, the fire department here sends three companies of firemen—enough men to stomp out the fire with their very boots.

Palo Alto is a dead end. To reach the view, one must skirt around the shrubbery to the right, being careful not to slip on the weathering shale. And you'll see it. The hill falls abruptly away in a steep grassy meadow to exhibit one of the pleasantest, most nicely framed city views in the city. The shrubbery shelters you from the wind, the grass is soft, and it's a serene and perfect place to savor a view with a bottle of white wine. (Note: be sure to pick up after yourself, the people on the block are fastidious; they'll have the cops on you for littering before you can make the corner—and rightly so.)

After you have finished viewing, stroll back along Palo Alto and up the road to the Sutro Heights Reservoir. It's a covered reservoir and one may walk on its roof. Farther up the hill, if the gate is unlocked, you can see one hell of a house.* Originally owned by one of the Sutros, it now houses the transmitting studios for three local TV stations. With its steep slate roof, high round turrets, and flagstone embellishments, it's so charming that you keep expecting Rapunzel to come to a window to let down her golden hair.

This is an especially nice outing for tourists because, when you go back to your hotel and someone asks you what you did today, you can say, "Well, I enjoyed a bottle of Riesling at Twin Peaks fire department reservoir, visited a charming house, and went walking upon fourteen million gallons of water. What did you do?"

*Or *could* see it. Unfortunately, it's been torn down since this was written.—ED.

Belgrave and Bigler

Further down the slopes of Twin Peaks is another splendid, but seldom visited, view. Drive down 17th Street toward the ocean, turn left on BELGRAVE, and again left on BIGLER. At the end of the street is a high, grassy knoll. Climb up and you'll find a lovely meadow with a fine northern view of the city. I don't know how long this view will be available so take advantage of it right away. There are "for sale" signs all around and it will probably be built upon soon.

Mount Olympus

Still on the slopes of Twin Peaks is another superb view. Coming down from Twin Peaks on Clarendon, go straight and you're on Clayton. Bear right and you're on Ashbury. Turn right up Clifford Terrace, go up a block to Upper Terrace, and right again to MOUNT OLYMPUS. This is a small city park that is located in the geographical center of San Francisco. A flight of steps leads to the pedestal that once held an early 40-foot electrifying statue called *The Triumph of Light*. Donated by Adoph Sutro, it was probably the most exciting statue in the city. But it is no longer with us. Devastated by ravages of weather and vandalism, it finally had to be torn down. The vandals left a perfectly wonderful pedestal, a ten-foot-high rock base above two flights of staircase leading to it. (It is now ringed with antivandal barriers, a fairly prosaic example of putting up the spikes after the statue has been torn down.) There is not a finer site for a statue in the whole of San Francisco, situated as it is on top of Mount Olympus, with sweeping views of the bridges and Bay.

Utilization of this wonderful pedestal is, of course, inevitable. My own preference for replacement runs to a forty-foot statue of Allen Ginsberg—naked and bearded, with beads and tambourine. He would be perpetually praying and chanting up there, and would serve as a fine talisman to protect the city from earthquakes and freeway-building politicians. A wonderful pedestal with nothing on it ought to be used before the Communists put up a clenched fist like the one on the Stock Exchange.

The walkway around the base of the pedestal provides many fine cameo views, perfect for taking professional pictures, framed views between buildings and trees, that will show you're not only a traveler, but a hell of a photographer as well. It's a pity they put antivandal spikes on the vacant pedestal. You could take pictures of yourself and your loved ones above and apart in a triumph of light.

Corona Heights

Although CORONA HEIGHTS is only one and one-half blocks from Market Street and barely a mile from City Hall, it is one of the most private views in the city—indeed, almost secret. Hardly anyone knows that it is not only city property and one of the larger of the midtown parks but has a surpassing view of the inner city.

Corona Heights lies directly southeast and adjacent to the better-known Buena Vista Park. Being somewhat lower, it benefits from the wind screen Buena Vista Park offers. And although it is lower, it has not only better views but more satisfactory views. At Buena Vista, the peak is so heavily wooded that one gets only glimpses of the city through the branches. On Corona Heights, you nearly always have the opportunity to savor the view in solitude. On Buena Vista this is not so. In the past several years, Buena Vista has become a favorite resort for the sylvan branch of the homosexual community (male). It became so notorious that the park department cut down most of the bushes. When you go to seek a buena vista at Buena Vista Park, you see fifty men walking their dogs and another fifty sitting in their cars in the parking lot enjoying the view of the parking lot. From my informants, I learned that it is divided about half and half—half back-to-nature homosexuals and half members of the police vice squad. It spoils what little view there is to be in the middle of such silent cops-and-robbers tensions.

The view from Corona Heights is so fine that it's best not to go unprepared with regard to food, and fortunately this area is one of the best places in the city to prepare you for a view. At Castro and Market streets you are in the heart of the Scandinavian section of town. You'll also find a Greek-Syrian delicatessen and gift shop and one of the finest Indonesian restaurants in town. The Chinatown Meat Co. at the corner of 15th Street and Sanchez Street specializes in Swedish Delicatessen. The Norse Cove on Castro right off Market and the Scandinavian Restaurant on Market at 16th are both restaurant-delicatessens that sell fine carry-out things to take with you up to Corona Heights, everything from a robust roast beef sandwich to a delicate smoked eel open-faced snack. All sell Danish beer.

While shopping at the delis and in the neighborhood, you might stop a moment at the Pilsner Bar on Church near Market. It's patronized mainly by Scandinavian merchant seamen. (You can always tell a sailor's bar from the number of phalanges or whole digits missing from the hands of the customers. For some reason seamen lose more fingers, or pieces of them, than any other worker.) The first time I visited the Pilsner, I walked through the door to be greeted by two Scandinavians who were Indian leg-wrestling among the litter and cigar butts on the floor. Nobody in the place paid attention to them except a fat lady who was screaming laughter and slapping her thighs . . . and the bartender, who was shouting at them to cool it, using cuss words in three languages. It was 9 AM on a Sunday morning. By no means stop to visit the bar in the basement of Norse Hall on Market at 15th. It is too comfortable, too pleasant and friendly, the home-made Swedish rye bread and pickled herring served as hors d'oeuvres too good to leave (*see* Chapter 5). If you stop, you never will get to Corona Heights.

There are several ways to approach the Corona Heights view and you can choose the one that best suits your athletic prowess, degree of encumbrance, and interests. For the full grand tour from the base of the hill to the peak, go north on Castro from Market to Beaver Street. Turn left on Beaver and the main entrance is found very close to 15th Street. Just inside the entrance is a geological wonder; a sheer cliff of chert polished to mirror smoothness by the rubbing together of the rocks in ancient earthquakes. This particular area lies in a dormant fault zone that runs from Hunter's

Point to Ft. Point at Golden Gate Bridge. The geological term for this polished cliff is "slickensides." This delights, amazes, and boggles me. When such a petrolithic discipline as geology employs as an official technical description a beautifully graphic, slangy English word, there is hope for all of us.

As we go through the playground to the path up the hill, we skirt one of the two tennis courts in Corona Heights. The one we pass now is the Sydney S. Peixotto courts on 15th Street. The Peixottos were a pioneer Jewish family who embellished San Francisco in many ways, including good works and leadership. The name still rings a social bell and once a player has used these courts, he can fret his fellow enthusiasts to death by dropping, "Pebble Beach is nice, of course, but you must agree that after you've played the Sydney S. Peixotto courts on Corona Heights, everything else is . . ."

The other set of courts on Corona Heights is high on the northeastern flank of the hill. The Flint Street courts are tucked away on three dead-end streets, up 16th from Castro to Flint, or at the end of Museum Way off Roosevelt. The Peixotto and Flint Street courts are good to keep in mind because they are so unknown. On the finest tennis day, when all the other courts in the city have waiting lines, you're sure to find an open court on one of them. The Flint Street court also has a view.

If you're completely unencumbered and interested in geology, you can take some of the many steep paths from the playground to the peaks. On the way up you'll see many fine examples of finely banded rutilated chert in outcroppings and fallen boulders. If you stopped at the delicatessen, though, you'll never make it up these paths, so drive up 15th Street to Roosevelt Way and turn left. At Museum Way, you'll see a chain link fence and a large unmarked gate. At the corner there is a sign pointing to the Josephine D. Randall Junior Museum. The large gate leads to the meadow below the peaks and is never locked. Although it looks like private or institutional land, it is a public park and the meadow is a fine place to picnic.

There are several mountain-goat-type paths straight up

from the meadow to the peaks. The path to the extreme right lets you hold onto the fence as you climb, but it is not recommended for the acrophobe because the chain-link fence clings to a sheer cliff. If you skirt the hill to the left, though, you'll find a gravel path that permits you to pursue the view more sedately and with less huffing and puffing. This path leads upward to a slight meadow-plateau beneath the peaks and it is here you'll find one of the two barbecue pits on the peaks—the other is on the other side of the hill. If you plan to cook, bring your own charcoal and equipment, for there is nothing else here.

The hike to the peaks themselves involves some careful work and real exercise, which makes this view special and exhilarating. I don't want to give the impression that it is an attack on El Capitan because a four-year-old or a determined grandmother can make it; although it's steep, it's safe. But you do have to work a little, so it's an especially pleasant outing for the city-bound native or the tourist who has been riding in planes and buses, staying at hotels, and walking on concrete for a couple of weeks. It's a short back-to-nature experience.

The view itself is interesting for several reasons. The overall view of the inner city is fine. Here, also, one gets a lateral view of some of the lesser heights that form boundaries of some San Francisco neighborhoods. In all cities, boundaries are formed between neighborhoods and some are very subtle. Here, they're not subtle at all. The valley streets are the boundaries. It takes a firm friendship indeed to trek down a 25-degree slope, cross Castro, and trek up a 25-degree slope to visit a neighbor. To the south and east you can see how the hills run down from Twin Peaks to Diamond, Castro Heights, Noe Heights over to the Dolores Street rise. All these hills and valleys are separate neighborhoods and good to drive through, especially the tops of the hills. The homes were put up mostly at the turn of the century and some are quite lavish and beautiful. One can get an idea of these neighborhoods by looking back toward Twin Peaks and examining the houses closest to us. Roosevelt Way is one of a number of terraced streets. (The others, with names like Saturn,

Vulcan, and Uranus, just beneath Mt. Olympus, we shall visit in Chapter 3, on monuments.) The houses were handsome when built and are handsome today.

Some of the landmarks you see beneath you from Corona Heights are the Basilica of Mission Dolores directly east, following the grid of 16th Street, and the U.S. Mint a little to your left on the pale green hill on the diagonal that is Market Street. But while it is interesting to pick out landmarks, it is more pleasant not to bother and simply sit and enjoy the view.

14th Avenue Muni Station

Although there are higher sites in the immediate vicinity, the view from the MUNI STATION at 14th Avenue and Quintara Street is one of the most extensive in Sunset Heights. The hill falls abruptly away at this point which permits a Western vista unimpeded by trees or houses. One has the whole view from beyond Golden Gate Park to the Zoo; a great part of the sweep of Ocean Beach. It is also one of the saddest lookout points in the city, for it overlooks the Sunset district —the city's most culturally deprived area. There, stretched beneath you, from Judah to Vicente, from 19th Avenue to the sea a mile and a half away, lie 321 square blocks of houses built on the principle that if one house is halfway well designed and livable, no one can complain of 321 city blocks of the same house. In the 3 square miles of the district, other than on the shopping areas along three streets—Lawton, Noriega, and Taraval—there are no corner grocery stores, no bakeries, no restaurants, no book stores, no specialty shops to look in the windows of, and even on the three main shopping streets, there are damn few places where a thirsty man might get something to drink. In 3 square miles, there are no public or private buildings interesting enough to walk a block to view. And although one of our finest churches, Holy Name, is located within the Sunset, it is one of the very few churches to be found in the whole district. In short, the Sunset is a residential desert.

Lyon and Broadway

Getting to the view at Lyon and Broadway is half the pleasure because it's right on the fringe of PACIFIC HEIGHTS and the Presidio of San Francisco. Everyone around you on the right and left is secure: the rich are secure in their riches, the military secure in their arms. You can't get there without enjoying the serenity of both, admiring the beautiful homes of Pacific Heights and the well-policed lawns of the Army post. The view from Lyon and Broadway is a charming cameo. You get a straight shot and beautifully framed view of the Palace of Fine Arts in the foreground and Angel Island in the distance—a wonderful place for photographs. And the viewing point is a comfortable one. Lyon Street dead-ends here above a four-level terraced pocket park with stairs from Vallejo leading in easy stages up the hill. One added point of interest in this view lies in a mansion of Catholic priests to be found directly beneath the Lyon Street viewing area. You can look down and often see the priests stalking back and forth on the terrace of their house muttering to themselves. I have never been able to find out just what the story was about this houseful of priests, whether they are merely being housed there, or are in training or retreat or whatever. From the kids in the neighborhood, I have found that if you're evil, you can shout down dirty things at them and safely flee before they can run up the stairs and get at you. I have observed that shouting down, "God bless you, Father!" fourteen times in various tones of voice usually gets some action.

Dona Ina Coolbreth Park

DONA INA COOLBRETH PARK on Mason Street between Broadway and Green Street is a lovely, private little park with benches and walks from which you can enjoy a narrow but interesting Bay view (as well as a peek into the windows of the high-rise apartment houses lower down). The only thing that spoils it is that in spite of a thousand signs, it is a favorite place for the people of the neighborhood to walk their dogs. It's not that I don't like dogs, but in the parks or in the streets, I find it a gross imposition to be forever minding somebody else's dog's business.

If you look across the street from the entrance to Dona Ina Coolbreth Park, you'll see flights of steps up the hill to even higher vantage points. These are public stairs, and if you are curious, you can climb them to the end of Vallejo above Jones Street. However, the views aren't particularly better than from the park lower down.

Coit Tower and Telegraph Hill

At the end of Lombard Street off Columbus. Follow the signs.

There's no telegraph on TELEGRAPH HILL now. And the telegraph the hill was named for was an unusual one. Not the dot-and-dash kind, it was a semiphore system. When a ship was sighted coming through the Golden Gate, lookouts on the hill would signal with the long, windmill-like arms the kind of ship to be expected. The ship's chandlers, boarding-house-keepers, and merchants would then send their agents rowing like mad in dories to be the first aboard so to have the first crack at the business of the ship.

COIT TOWER is the crown of Telegraph Hill. It's the second most popular view in the city (after Twin Peaks). It's lower than the Peaks but affords a better view. It's also harder to get to in the middle of a summer day. A narrow, two-lane road leads up Lombard Street to a 30-odd-car parking lot. Those below can't get up until someone on top leaves. At the height of the tourist season, this might mean a thirty-minute stop-and-go wait on the steep street up, breathing all the auto fumes and worrying about your car's getting overheated. The fret can be avoided by boarding the Coit Tower Bus at Union and Columbus, but the wait will be the same.

Once up, though, you'll have a glorious view of some of the most exciting parts of San Francisco. The Embarcadero's docks and ships are directly beneath you and if you're lucky and one of the uncontainerized freighters is on this side of the Ferry Building, you'll be able to see the very complicated movements of the ship's booms loading and unloading cargo. The curious ball on a pole in the parking lot is a replica of one that existed during the early days. It was a service of the port, a clock. Precisely at twelve noon, the ball would fall, letting the ships check their chronometers.

Coit Tower parking lot is several hundred feet lower than Twin Peaks and often when it's foggy up there, it's clear here, giving you dramatic views of the bridges and Bay islands with the fog above. To the west, you'll see crooked Lombard Street; to the south, a very fine cityscape. The twin towers of the church beneath you belong to Sts. Peter and Paul on Washington Square in the heart of North Beach.

Coit Tower itself is another thing entirely, and curious indeed. To show that a good view is not necessarily dependent on height, take the elevator to the top, 210 feet above the parking lot. One would imagine that the higher view would surpass the lower one, but it isn't so. The windows in the tower segment the panorama so you don't get the magnificent sweep you do farther down. The tower was built in the thirties through a bequest from Lilly Hitchcock Coit (*see* Chapter 3). The base of the tower, though, was decorated with murals by WPA artists. They're closed off pending vandal restoration work—that's been going on for at least three years—but it's still interesting to look in the windows to see what was painted. It's all social realism of the "only the left is right" school, stalwart farmers, workers, and engineers that cover the whole spectrum of California's labor force. Most interesting is the mural putting everything into a San Francisco street-corner scene (toward the back of the base). It could be today except for the lack of black and Oriental faces. The wind is blowing up girls' dresses; on the newsstand, the vendor is selling the *Examiner* and *Chronicle* and the *New Masses* and the *Worker* (substitute the *Berkeley Barb* and any other "underground" paper); a citizen is getting robbed—by two white men; working stiffs are pushing around goods on hand trucks instead of fork lifts; *City Lights*, the avant-garde movie, is being advertised on a billboard.

The only thing that doesn't make it contemporary is the fact that all the men (and women) are wearing hats and 1930s fashions. It's a mural full of action, painted forty years ago and things are not less full of action today—the same fuss and fury.

The slopes of Telegraph Hill aren't as rich in views as Twin Peaks (having been usurped by rich apartment houses), but there are two worth viewing. You have to come back down Lombard to Stockton, turn left, then left again up Union Street to the top. Park, if you can find a space, and check the views at Union and Montgomery streets, and Montgomery at Alta. These are cameo views with some surprises. As you look down from one, you will see an amazing thing. There, on top one of the many warehouses beneath you, is an aerial lawn. It's not quite a penthouse thing with fancy gardening, but more a suburban plot of grass and trees on a roof. I keep imagining unwanted neighbors climbing up the fire escapes, pulling themselves over the edge of the roof, and confronting the owners in their lawn chairs: "Hi, we just moved next door and I wonder if I could borrow your lawn mower?" Or a human fly (you don't hear much about human flies lately; I wonder why) scaling the three stories of brick to an enthusiastic cheering audience below, and being beaten on the head with a garden trowel when he reached the top and forced to retreat by a lady in shorts and sunbonnet. It's a nice place to look down upon.

Russian Hill

RUSSIAN HILL offers many surprises. One of the most popular views in the city is from Russian Hill at Lombard and Hyde, where the cable car takes that nerve-shattering three-block drop down to Bay Street—everybody clinging on for dear life and praying that the brakes hold. Here also begins the descent to the "crookedest street in the world"— the block of Lombard between Hyde and Leavenworth. It's a great place for dramatic cable-car photos—with a gorgeous sweep of the Bay. Try the "crookedest street" once. It demonstrates the inflexible square grid plat the original mappers imposed on the city, come hell or 30-degree grade. Seven tight hairpin curves down a red brick landscaped street that turns your car into a roller coaster: halfway down, you'll wish you hadn't, but the kids think it's thrilling. Another spooky hill is Filbert Street from Hyde to Leavenworth—this scares even the natives to death.

If you have time to explore, Russian Hill is also a great place to walk around. The real estate is extremely expensive, but on the hill, you'll find small homes off cobbled lanes and you'll think you're in the country—or a small village. Macondray Street is the best example, off Leavenworth between Union and Green streets. It has steps instead of sidewalks. Again, a beautiful view is Jones and Vallejo. Going up Vallejo from Leavenworth, you'll find it seems to end at a high wall with two ramps coming down onto Jones. Go up one of the ramps and you'll find that Vallejo continues another half block and really ends in a balustrade at the end of the street with an elegant East Bay view. The homes around and beneath you are handsome indeed. Not many people know of this view, although it's in one of the most populous sections of the city.

Lafayette and Alta Plaza Parks

Pacific Heights is a series of ridges and knolls (perhaps truncated knolls) along the north-central edge of San Francisco from the Presidio to about Van Ness Avenue. The prospects from Pacific Heights are grand and serene. There is little commerce or industry and few grubby shipping wharfs along the waterfront to disturb the foreview. The Bay views from Pacific Heights, with the exception of Crissy Field along the Bay edge of the Presidio and the Marina Yacht Harbor, are almost as pristine as the views of fifty years ago. Broadway, Pacific, Jackson, and Washington streets from Van Ness to Lyon all offer very fine intersection views with the best being at Broadway and Fillmore. We will be visiting these streets when we view the rich in a later chapter, but for now, we will look at two city parks.

It's amazing that either is there at all. Both are fair-sized parks with tennis courts and children's playgrounds, and both occupy prime-view real estate in fashionable neighborhoods. There must have been powerful pressures upon the city fathers to sell the property and realize several millions for the city. Doubtless, also, there were balancing pressures from the residents already in the neighborhood to prevent it.

LAFAYETTE PARK, at Washington and Laguna, has many park benches along the northern side where one may sit beneath the trees and enjoy narrow but pleasant views of the Bay. Here, also, one may look down into the windows of the Spreckels' mansion for a *House and Garden* view of the interior.

ALTA PLAZA PARK, at Scott and Jackson, is also pleasant and offers great Bay views from the tennis courts.

Golden Gate Bridge

There is a complex of sweeping views from the bridge and around it that shouldn't be missed. The walk across the GOLDEN GATE BRIDGE is a thrilling experience in itself. The views are unsurpassed and you understand why bridge builders and workers become so attached to bridges. The Golden Gate Bridge is a living thing. The wind whistles through the cables, the lamp posts vibrate, you can almost feel the give and sway of this tremendous structure as it carries the great weight of the roadway and hundreds of speeding cars, and yourself. Driving on it, you're too busy watching traffic to appreciate it as much more than a convenience. When you're walking on it, though, it inspires a kind of primitive disbelief that this could be constructed by ordinary men— they must have been giants, and you are stirred by a feeling of awe, not pride.

There are also excellent views on either side of the bridge. The first is under it, in the parking lot—park beneath the toll plaza. If you're going out highway 101 toward the bridge, keep in the right lane and watch for the signs as you approach the toll booths. There is a cut-off that will lead you to the view area. This offers a sweeping lateral view of the city and some other interesting features. Here is a statue of the architect of the bridge and a section of the cables from which the span is suspended. You get a look here of the complicated system of girders beneath the roadbed of the bridge. If your timing is lucky, you'll arrive in time to photograph a great passenger ship, such as the *Oriana,* or a large warship as it is passing beneath the bridge. On any weekend, you'll have a chance at beautiful "sailboats on the Bay" photos. The toll plaza restaurant serves snacks, sells souvenirs, and has public rest rooms.

On the Marin County side of the bridge, another view area offers a beautiful look at San Francisco's skyline and a new perspective of Angel Island and Alcatraz.

Presidio

Even nonmilitarists must conclude that the Presidio of San Francisco has been a blessing to the city. The strategic importance of guarding the Golden Gate has kept this north-western tip of San Francisco from being developed, and, thus, largely wild and green. It has to be one of the most beautiful military bases in America. Those of us who were in the army can hardly believe that the Presidio *is* a military base. There's no sprawl, the grounds are carefully landscaped. The enlisted men live in three-story brick barracks reminiscent of private school dormitories. The duplexes up Arguello Boulevard house the noncoms and lower officers who have made the army their career.

The Presidio is one of the oldest continuous military establishments in the country. San Francisco was founded in 1776, the Presidio established two years later, and it has been in operation ever since. It has always been a defensive army camp, not a training camp (that requires more space and a general messing up of the landscape). The fact that it has long been the headquarters of the Sixth Army and the site of a national cemetery and military hospital has also led to permanent construction and careful consideration of changes.

The Presidio and the city have always maintained a curious rapport and interaction unique in America. Some of the greenery of the Presidio was planted by schoolchildren in Arbor Days of long ago. The Presidio has always been (except in wartime) an open army base, and within its limits are two city parks—Bakers Beach State Park and now the Fort Point Historical Monument and museum. There has never been an abrupt city-army separation, such as occurs in so many other city-army situations. Drive through it. The military police office near the Lyons and Lombard streets gate can give you directions to the points of interest. Drive carefully. The MPs are zealous in making sure you follow the speed limits. Again, *never* litter when you're in the Presidio. It's still the Doggies who have to pick up, and they have enough to do as it is.

Lincoln Boulevard in the Presidio follows the crest of the heights from 25th Avenue to Golden Gate Bridge. Two pullouts, one near Pershing, the other near Washington Boulevard, offer superb views of the approach to the Golden Gate and the Marin headlands. To reach Lincoln, take Highway 101 to the bridge, turn right into the toll plaza parking-view area, under the tunnel beneath the highway and straight ahead (do not get back on the highway) to Cranston and Merchant roads (short streets that will take you right to Lincoln). If you're at the Cliff House coming back, turn to your left on 25th Avenue (near the gold-domed Russian cathedral) and follow it to the end and turn right.

Palace of the Legion of Honor

The PALACE OF THE LEGION OF HONOR is one of the many grand gifts to the city by the Spreckels family, let their name be praised. When you see a gift as elegant as this you muse on the shabbiness of spirit that characterizes the rich today. Before, the rich gloried in their richness and endowed the community with beauty and culture. Today the no less rich prefer a low profile in order not to call attention to themselves and have their tax refuges taken away. Avery Brundage has recently given the city the magnificent Center of Asian Art and Culture, but he is certainly a rare bird among so many others with golden feathers.

The Palace of the Legion of Honor is an elegant setting for elegant views. One finds beautiful cityscapes from the balustrade near The Shades in the parking area; Golden Gate and bridge views from the museum lawn near El Cid. There are many, many subsidiary views; bring your camera.

Behind the Legion of Honor there used to be a scenic road, El Camino del Mar, an extension of Lincoln Boulevard in the Presidio and Sea Cliff Avenue. It went through Lincoln Park to Observation Point in the Cliff House area. Recurrent landslides have blocked the road and there is usually a mounted policemen in the area to warn against venturing near the cliffs. You see well-trodden paths going down the hills to Lands End, but don't be tempted to follow them. Lands End is a jutting point of land into some of the most treacherous water of the Golden Gate. Many lives have been casually lost by those who have perched, safely, they thought, above the waves only to be pounded away into the ocean by a chopper (here several wave chains converge, sometimes enforcing each other to create a sudden mountain of water).

Pt. Lobos Observation Point

Off Pt. Lobos Avenue (an extension of Geary Boulevard) near the Cliff House, turn right on El Camino del Mar to Observation Point for sweeping views of the Golden Gate and the Marin headlands, probably the best in the city. That flat-topped round building beneath you in the ocean is a lighthouse. These are treacherous waters at the entrance to the Golden Gate, bad tides, bad currents, often completely shrouded with fog; many ships have foundered here. The lighthouse was built and must have been the most curious Coast Guard duty anywhere. The six men who manned it were as isolated, several thousand yards from this populous city, as if they had been a thousand miles out to sea. Supply

boats visited once a month. The lighthouse is now fully auto-
mated and the flat top is a helicopter landing field for main-
tainance crews. Ten-cents-a-look view-telescopes let you scan
the whole thing.

In the observation area to the west is the command bridge
of the cruiser *USS San Francisco*. From there one gets a fine
view of Seal and Bird Rocks off the Cliff House. The bridge
of the *USS San Francisco* is also the most moving war
memorial I've ever seen—a monument to heroism with no
sweetening, no idealizing.

When you stand on the bridge you see where enemy shells
punched holes in the half-inch steel armor and exploded at
leg level. Not one but twenty-four direct hits. The whole ship
was raked with this kind of fire. We have all seen newsreels
of battles and think that we know something of it, but
the command bridge is no newsreel. You keep gingerly placing
yourself so that you will keep out of the way, but there is no
place to be safe, no place to escape the danger.

Nearby, down the hill at the end of Golden Gate Park, was
another such monument to man's heroism, Roald Amundsen's
ship the Gjøa, a counterpart of the *USS San Francisco*. It's
gone now, taken back to a place of honor in the Oslo Maritime Museum in 1972. On that little-bitty boat, 60 foot long
and 20 foot wide, Amundsen and a crew of six, in a three-year
journey, forced the Northwest Passage in 1906. A similar
journey was not made across the top of the North American
continent until the *Manhattan,* an icebreaker–oil tanker did
it in 1969, with the help of sonar, radar, and helicopters.

San Francisco was lucky to have had the Gjøa as long as
we did, because there are few so eloquent monuments to man's
heroism. The *USS San Francisco* in war, the Gjøa in peace.
Both made you wonder about heroism: what makes heroes?
Both made you realize why ordinary men raise monuments
to valor.

Sutro Heights

The northwest corner of San Francisco is fascinating. The
city meets the open ocean here in a setting that is almost

absurdly dramatic. At the CLIFF HOUSE and the heights above, two-hundred-foot cliffs drop abruptly to level sand beach that is almost five miles long without interruption. And Ocean Beach is all public park land. Directly off the point beneath the Cliff House, Pt. Lobos, are two weatherbeaten islands, Seal Rocks and Bird Rocks (somehow always in the plural). Despite the pollution, surfers, and immediate proximity to a great city, the seals (sea lions really, huge beasts as big in their body as a cow) come back every year to Seal Rocks to hump themselves up on the rocks for sunbathing and honking, and general sea-lion carryings-on. Wild buffalo don't congregate in the outer suburbs of Omaha. Caribou don't traipse through the outskirts of Nome, but huge wild sea mammals still come to pleasure themselves on the rocks a hundred yards off San Francisco.

Of the hundreds of thousands of people who enjoy the view from Cliff House, only a few realize that there is a grander view immediately above them in SUTRO HEIGHTS, a public park. You get to it from a parking lot beneath or turn off Pt. Lobos Avenue to 48th Avenue and Anza. The property used to belong to Adolph Sutro, the ingenious engineer who drove the then impossible tunnel into the Comstock Lode to drain it of water so more millions in silver ore could be gotten out. The gardens of his estate are maintained by the city and, above, you enjoy a grand view of the Pacific and Ocean Beach from the foundations of his mansion. The mansion was destroyed by fire, but the view remains, and is a must for every visitor.

Golden Gate Park

There are two lovely views in GOLDEN GATE PARK that are generally missed by the average tourist—indeed almost unknown even to the residents of the city. The most striking is from the peak of Strawberry Hill in the middle of Stow Lake. It used to be one of the most-visited features of the park.

STRAWBERRY HILL is smack in the eastern-middle of the

park, very near the Music Concourse. (*See* No. 7 on map, page 90.) Stow Lake is still popular, the lake around the base and of the hill is still full of rented canoes, rowboats, and low-powered electric motor boats—and is curious in itself. It's the only in-town, dummy rent-a-rowboat lake I've ever seen that can give you the apprehension that you're getting lost on it, even if you're just going round Strawberry Hill. You don't just row from here to there, you row from home to adventure and thank God you've made it back.

There are two bridges across Stow Lake to the path up Strawberry Hill. One is an ordinary reinforced concrete bridge near the boathouse and the other, along to the north—an extraordinary Victorian rustic bridge, studded with huge boulders and beautiful in its flamboyance—leads directly to the gentle walk up Strawberry Hill.

The view from the top of the hill is delightful, the highest point in Golden Gate Park, but unsettling. In pre-earthquake days a pleasure resort occupied the peak. The windmills along the ocean pumped the water up to the still-existing reservoir, whence it cascaded down a man-made waterfall and supplied the various lakes in Golden Gate Park. On top of the hill, you'll still see a ruined dance pavilion, and an empty decorative pool of generous dimensions.

Everything went kaput in 1906 in the earthquake. The pool cracked, the falls were disrupted, and the pleasure resort never got back into business. It cries for development and refurbishment. With the pool repaired, a funicular up the site of the former falls, a beer garden with strolling musicians, it could be a superb new attraction in the park, repaying any investment in a single summer. It is to be hoped that something is done about it.

HORSE SHOE COURTS. Enter the park from Fulton and Willard or a little above the Conservatory. Here is a good inner-northern view with two pluses. On the side of the hill at the horseshoe courts, you may marvel at a 20-foot-tall reinforced concrete bas-relief of a speckled horse. Nearby is an imaginative children's playground, and, on the walk up the hill, there are great trees for little kids to climb on.

Grand View Park

The most glorious western view in the city is to be found at one of our most secret parks, GRAND VIEW PARK. It's a little tricky to get to and many of the neighborhood residents don't even realize that it is a city park. It has the special attraction of being a geological phenomenon, the highest sand dune in the city. When you learn that it is almost 400 feet above sea level, you have to say that it's quite a sand dune.

The easiest approach is off Lawton at 19th Avenue. Head up the hill to Lomita, to Aloha, to 14th, and go as high as you can. It's not for heart patients·because there must be six flights of steps up from 14th Avenue, and a further sandy climb up from there. Once there, though, you'll see that the climb was worth it, exquisite. This is one of the very finest views in the city and seldom seen by either natives or tourists.

Diamond Heights

DIAMOND HEIGHTS is a series of foothills leading to Twin Peaks to the south. It is good to know of these views because they are very fine, offering a lower perspective of the views seen from Twin Peaks, but like Coit Tower, they are often clear when Twin Peaks is covered with fog.

I offer these views tentatively because building is going on at a furious rate. What may be a nice vista today may be a wall of apartment houses in a year or two.

To reach Diamond Heights go west on Market Street to the intersection of Burnett and Clipper (it's not hard to find: you're at the top of the hill, Twin Peaks is to your right, Diamond Heights to the left). Turn left, then right at the first street, Diamont Heights Boulevard. There are excellent views the first block down the street, Duncan, and up Red Rock. Also, if you follow Diamond Heights down a few blocks to Gold Mine Drive, turn right then left on Ora or Topaz.

You may be curious about the long area of greenery beneath you to the south. This is Glen Canyon Park and looks for all the world like a locale for stagecoach scenes in old Western movies. No cars are permitted in it; novice mountain climbers use the rocks for practice; and the city has an extensive day camp program there during the summer. There is the romantic legend that early smugglers used secret caves in Glen Canyon to hide their booty and some is still hidden there somewhere. It can't be believed because at least fifty thousand kids swarm all over the place each year and if they haven't found anything, nothing's there.

Mt. Davidson

MT. DAVIDSON is our highest point, higher by about 40 feet than Twin Peaks, but is largely ignored by native and tourist alike as a view point. Indeed, except for once a year, the park is used only by people in the neighborhood, mainly because there are no roads to the top; you have to hoof it, and it's a climb.

On Easter Sunday morning, however, crowds do gather and make the walk up to the traditional sunrise services at the base of the cross atop Mt. Davidson. The cross is something special. At 150 feet high, it is the tallest reinforced concrete cross in the Western Hemisphere. It is amazing that so venal a city as San Francisco should boast the biggest cross in the Americas, but facts are facts. The cross does cause some problems in that it presents a challenge to the mountain climbers. Their sense of accomplishment in climbing the sheer face of the cross and sleeping overnight on one of the arms overcomes their fear of a bust for blatant cross-climbing. At least once a year, one sees newspaper photos of climbing nuts hauled down off the cross and they don't look a bit guilty of their sacrilege. I understand that there is a secret fraternity of those who have successfully assaulted the cross. Of course, climbing nuts would attempt an assault on a 150-foot statue of their own mothers if the climb were sufficiently difficult.

Mt. Davidson does offer magnificent southeast and north-east panoramas of the city and Bay—the westward view is largely blocked by dense trees. To get to it, turn off Portola

Drive (Market Street after it goes past Twin Peaks) onto Miraloma (keep in the left lane, you'll see a fire house to the left as you go down the hill) then left to Marne, Juanita, and Dalewood. At either of the entrances, you'll have a hike up the hill, but it's an excellent picnic spot and the views are worth the climb.

John McLaren Park

The second-largest park in the city, JOHN MCLAREN PARK, has long been a kind of stepchild in the Rec and Park situation. Because of lack of funds and political pressure, the park was kept in its natural state until several years ago. There probably was no pressing reason to develop it, as that part of the southeastern section of town was also largely undeveloped until recently. This is the true banana belt of San Francisco. Fig trees and poinsettias grow lushly here. The area was famous for truck farms and greenhouses that generated in 1969 a gross agri-floricultural revenue of some $800,000 within the city limits of San Francisco. That's a lot of vegetable-flower money to be raised in one of the most densely populated cities in America. With rising taxes, though, and pressing need for more housing, most of the greenhouses have been razed to be replaced by homes. The homes mean more kids and so McLaren Park is being developed. It's turning into one of the finest parks in the city.

Roughly bounded by San Bruno Avenue, Visitacion Valley, and the Excelsior districts, it's interesting to visit because of the neighborhoods. Truly international, one of the local savings and loan offices advertises that its tellers speak German, French, Spanish, Italian, Portuguese, and Maltese. In one short stretch on San Bruno, you'll find a bar with the beautiful name Club Firefly, and an Italian bar with a *bocce* ball court. If San Bruno weren't so far out, it could easily become another Union Street.

There are two very fine views in McLaren Park. From the water tower off Shelley Drive or from La Grande and Avalon, one gets a sweeping view of the northeast quadrant of the city;

from Mansell and Visitacion, a grand view of south of the Bay and San Mateo County. McLaren Park is a wonderful place to picnic. The delicatessens in any of the adjoining neighborhoods are as good as any in the city.

Bernal Heights

BERNAL HEIGHTS is right in the middle of the Mission District and offers such unimpeded views of the inner city and Bay that Pacific Telephone put their microwave relay station on top of it. Go straight up Folsom Street to Bernal Heights Avenue. The views are good and, when you get up there, are made even better when you realize that Bernal Heights was the site of the only gold rush inside San Francisco. In the late 1870s a pranking Frenchman announced, "There's gold, *gold in Bernal Heights!*" About a thousand fools went gallumphing out there and began digging holes in people's back yards. At that time, the area was largely rural Irish and the locals didn't know whether to encourage the tearing about or chuck the beggars off for disturbing their gardens and livestock. After a week of high excitement, the gold rush petered out. The Frenchman, it is said, took a short vacation for his health, for those who had been "had" were looking for him with pick handles. Those who weren't caught enjoyed a nice chuckle and "There's gold in Bernal Heights!" was a temporary local catch-phrase indicating exaggeration.

Bay View Park

BAY VIEW PARK, above Candlestick Park, is perhaps the most secret view in the city, and one of the most glorious. On the extreme southeast corner of the city, it rises one to two hundred feet abruptly above Candlestick Point (for which the baseball park was named) and surveys the whole of the East Bay and South Bay. According to the original plans for Candlestick Park, Bay View Park was to be protected, beautified, and enhanced by the contractors. What the bulldozers are doing now is tearing down the sides of the hill to provide fill for more parking space for the ball park. None of the city maps presently available gives the correct approach to the park because it changes every month or so. They haven't touched the park on top, though, and, through neglect and lack of access, it has become one of the most unused parks in the city, still providing the best East Bay view in a sylvan setting that almost seems theatrical, it's so fine.

At this writing, the best approach is off 3rd Street left to Key Avenue and up. If the road isn't there, look around for several blocks on either side. I almost didn't include this view in the book because it is so private that you almost think you own it when you have it all to yourself. I'm afraid, though, that if it isn't publicized, they'll tear down the whole thing for fill and it would be lost to everyone.

3
The Spirit of a City as Revealed through Its Monuments

One of the most charming features of San Francisco, and a mark of any great city, is its wealth of statues and monuments. Curiously, an examination of the monuments of San Francisco, public, commercial and institutional statuary, has never, to my knowledge, been included in any guidebook of the city. I intend to correct this omission for several reasons. Public statuary not only embellishes a city but reveals a great deal about the essence, the spirit, the historic sense of a town, if only in a study of the statues the city suffers to let stand in its public places. Think of what it means to raise a statue. First, there is the person with an idea. The Italian community wants to glorify itself by presenting a monument to the city. Everybody in the Italian community thinks this is a hell of an idea and the money is raised . . . and then come the problems. Who, of all Italians in history, shall be immortalized and set before the world as the essence of the best that is Italian? Some say Garibaldi; some say Dante, Julius Caesar, a Medici, a pope, a saint, a Columbus, a Michelangelo. The interest that the Italian community has in the statue reaches the politicians and they count the Italian vote. Since the Italians are a substantial portion of the voters, the politicians say that nothing is too good and they assign one of the most prestigious statue sites—on the Music Concourse in Golden Gate Park. This logically narrows the selection to Italians of musical genius. After huge and fearsome shouting and infighting, Verdi is chosen. We will not talk about the choosing of the sculptor. What finally emerged was the Roman-like, naked-to-the-collarbone Verdi-Caesar bust being hailed by a combination of naked Dantesque-Michelangelo men raising Garibaldi flags to the genius of Italy!

It takes a huge helping of honest self-esteem to erect a statue to declare to the world, "I believe this sentiment eternal enough to memorialize in a work of art; I think this man great enough to honor with a monument!" Even if the sentiment is sentimental to the nth degree, sticky and/or foolish (e.g., Lilly Coit's firemen in Washington Square) the deep conviction of the person or group commissioning the statue, and the respect by the city of that conviction, often tells more about the city than the listing of its famous sons. Unfortunately, honest self-esteem seems to be waning. In the private sector, one sees no statues of "The Founder" being sculptured any more. The founder, if he is living, is too afraid of stockholder reaction to the expense to bull it through as he would have done in earlier years. And if he is dead, the money which should have gone into a statement of respect for the man who built a business is spent on recognized art masterpieces in order to get the tax benefits, or a committee-decided abstract in order not to offend. A prime example is the Noguchi statue of the huge augury liver in front of the Bank of America building. Dead wrong. Here is one of the tallest buildings west of Chicago, brand-new, built to house the biggest bank in America, and they put a huge liver in front of it. Ridiculous because the Bank of America was built by one man, A. P. Giannini—from nothing, in this century—a hell of an accomplishment. A fitting piece of statuary, if they were going to have *any* piece of statuary in front of this headquarters for the bank, would be a monumental A. P. Giannini, three or four stories high, blessing this California that he helped to build and the piles of dollar bills in his vaults. But they didn't do it. The bank went and got Noguchi to sculpt a liver because if the bank ever went bust, a Noguchi liver would be easier to liquidate than a four-story A. P. Giannini.

This cash-register approach is wrong because it leaves no shining examples for the industry or public; it glorifies things, not men or ideals. And, with few exceptions—notable exceptions to be sure—public statuary has fallen into the same sad condition. Noble sentiments are no longer memorialized except in such abstraction that the sentiment is lost in fuzzy consensus. Notable personages are rarely honored by monuments now unless they are so long dead that they are politically, morally, socially, religiously, and historically safe, without the slightest danger of any controversy to be reflected upon the committee. This is why committees prefer abstract sculpture now. They prefer not to stand the heat that a statue of, say, Harry Bridges or Dr. Fred Schwartz or General Westmoreland would generate. It is much safer to purchase "Formulation of Sunset Mantra Number 5," and inflict it on the public. The criticism will be strictly artistic and with modern art, everybody in the whole world is as valid a critic as anybody else.

The problem with this approach is that a huge amount of fakery and foolishness is foisted upon the public. With abstract sculpture, there is no guarantee that our children will not look at the statue, realize it is awful, and simply throw it away—something that never happens to realistic sculpture; as it ages, it grows more quaint. The second argument against abstract statuary for public monuments is that it is simply dead wrong for public viewing. One must bring too much to it for adequate enjoyment. Public monuments should work the other way around; bringing a positive message to the public first, artistic considerations of secondary importance.

We have two very fine examples of what I'm trying to say that arc very close together on Market Street: the abstract fountain and statue at the Crown Zellerbach Plaza at Market and Battery, and Douglas Tilden's monument *The Mechanics* half a block down the street at Front. Both the huge dancer in the lobby of Crown Zellerbach and the fountain outside are aesthetically pleasing. The dancer, rather bird-faced, seems to soar. The fountain presents a masterly combination of forms, lines, symmetries, and textures. Our minds are led to an appreciation of the construction and welding involved in its fabrication. But at this point, the appreciation ends. We are not instructed.

The Tilden statue, on the other hand, goes far beyond this beginning. We also admire the form, juxtaposition of the dynamic lines of the six seminude mechanics with the static lines of the machine—a huge punch. The male figures, ranging from youth through old age, are excellently sculptured. But as we look at this monument, we are confronted with what it depicts and are forced to contemplate its message. Close examination reveals this naked old beggar directing a passel of simpletons who are furiously endeavoring to punch a monumentally useless hole in a piece of metal which can have utterly no application in the construction of any device known to man—except possibly the erection of a short, oddly-shaped metal gate with a hole in it. The manner in which the mechanics are operating the punch shows that *nobody,* including the old man, has a prayer of an idea of what the hell he is doing or how he should do it. We learn a great deal from this monument. One, that gray hairs do not wisdom make. Again, that as long as there is somebody around to give foolish orders, there will always be damn fools to follow them. We are instructed by this monument while merely titillated by abstracts. With that out of the way, let us look at the statuary of San Francisco.

James Lick Memorial

The most elaborate statuary group in the city is the JAMES LICK MEMORIAL at the corner of Market and Hyde streets near the CIVIC CENTER. This monument is interesting not only for the reasons mentioned in Chapter 1 but for its sheer artistic exuberance. This single monument exhibits ten life- or over-life-sized figures, four low-relief portraits as medallions, and four high-relief insets in the central column, as well as other embellishments. It is an amazing exhibition of a single sculptor's virtuosity and speaks worlds for a classic art education. Frank Happersberger showed himself such a master of every sculpture technique and such a superb artist that this crowd of statues, symbols, and sculptured ornaments fitted together perfectly to make a beautiful and dignified monument to the pride men felt for California and in being early Californians. It is a lusty statement and a delight to the eyes. But on to the monument.

Rising from a two-tiered central column is the heroic figure of California with her shield and beribboned spear, the California bear at her knees. She stands so sternly noble that she is, unfortunately, almost a caricature of Nobility. This is too bad because, as often as not, there is a seagull perched smack on her head. As you know, there is probably no more proudly standing bird than the seagull, which makes for an uncomfortable clashing of nobilities, like two Napoleons in the same asylum.

California stands noble guard above four piers which project from the base of the column. On two opposite piers are two more ladies, both seated. The lady on the pier labeled "In '49" is seated upon a stylized boat and represents the goldseekers who came by ship. The other lady exhibits a cornucopia which symbolizes "Seated Abundance," I imagine, or perhaps, "Fruitful Earth." All the ladies, standing or seated, are plush, saftig,* full-bodied women and a pleasure to look at.

The most interesting part of the monument are the two tableaux on the remaining piers. The one facing Market Street shows three miners panning gold; its opposite member, labeled "Early Days," shows a *vaquero*, a priest, and an Indian. The reason they are so interesting is that they are so dead right. The Early Days tableau shows a *vaquero*, saddle at his feet, handling a wire rope. That man is not out of the cowboy movies. He is a tough, fierce, hell-raising man, you can tell by looking at him that he spent his year's wages in one wild fling on whores and whisky. He would leave cow punching in a minute to join a filibuster or a raiding party on a Protestant wagon train. The hooded priest is as crazy-eyed a figure as has ever been sculptured—probably the finest re-

---

Saftig in German means merely "juicy" but when it is applied to women it means something more.

ligious fanatic ever done in bronze. There is that mild mouth under those spooky eyes that perfectly depict that breed so lashed by God that they would walk through hell itself to baptize a heathen—and, if he didn't want to be baptized, to burn him as a good example. The Indian, to be nitpicking, strikes the only wrong note in the whole complex. He should be a California Indian, but he is obviously a Plains Indian with breech clout, and braided hair with two eagle feathers. The California Indians were much different. They went around bare-bummed and wore peculiar hair styles: sometimes they shaved half their heads, either front to back or side to side or sported big bushes or top knots, and, in the main, they used baskets for headgear. This is a minor point, for Happersberger depicts the Indian perfectly as most of them must have felt at that time. He lies at the priest's feet in a bemused, "What have I done to deserve this?" attitude. His face shows that he is as overwhelmed as the man who gives a thirsty stranger a drink of water and suddenly finds that he has bought a set of encyclopedias and is already one payment late.

The tableau of the three miners working a claim is equally remarkable. Nothing has been done to prettify the men. They have been grubbing for gold and that is dirty work. Their faces, though, are extremely arresting. They are gazing at the nuggets in the pan with the rapt devotion usually seen on the faces of heroes in the last few moments of movie extravaganzas—where they seem to glow with an inner light and say, "This land is good land and here we will build our nation." These miners have that sort of glow, but they are glowing with the inner illumination of the sudden acquisition of money. It is a rare statue that is devoted without apology to the honest statement, "Lord, ain't it *fine* to be rich!"

The other features of the monument are well worth considering, both to admire Happersberger's skill and to see what was considered important enough to memorialize. The four high-relief insets on the central column depict fairly complicated scenes of a covered wagon with men working to raise an ox that fell; a scene showing the wealth of California—

shipping, agricultural, et cetera; a scene of the early *vaqueros* punching cattle; and a scene depicting trading with the Indians (again, the Indians are Plains type). Happersberger is very good with high relief; the depth is fantastic—it's like looking into a fancy Easter egg. His low-relief portrait-medallions are more interesting for whom they portray than for the portraits themselves. Sutter, Father Junipero Serra, Sir Francis Drake, and General Fremont were felt worthy of the honor, with James Lick himself shown as the most honored of them all—his medallion is wreathed and occupies the place of honor facing Market Street.

Most of those honored rightly deserve their place there. Sir Francis Drake touched land a few miles north of here in the sixteenth century, Father Junipera Serra founded the Mission Dolores in town, General Fremont fomented the Bear Star Rebellion in Sonoma and liberated California for a while, and gold was discovered at Sutter's mill. James Lick, though, was another matter. He was certainly not historically important, as the others were—he was no innovator or shaker and mover in the state. But he did make piles and piles of money and donated a large amount of it to the city and the state. This monument, for example was built with $100,000 of his money and the Francis Scott Key memorial in Golden Gate Park with $60,000 more. The Conservatory in the Park was another of his gifts, as was Lick Observatory on Mt. Hamilton. On this monument, Lick's name is slightly larger than those of the others and equals in size the name of the city. But why this man was so honored is a very fine example of what was highly and honestly regarded; an early Californian who made huge amounts of money and gave it to the city and state.

It is interesting also that he is listed with the very great and legendary, while those who more fittingly could be described as founders of California—the explorers and developers of the state—were given honor only by inscriptions around the main column. These are Larkin, Cabrillo, Portola, Sloat, Marshall, Vallejo, Castro, and Commander Stockton. All in all, it is a very fine monument and well worth viewing.

Stock Exchange Statues

Ralph Stackpole's massive statuary groups flanking the steps of the PACIFIC COAST STOCK EXCHANGE at Pine and Sansome streets is of great interest for many reasons. It was completed in 1932 and is one of the very few examples of the social-realism school of art to survive the prosperity of the workers. Most of the art work of the Depression, pictorial as well as sculpture, has not stood the test of time. They were so mannered, so propagandizing, that when victory for the worker came, they were left far behind. The art still preaches that it is well to die for the ten-hour day to the worker whose concern today lies more in the direction of whether to spend his three-week vacation at his cabin on Russian River or go to Hawaii. When the message is delivered, the sculpture or painting becomes mere historical curiosity. We can see this in San Francisco in a few places. The apartment house across from the Shadows Restaurant on upper Montgomery Street is decorated in the most chi-chi 1920s style. It was undoubtedly the cat's pajamas then. The ultra-modern abstract mosaic on the Medical-Dental building on Sacramento at about Buchanan will probably be stuccoed over in a few years when the owners uncomfortably find that though it is "modern" it is ugly.

There are many homes in San Francisco that proudly display Andy Warhol Brillo boxes and paintings of soup cans. It is interesting to contemplate the fate of these works of art. I mean, hell, you just can't throw away something that cost in excess of one thousand dollars, even if it is, when you get right down to it, a representation of a box of Brillo pads or a painting of a can of soup. I predict that in the near future, our museums will be stuffed with these works of art donated by high-minded and civic-oriented art patrons who prefer to share their treasures with the world (and take the tax deduction) than selfishly to keep these wonders hidden in their homes.

Ralph Stackpole's statuary groups, though, still hold up. They are massive and wonderful. The two groups, women on the left, men on the right, stand proudly, forcing the attention of the stock brokers and passers-by. The women represent "Earth's Fruitfulness," the men, "Man's Inventive Genius." The groups are commanding. It's not a piece of art that makes you melt with the sheer beauty of it; it is raw power that grabs you.

But when you simmer down, you see the zinger of the group, a detail that tickles you to death and makes you want to show it to all your friends. There, at the portals of the building in which the most blatant kind of capitalism is practiced, is the sturdy little boy with his fist raised and clenched in the Communist salute!

I don't know if Stackpole's sketches of the completed group included this detail when he submitted his bid for the work. I hope it wasn't because it gives rise to all sorts of delightful imaginings. I can see the Embellishment Committee fretting themselves to death about it after the unveiling.

"What in Christ's name are we going to do about it?"

"Tear it down! And immediately!"

"Think, man, the goddamn thing weighs thirteen tons!"

Well then, chip off the arm—or make it hold a flower or a wrench—any damn thing!"

"Can't do it. Checked with our appraiser. Said we bought it at thirty-five in the works, now worth fifty completed and chipping off an arm will drive it down to seventeen."

"I got it!" says one of the younger members. "Don't chip off the arm. Take the clenched fist and alter the first three fingers so that he is no longer a Commie, but he is giving the Boy Scout Salute!"

Tumult and exclamation until one of the older and wiser heads says gravely, "What would a Boy Scout be doing gracing the entrance of the Stock Exchange? They're supposed to be trustworthy, loyal, thrifty, clean, reverent, and so on and so on. I think, gentlemen, that that kind of thinking would be hugely more detrimental than leaving the little Commie sonofabitch where he is. I've found in my long experience that it's much better to spite a statue than make excuses for not living up to it."

A Communist salute greets all those rampant capitalists every blessed morning. Amazing.

It might be mentioned that the rich of the Depression were in a peculiar bind because of this kind of sabotage by Depression artists. Most of the great artists were flaming revolutionaries—usually Communists, such as Diego Rivera and Pablo Picasso. But they were also recognized masters whose works were perfect investments—much better than blue-chip stocks, even better than gold in that they grew in value with every passing year. The problem was that the artists played dirty. Rivera was especially troublesome. Just as the Rockefellers in New York have a screened-off Rivera because he incorporated a portrait of Lenin in the piece, so SF has a secret Diego Rivera in the inner sanctum of the Brokers Club in the Stock Exchange. The work, a mural, portrays Rivera painting a mural, a self-portrait of his back being part of the composition. It must be uncomfortable for the men whose lives revolve around the premise that money *buys* to have the Stackpole statuary and the Rivera mural as constant reminders that a few people are more powerful than money—and not only that, but they flaunt it at you.

Hidalgo and De Anza

Although the statues of Hidalgo and De Anza are not in close proximity—are separated by about a mile—they will both be considered together here because of their many similarities. They are two of the most recent pieces of monumental public statuary in the city, the Hildago erected in 1962 and the De Anza in 1967. Both are worth going out of your way to see.

Juan F. Olaguibel's magnificent MIGUEL HIDALGO Y CASTILLA dominates MISSION PARK. A gift from San Francisco's Spanish-American community, Mexico's "Father of Independence" is presented in a kind of softened social-realism style. By this I mean that the statue is not overwhelmed with propaganda. Hidalgo is a superhero, but still a man, and not a god. The statue, in its sweeping robes (Hidalgo was a priest), is the epitome of dignity, pride, and strength, an excellent example to those who would sculpture a monument to a notable personage. The only problem with the statue (it is probably one of the most "unknown" major statues in the city), is its position high above the main part of the park. The only way to reach it, if you don't want to climb the equivalent of five stories up from Dolores Street, is from Church Street at about 19th Street; cross the bridge over the streetcar tracks. It's impossible to find a parking place up there. Once you reach the statue, though, you'll find it in a pleasant recreation area given to sedentary pursuits such as benches and card tables. Since it's usually sunny, you'll find that it's a very nice place to sit and relax, with a sweeping view of the green lawns of the park, the trees, the rooftops of the Inner Mission, the palms of Dolores Street. It's an especially nice place to drink beer.

Julian Martinez's equestrian CAPTAIN JUAN BAUTISTA DE ANZA near the Ferry Building in the EMBARCADERO PARK was a gift from the state of Sonora, Mexico, to San Francisco in 1967. The statue itself is a little disturbing. At a distance, everything seems in order, but the closer you get to the monument, the more you feel that something's wrong.

De Anza, in later Conquistador costume under a huge slouch hat, is astride a gigantic horse—it must be an early combination of Arabian-Percheron or Arabian-Clydesdale. His face is fierce and brooding and uncompromising. When you look at the face, you're positive that today he would be locked up in an instant. There is a man that you don't mess with. The problem, though, is that his legs are too short. His trunk is at least as long as his legs. It could very well be that he was built that way, but it transforms the whole aspect of the monument and makes you uncomfortable.

But flawed or not, the De Anza is a curious and historic monument in several ways. For one thing, it is probably the only *equestrian* monument erected in the United States (as far as that goes, in the whole world) in the last thirty years, at least the last twenty years, most certainly the last ten years. People no longer ride horses for any serious purpose and the lack of a horse is a great loss to sculptors. For, when you think of it, a man can be depicted only seated, standing, or in action. In sitting, there comes an impasse if there is no horse about. There are only three things a man can be shown to be sitting upon: a chair, a rock, or a horse. Man's most usual seat, in an automobile, can't be used because cars are dreadfully hard to sculpt and they keep changing the models on you. Airplanes are simply out of the question.

The horse has always been one of the most useful of statuary adjuncts. It is very fine to see that San Francisco has a new equestrian monument even if it isn't perfect.*

The Hidalgo and De Anza statues have an immediate classical and historic significance in that both are probably the dying flicker of the ancient and honorable practice of donating statues to the city by an interested group.

Statues at Washington Square Park

The two monuments in WASHINGTON SQUARE PARK at Columbus and Union are worthy of examination because both have messages for us. The "FIREMAN SAVE MY CHILD" tableau by Haig Patigian depicts three firemen in furious action. One mans a hose; one, clearly a hero, holds a little girl rescued from a certain fiery death; and the leader, shouting through his trumpet, directs unseen others in fighting what certainly must be a conflagration equal to the burning of Chicago. I would have said, "burning of San Francisco," but all the men are in period dress of the volunteer fire brigades who served the city before regular fire service was offered in 1865. The only discrepancy in precise portrayal is that the hoses depicted are smooth, not the rivited buffalo-hide hoses used in those days (as seen in the Pioneer Fire Museum). It has to be the schmaltziest of sentimental sculptures and what makes it interesting is that it was erected not in

---

*The author realizes that the motorcycle as a logical modern substitution for the horse has not been touched. This is a deliberate omission. Certainly the motorcycle has animation, power and grace, just like a horse. The problem is that a motorcycle simply doesn't have class. One can sculpt any jerk and put him on a horse and he is ennobled. But even if you sculpt the most noble of men, say George Washington, and put him on a motorcycle—well, the result is bound to be unfortunate.

the 1800s, as one would expect, but in 1933 in the depths of the Depression. Of course, it was built through a bequest of Lilly Hitchcock Coit, a favorite of the city, but it is indicative of San Francisco's love for its past that such a sentimental piece of statuary was permitted to stand at the same time William Randolph Hearst was roundly damned for spending money in Europe to buy up antiques cheaply. In any other city, it would have been torn down by angry, unemployed workers and sold for its scrap value.

BENJAMIN FRANKLIN. In this work of art, also found in Washington Square Park, Franklin is portrayed a little over life-sized on a pedestal shaped like an old-fashioned mailbox. The base of the pedestal is fascinating for it combines not only arrant fraud but one of the most mordant inscriptions to be found on any monument in the world. At the base of three of the four sides of the pedestal are inscribed pavingstones that bid "welcome" to those who would refresh themselves from the drinking fountains that used to be on the sides of the pedestal. The taps of the fountains are labeled Congress, Vichy, and California Seltzer, but the only water that ever flowed from those taps came from the single pipe leading from the water main on Columbus Street—a blatant piece of fraudulence. The inscription on the statue reads:

> Presented by H. D. Cogswell to our boys and girls who will soon take our places and pass on.

I have seen no single sentence in my life so perfectly designed to make one feel miserable. It is guaranteed to ruin even the most perfect day and make you feel out of sorts and moldy for the next few following. The only thing that saves the reader will be the information given in the San Francisco Art Commission's report on local art works. One learns that Cogswell, a dentist made good, eccentric and a temperance nut, built fountains all over the United States, many carrying his likeness. The report says, "All but this were destroyed by public acclamation." It is hard to feel spite for an obscure and long-dead dentist, especially one who was also a statue-builder, but this knowledge makes me feel warm and happy in my stomach. He must have made multitudes unhappy by his wowserisms and it is a pleasure to see that his only remaining work is in the single city immune to his kind of moral foolishness.

Across the street from Washington Square is a little island of greenery at Union and Columbus. This is Frank Marini Square and offers two pieces of sculpture that deserve attention. The first is the fountain of the bearded man who is supposed to be drinking. This bearded man, a handsome statue in itself, is vomiting water into his cupped hands, whence it flows to a pretty little pool.

The other piece of sculpture in the park is a bust of Frank Marini. Though not particularly distinctive, it is an honest bust showing an Italian businessman with a mustache wearing the wide-lapeled suit of the 1920s. It would be a typical bust of any prominent man except for the single word beneath his name and date. It reads "Benefactor." There are few one-word epitaphs so arresting; words that convey so much love and esteem. When you think of it, there are few one-word pejoratives that carry so much power, that epitomize a man so completely. When reading the inscription, "Benefactor," one feels a great regret at not having had the opportunity of knowing Frank Marini—much more regret than from an inscription listing a man's mighty deeds and high offices.

Seamen's Memorial

Two of the finest portrait busts in the city are in front of the SEAMEN's UNION of the Pacific headquarters at the corner of Harrison and First streets. The busts of Andrew Furuseth and Harry Lundeberg are special because they are monumental in impact. The only other modern portrait bust in the city that stops you cold, as these do, is the bust of Angelo Rossi in City Hall, and this is perhaps a good place to pause to examine just why.

These are not like the usual City Hall likeness in which the sculptor reads so much dignity, respect and high ideals into the image that the person depicted is left far behind. Angelo

Rossi is smiling, one of the few smiling portrait busts extant, and, like his, the Lundeberg and Furuseth busts are uncompromisingly human. Lundeberg is shown as the commonest of common men, a broad-faced worker wearing a flat cloth cap. Though he is pleasant-faced, you can see that he was hard as nails. (The union still places wreaths before the bust on the anniversaries of his birth and death.) Furuseth's bust shows a sour, thin-faced, mean-mouthed, frowning, worn, bitter man. There is no attempt to soften or idealize his features. His bust has such power that you almost feel sorry for the ship-owners who had to deal with him.

The inscription on Furuseth's bust reads:

You can put me in jail, but you cannot give me narrower quarters than as a seaman I have always had. You cannot give me coarser food than I have always eaten, you cannot make me lonelier than I have always been.
Emancipator of Seamen. Erected 1941.

The pedestal (by the way, both busts are perfectly pedestaled) is so weathered now that the inscription is almost illegible. This strikes me as strange and sad. The pedestal is of slabbed black and white granite and was erected only thirty years ago. San Francisco weather is hard on stone, but it is a shoddy stone for union members to erect for a man who spent his life bettering working conditions for seamen.

Shriners Hospital Fountain

The SHRINERS HOSPITAL FOR CRIPPLED CHILDREN at 19th and Moraga is a Good Work in capital letters. But while the Shriners Hospital graces our city, the statue in the fountain gracing its front lawn is runner-up for the worst piece of statuary in the city. All the elements of what should be in front of a children's hospital are there. It's a fountain, for one thing, and there are statues of little boys and girls and squirrels and bears. The problem with the porcelain figures is that the sculptor didn't know how to do children and had no conception of what to do with water after he had the figures. So here we have six squirming and enormously evil kids. The boys have the faces of hoodlums and are so well endowed genitally that it is shame and affront to ordinary citizens; the little girls are as curvacious and seductively posed as any flock of Delacroix odalisques—all are cavorting under thin but powerful squirts of water, which one should avoid at all cost in connection with sculptured little children. Even the squirrels and bears look evil. I have a feeling that the reason the Shriners let the fountain stay and did not denounce it to the vice squad is the old "emperor's new clothes" syndrome. They had to accept it and keep it because it was already built and paid for.

First to the Front

Douglas Tilden's wonderful statuary group at Dolores and Market streets is an excellent example of how a heroic statuary complex should be built. This monument commemorates the little known fact that the Volunteers of California were the first Americans to engage the enemy in the Spanish-American War. Long before Theodore Roosevelt and his lot were fighting in Cuba, Californians were fighting with the Spanish in the Philippines. That seems curious because Cuba is only 90 miles from Florida while the Philippines are thousands of miles across the Pacific.

The monument depicts one hero fallen, one raging, both led by a ferocious woman on a winged horse—either the Spirit of Victory, the Spirit of War, the Spirit of an Aroused America, or perhaps the Spirit of William Randolph Hearst Vindicated. The lines of the statues are in perfect balance, every sword, wing, muscle, flying drapery emphasizing an unshakable and heroic will to win or die. The perfection of the statue in expressing this ideal can be felt in the timelessness of the monument. This monument might apply equally to any war ever fought from the Revolution to

Prohibition and for either side—which indicates exemplary efficiency in monument building. One little-known fact that ties this monument to that particular war is that the Spirit's sword lies on the exact compass bearing from the intersection of Dolores and Market streets to the geographical center of the Philippine Archipelago.

The primary importance of this statuary complex, though, lies in the lesson of how a statue can enhance a neighborhood. Dolores Street is a very curious street indeed. Being the only boulevard in the city graced with towering palms, the most venerable building in town, and the lush green of Mission Park, it in all rights should be one of the grandest streets in the city. But it is not at all grand. The whole street, from Market to Mission, is built edge to edge with mean buildings —two-story flats, five- to six-unit apartment houses. There is not one handsome private residence on the whole street, although there are on the adjacent streets of Guerrero, Valencia, Fair Oaks. The only feature that saves Dolores Street from being as characterless as the Marina district or the Sunset is "First to the Front." You get a shot of grandness that carries you past all the banality right to the history of Mission Dolores, where that occupies your mind. You are sort of bounced over the dumbness of the street by that first exhilaration of the monument. Developers of dreary tracts could do much to ease the criticism by erecting monumental statuary groups about every six blocks. Classical approaches are best because they offer no handholds for criticism and give no offense (as is seen in Forest Lawn Cemetery). Abstract is safe as aces if it is big enough because everybody knows that no one would put money in six or seven tons of material if it weren't worth it. Contemporary scenes could be handled just as well and inoffensively if they were vague enough. On an island between the four lanes of highway entering Crestview Knolls could be a statue depicting an imaginary debate between Richard Nixon and George McGovern. Both could be shown triumphant, but both with shoulders slumped enough to show either that the other had made a telling point or they were bowed with the burden of championing their causes. Look at how *First to the Front* has lifted Dolores Street. The area is one thousand times more embellished than if it were not at the intersection of Dolores and Market.

Lotta's Fountain

Geary, Kearny and Market streets. In any guide to San Francisco, LOTTA'S FOUNTAIN must be noted because, even if it is one of the least beautiful articles of street furniture to be found anywhere, it is of great historic, romantic, and philosophical interest. The "fountain" consists of four drinking fountains at the base of an ugly cast-iron pillar. Usually, none of the drinking fountains work, or one works too well and leaks all over the intersection. It was given to the city in 1875 by Lotta Crabtree, an extremely popular singer-entertainer, who, even more than Lola Montez, was the darling of the city. In the early Gold Rush days, she performed in the Sierra mining camps when "entertainment" meant mostly whores, gambling, and booze. She brought a great deal more and was amply rewarded in money and popularity.

Affixed to the fountain is a plaque stating that Louisa Tetrazzini sang nearby in 1910. Now, Tetrazzini was an operatic diva, not a music-hall entertainer, but she got her start in San Francisco and on a memorable Christmas Eve in 1910, she gave a free concert to a multitude of admirers at about Third and Market; thus the plaque on Lotta's Fountain. What's philosophically interesting and typically San Franciscan is that the opera singer didn't object to having the commemorative plaque attached to a fountain donated by a popular singer.

Victory

Union Square, by R. I. Aitken. THE DEWEY MEMORIAL. The lady standing on her toe, holding a victory wreath atop an eight-story pillar in Union Square, is a tribute to the gallant men who won the Spanish-American War. Although Teddy Roosevelt and his Rough Riders glommed most of the glory in that war when they invaded Cuba, it was the valiant naval forces of Admiral Dewey and the California volunteers who conquered the Philippines. The relative worth of the two assaults may be seen in the fact that Cuba doesn't give a damn about us, and some in the Philippines want it to become our fifty-first state. President McKinley broke the ground for this monument, and Theodore Roosevelt dedicated it.

It was in Union Square in the fall of 1972 that Joan Sutherland, prepetuating a tradition spontaneously started by Tetrazzini in 1910, sang to a rapturous audience of five thousand to mark the opening of the fiftieth anniversary season of the San Francisco Opera.

St. Anne of the Sunset Church Sculpture

St. Anne of the Sunset Church. 850 Judah Street (on the streetcar line at Funston and Judah). Here is one of the most ambitious statuary groups in the city. It's 100 feet long and 4 feet high and depicts the establishment of the Church of Christ prefigured by the children of Israel. Designed and cast by Sister Mary Justina, it presents at least 107 major high-relief figures including men, women, children, camels and donkeys in a great frieze across the entire front of the church, and many minor figures. It is not a great sculptural work, because all the faces, whether of men, women, or angels, are the same. It's sort of cookie-cutter art, but the sheer sizc of the thing makes it impressive.

Sun Yat-sen

St. Mary's Square on California Street off Grant, downhill, to the right. Until recently, the Chinese community in San Francisco has been one hundred percent pro-Chiang Kai-shek and the Republic of China. It was in San Francisco that Sun

Yat-sen and fellow revolutionaries planned the overthrow of the Manchu Dynasty of China. Bufano's twelve-foot stainless-steel and rose-granite statue of SUN YAT-SEN shows the reverence for that man in this city. Serene and strong, the statue is a great one, as the man was. It's interesting to note that Bufano's use of stainless steel here was the first ever attempted in a major sculpture.

Civic Center Monuments

As if not to distract from the glory that is our City Hall, there are few statues around it, none inside (busts excluded).

On the McAllister Street side of City Hall (directly opposite the Society of California Pioneers Museum) is R. I. Aitken's standing HALL MCALLISTER. Erected in 1904, it perhaps typifies all the honored statesmen statues through the length and breadth of the land. Rather obscure, spattered by pigeons and stained by time, the statute of Hall McAllister, a regional, not a national statesman, is only an ornament. Around the corner to the left of the entrance on Polk Street is Haig Patigian's SEATED LINCOLN—copied from the better one in Washington, D.C.'s Lincoln Memorial. This is a little more significant in that the subscription for the statue derived from the pennies of schoolchildren. The statue was raised in 1927. This is part of the lost "good old days," remembered by our elders. Community, grass-roots efforts like this were common then.

The rise of charity as big business, among other things, killed that spirit and lessened community effort. The deduction of your "fair share" from your pay check is a cold-hearted operation and breeds cynicism—you wonder how much of your one dollar a week (after bookkeeping expenses, head bookkeeping expenses, area coordinator, regional disperser, advertising, and other expenses) finally trickles down to buy a warm overcoat for a cold, poor child.

Immediately within the entrance of City Hall are two Haig Patigian busts of former MAYORS PHELAN AND ROLPH. Both are severe, Roman senator, lifeless things—from looking at

Rolph's bust, for example, you'd never realize his nickname was "Sunny Jim." A little farther into the foyer, though, is the most charming bust in the city. It is of ANGELO ROSSI by R. Cravath. (She signed it R. Cravath to conceal the fact that she was a woman—shades of Malvina Hoffman!) Angelo Rossi was one of the most beloved of San Francisco mayors, a jaunty, honest, smiling man who sported a carnation in his buttonhole—a trademark. There is a street and a municipal park named for him. Cravath depicts him as he was. One of the few smiling portrait busts of politicians in the world, it is a jewel.

This leads you into City Hall. You can't experience our City Hall without bursting into superlatives. The architects were Arthur Brown, Jr., and John Bakewell, Jr.; it is a monument in itself. What I remember is the House Un-American Activities Committee hearings here in the middle '60s. The hearing rooms were packed with pro-Committee ticket-holders and there were thousands outside trying to get in. The grand marble staircase was stormed by the anti-Committee people and they were washed down the steps by firehoses. The rotunda was full of screams and invective and the stormers bounced down the steps on their butts, pushed by streams of water. It was an outrage, but what a gracious staircase to be pushed down by streams from firehoses!

There's a grandness about City Hall, a magnificence, from the great dome, which, by design, soars higher than the Capitol dome in Washington, to the careful attention to the gilt work outside on the fences and lamps. The crazy thing about it is that it is a working building, housing the Assessor, Civil Service, Superior Courts, Registrar of Voters, Mayor's office, and all the rest. I doubt if there is a finer public building in all America.

Across the street, in the Veterans Memorial Building (where the two most incongruous civic entities imaginable, the American Legion and the San Francisco Museum of Art, are housed), is one of the most beautiful statues in the city. In the lobby is a copy of Houdon's GEORGE WASHINGTON. Jean-Antoine Houdon sculpted Washington from life. This statue, donated by the Daughters of the American Revolution, had to be approved by the Virginia Assembly before the copy of the original (which stands in the Statehouse at Richmond) could be cast. It's a unique piece and San Francisco is lucky to have at least three such reproductions. The Houdon *Washington* is one: the bust of *Shakespeare* graces our Shakespeare Garden in Golden Gate Park, and Rodin's *The Thinker* at the Palace of the Legion of Honor was one of five in the world cast from the original mold.

Commercial Art

The history of the business approach to fine art is easy to see in San Francisco. When the new office buildings went up after the quake-fire of 1906, the old tradition prevailed. Private companies embellished their office buildings and factories to show pride in the firm. There were fancy cornices, fine brickwork, inlays, and appropriate pieces of sculpture. The capital going into the building was a visual affirmation of the firm's economic strength. With the rise of the mega-corporation, the conglomerate, the sudden discovery of efficiency, these embellishments were re-examined and discarded as needless frills, a waste of utilizable space. There was a long spell in which glass boxes were built without grace, charm, art, or morals.

Two things stopped this rush to utilize without conscience every inch of prime space. First and greatest was the public reaction against the boxes. A statement of former governor Pat Brown (sane in nearly every other way), reflected the feelings of the big guys when he said of the Embarcadero Freeway, "It's beautiful!" The mayor thought the same, but they were so ridiculed in the papers and on the street that grass-roots pressure stopped the freeway building and instituted a very tough zoning ordinance outlining the space a building could occupy on a given lot. Public muscle exposed, the builders went out of their way not to induce any more bad publicity and subsequent restrictive limitations.

Then there was the sudden aesthetic re-evaluation of fine art by the builders. In the early '60s, a Rembrandt was selling for one million bucks, a Van Gogh for two hundred thousand. The value of a painting, mural, statue was what are critics said it was—art being a commodity the purchaser couldn't check in any other market. Big business embraced the arts with a vengeance: there have been more company-bought major sculptures available to the general public in the last ten years than there were in the previous twenty. And the list is growing. There is a difference in the *new* company art and the *old*. The old company art was incorporated into the structure of the buildings, the new is more or less portable.

The good commissioned sculptural decorations on commercial buildings can be seen in a short walk down Sansome and Montgomery streets between Bush and California. A lot of money was spent in decorating the façades. The two best examples of old-time pride in building, though, are seen in the following.

THE OLD KOHLENBERG CADILLAC BUILDING, 1000 Van Ness Avenue (Van Ness and O'Farrell). Now the San Francisco Lincoln Mercury agency, the whole building is one of the most exuberant commercial buildings in town (the second must be across and down the street a block at the Chrysler and Imperial agency). It, and the other down the street, are so outrageously elegant that it makes you feel good just to look at them—like the old-time movie palaces. They certainly displayed pride in the product they were pushing (Kohlenberg had a discreet sign in the main display room that led to the "Salon of Previously Owned Cadillacs"). Atop the marquee above the entrance are two sculptures done by the same Jo Mora who did the exquisite *Cervantes* in Golden Gate Park. These are two heroic figures, one representing Industry and the other Transportation. I must say that they aren't as captivating as Mora's other work, indeed they are the most languid, uninterested male sculptures around. Beneath, though, are two pedestals upon which are perched *Smiling Bears*. They are delightful—the best bears outside the Zoo. Although the Kohlenberg statues aren't masterpieces, it is an indication of how things were in the '20s when even automobile sellers commissioned major sculptors to embellish their buildings.

SOURCES OF POWER, by Robert B. Howard. Pacific Gas and Electric Substation, 8th and Mission. As a public utility, the Pacific Gas and Electric Company has done more to beautify utilitarian buildings than most commercial firms. Of course, to a degree, they must. An electric substation must be built as a fortress against dust and dirt that could foul the complicated switching works—and to keep people from wandering in and electrocuting themselves. The buildings are necessarily blockhouses. PG&E has done a lot to beautify the buildings, though. The smaller ones resemble fine mausoleums—discreet, clean, and unobtrusive. The substation at 8th & Mission is three stories high. In front of the building are black granite pillars for lighting the façade and on the façade itself are two huge bas-reliefs, also in black granite, by Robert B. Howard. They represent the sources of power, one above ground, one below ground, and although the symbolism might be a little heavy, the bas-reliefs aren't. It is growing more and more unusual to see major bas-reliefs incorporated into the architecture of a building. These are worth viewing.

The New Wave. A new complex of office buildings, apartment houses, and town houses arose on the redeveloped rubble of the old produce area (to the Embarcadero side of the financial district). This is part of the striking change in San Francisco's skyline between the middle '50s and now. EMBARCADERO CENTER and MARITIME PLAZA were carved out of this area and with the new buildings came new and excellent art. The best place to start is at Battery and Sacramento streets at Maritime Plaza. Walk into the building and you are confronted by two huge stainless steel forms in the middle of a pool, by Michael Bigger. On your way in, you'll see two sheet-iron works by Willi Guttman. Walk up the stairs and over the bridge across Clay Street, and you're in a large garden of sculpture, each to its own little corner, the Golden Gateway Center Collection of Fine Art. First from the bridge is a kind of involuted bronze geodesic dome entitled *Icosaspirale*, by Charles Perry. Nearby is *Standing Figure Edged*, by Henry Moore. At the time of my visit, eighteen works by Bufano were bunched, unpedestalled, waiting for exhibit. *Bronze Horse* by Marino Marini is toward the Alcoa

Building and to the left. Directly before the building is the famous fountain by the Australian sculptor Robert Woodward. It looks for all the world like a dandelion blossom gone to seed and just ready to puff for a wish. There are benches and quiet corners everywhere here. It is a perfect place to eat a peaceful brown-bag lunch (as do the office workers). It is also one of the few places, outside of museums, where so many fine sculptures are available to the public.

It's not stopping here, certainly. As the new buildings go up, more art will appear. There's a whole new complex of buildings rising around the foot of Market Street. By the time this book is on the stands, some should be completed and it will be worth your while to explore them to see what they have to offer.

4
The Miracle of the Dunes—Golden Gate Park

San Francisco's park system is one of the major factors that make it a delightful city. Compared with other cities, San Francisco might seem a little topheavy with parks. There are 3,575.3 acres of maintained park land and recreational facilities within the city limits (a ratio of 5.5 square miles to 46 square miles of city). But then again, at 20,000 beings per square mile, San Francisco is topheavy with people. Only the easy accessibility to our parks and the sheer bulk of park space prevents the pressures of claustrophobia. The folks who have moved to the suburbs realize to their distress the loss of this most gracious of urban amenities when they have to drive the kids ten miles to find a playing field.

The scope of the park system and recreational facilities is immense. The guiding principle for the system is that no mother with preschool children should be more than a quarter-mile from a playground with sandbox, slides, and swings; and no family should be more than a half-mile from a supervised playground with play facilities that range from story-telling to organized activities such as basketball teams for the older children. By and large, this ideal has been accomplished and, curiously, our park system is still growing.

Within the city limits are 144 park-recreational-cultural facilities that range from tiny pocket parks (even a movable park for streetcorners) to Golden Gate Park itself; from baseball, football and soccer fields to the Zoo, museums, fresh and salt water marinas, stadia for professional sports and 2.5

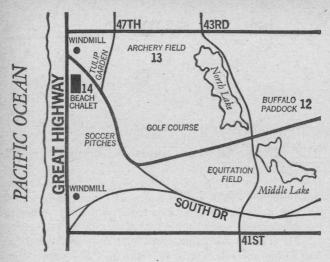

miles of public ocean beach. There are two public nine-hole
and two eighteen-hole golf courses within the city limits (and
another eighteen-hole course right over the city limits in
Pacifica); 10 municipal indoor swimming pools, and the
largest outdoor swimming pool in the world (1,000 feet long,
150 feet wide).

The glory of the park system, indeed one of the crowning
glories of San Francisco, is Golden Gate Park. Four miles
long, one-half mile wide, from the imposing McKinley Memorial at the beginning of the Panhandle to the WPA murals
above the bar in the Beach Chalet on Great Highway, Golden
Gate Park is one huge pleasure. Within it are found so many
points of interest—floral, faunal, cultural, athletic, aesthetic,
historic, even erotic—that it's not surprising that even native
San Franciscans don't know all the wonders it contains. It is
a fantastic place, made even more fantastic with the knowledge that this huge, lush green area is almost entirely man-
made.

There was *nothing* here in the late 1860s when the city
acquired the land; nothing but a waste of sand dunes and a
few marshy lakes. On the old maps, the western edge of the

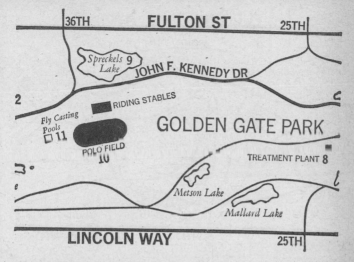

city was labeled "uninhabitable." Every tree you see, every bush, every blade of grass was planted by the hand of man. William Hammond Hall (the designer of Central Park in New York City) laid out the over-all design and John McLaren carried out the plan. Ambitious from the start, and decried from all sides as impossible, the park came into being through the work of men—an undertaking, seen now in its completion, as ambitious and monumental as the building of bridges across the Bay.

How they did it deserves a short explanation. It was thought impossible to make things grow on the windswept dunes because nothing grew before. Through an accident, McLaren's horse's nosebag fell down and sand got into the oats and the horse wouldn't eat it so McLaren dumped it out. The oats sprouted and grew, holding down the little patch of sand around them, so McLaren knew he had a starting point. He sowed oats to give shelter to imported beach and dune grasses from Normandy, which in turn sheltered quick-growing trees —pines and eucalyptus—which gave shelter to the slower-growing cypress, live oaks, and lawns. So grew Golden Gate Park, the typical San Francisco story of luck and pluck. At

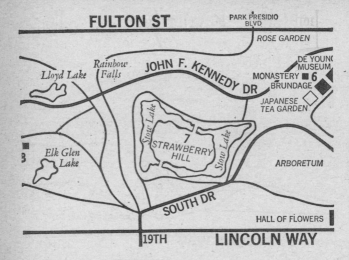

first there was huge skepticism, then begrudging appreciation, and ultimately great pride. The park developed so rapidly that it was chosen as the site of the Mid-Winter Exposition of 1894. A couple of blocks to the south, the Sunset District remained sand dunes for nearly fifty more years, until the late '30s, early '40s, when development houses were started there.

The major attractions of Golden Gate Park are found around the Music Concourse. This is where the tours go, and rightly so, for the area is well worth visiting. It comprises a cultural complex unique in the world; and most of the features are free—those with admission fees are well worth the modest tariff.

The Music Concourse is a long, oval avenue containing a sunken, tree-studded open auditorium fronting the band shell. Acoustically perfect, the band shell is capable of holding 100 musicians. About 2,500 people can be seated on the fixed benches (the whole bowl has held 15,000 on occasion), and there is nothing finer than to sit under the trees at 2 PM of a Sunday afternoon and listen to the free concerts provided by the Municipal Band (another urban amenity and

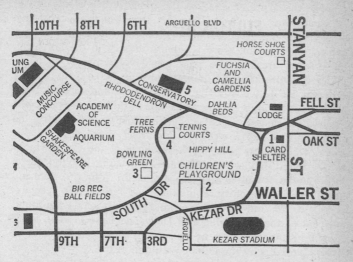

anachronism found in San Francisco) or staged by the various
ethnic societies of the city. Nearly every cultural group here
celebrates its national day by performing a concert in the
park. Many tourists hear the music and drift toward the shell,
nervously looking around for ticket-takers. It's still free here
and the same kind of thing used to be free in nearly every
town in America. It's not necessary for a city to have a
minicipal band, but it's one of the most pleasant things a
citizen can pay taxes for (incidentally, in San Francisco it's
pronounced MU-ni-sip-ple—from street cars to band).

Around the Music Concourse are three of the five major
museums in San Francisco; the De Young, the Brundage,
and the Academy of Arts and Sciences (*see* Chapter 6).

The Japanese Tea Garden lies just west of the De Young–
Brundage museums and is an incredible conjunction of the
formal and informal. Somehow the contemplation of the
artfully contrived plantings, the view brought to little, the
gracious goldfish brooks and squirrels eating peanuts from
your hands beneath red-leafed maples doesn't clash with the
hundreds of noisy kids climbing the moon bridge and fifty
adults drinking tea in the teahouse not 30 yards from any

point in the Tea Garden. The Japanese Garden is always full of people, but rarely do you get the feeling of crowding.

As is to be expected in a park in which all plantings were made by man, there is intense interest in the botanical, and several areas of the park are devoted purely to horticultural features. One of the most obvious is the Conservatory on John F. Kennedy Drive, which we will deal with later. Between McLaren Lodge and the Conservatory are the Fuchsia Gardens (an exotic plant in most of the country, the fuchsia grows like a weed in this area). Here also are displays of camellias. Near the floral clock at the Conservatory can be found dahlia beds. The John McLaren Rhododendron Dell can be found behind his statue on John F. Kennedy Drive. Strange, prehistoric-looking tree ferns (you keep expecting to run into dinosaurs around the next bend) are found adjacent to the Rhododendron Dell. The Rose Garden is off John F. Kennedy Drive at Funston. The Queen Wilhelmina Tulip Garden is by the Dutch Windmill at the very end of the park near the ocean. At each of these specialized floral areas, you will find beautiful and costly displays of the finest varieties of each subject plant. They are very popular, great places to meet fellow aficionados from all over America with whom you can exchange mulch recipes.

The premiere horticultural feature of the park is the Strybing Arboretum and Botanical Gardens just off South Drive at 9th Avenue (a short block from the Music Concourse). A delightfully refreshing place (really a park within a park), it's a fine place to recover from museum feet. The 40-odd acres are a botanical wonderland with more than 5,000 rare specimens from all over the world openly displayed on lovely paths through rare trees and around the two lakes. Two features within the Arboretum are of special interest.

Near the entrance, *Sunset* magazine has built an interesting display of garden and patio designs that is helpful for anyone who is working on his own back yard. It shows the end product of the excellent "how-to" books it publishes, including a curving pavement that incorporates almost twenty different brick, stone, and pebble mosaic designs that you can make yourself. Various examples of garden benches and windscreens are also seen.

Deeper into the Arboretum, but still near the entrance, is the Garden of Fragrance, a botanical display created for the enjoyment of the blind. Atop a curving stone wall (all specimens are at touch level), is a collection of plants gathered for their unusual texture, taste, or fragrance. The labels of the plants are both in Braille and written, a very thoughtful and ingenious display.

This has been a quick look at the major features of the park. It might seem hard to improve on such richness, but in the last two years, the city has done just that. Traffic congestion in the park was assuming dangerous proportions, so with unusual wisdom in dealing with the obvious, the main part of the park was ordered closed to auto traffic on Sundays. It was just like getting the park back again. It's wonderful walking there now—just watch out for the bicycles. In the summer of 1972, the Recreation and Park Department instituted a new service. Every fifteen minutes, a bus leaves McLaren Lodge for the high points of the park. There are six stops from the Conservatory to the buffalo paddock. The fare is 60 cents for adults, 30 cents for children, and one may get off the bus at any point, spend as much time as he wants, and reboard the bus to visit the next point of interest. One ticket lasts all day.

And now that we've seen the main attractions, let's get into the rest of Golden Gate Park.

Card Shelter

Decorated with a chess motif—chessmen support the roof and form legs for the tables—the CARD SHELTER right off Stanyon near Haight (No. 1 on map, page 91) is always an exciting place to visit. The dedication of the habitués is positively electric. On the bleakest, coldest, rainiest, most miserable day, you'll find them huddled around the tables playing like crazy. It is, indeed, one of the very few places where one can witness such pure and intense devotion to purpose. The only other place where one can find such a number of people united in this kind of furious dedication is at the racetrack.

Two notes of caution for those who would play at the shelter. First, it has been rumored that on occasion, though strictly unlawful, money is suspected to have changed hands on the outcome of a chess game—especially lightning chess. I would not suggest that the city is maintaining a gambling hell or anything like that, but merely to urge prudence when playing with strangers. It's amazing how much money you can drop in twenty minutes, playing only a buck a game—especially when you're fairly sure you know something about the game. As in billiards, the most fumble-fingered duffer can become magically transformed into a Minnesota Fats, or in this case a Bobby Fischer, when money is on the table.

Children's Playground

CHILDREN'S PLAYGROUND, which is about two blocks into the park from the Haight Street entrance (No. 2 on map, page 91) is best approached in a circular way because there are several nice things to see on your way there. One of these is the fountain outside the Park police station on the South Drive by Kezar Stadium. To my knowledge, this is the only drinking fountain in the city dedicated to a specific dog. There is a horse drinking fountain at Horseman's Retreat in the Park, a curious round thing, like a very thick loving cup, but that is dedicated to the Noble Horse—all noble horses (erected, I understand, by a famous dogfood company). No names are mentioned on the horse fountain, but the inscription on the dog drinking fountain reads:

TO THE MEMORY OF A DOG
Drink to the memory of "Schultz" today.
His friendliness to man did him betray.
1948

Now, that is a handsome piece of doggerel and apparently is a memorial to a long-time pet of the policemen at the station there who was done in because he trusted too much.

Unfortunately, all I could get out of a policeman I questioned was, "I think he used to hang out around here and somebody ran over him." I questioned that policeman two years ago, before the Park Station was bombed and a policeman killed in the explosion. To view the fountain and muse upon doggy luck and the results of love and trust, you now have to pass through ten-foot chain-link fence gates that tell you to stay out unless you are on official business. You can muse upon much more there now.

The Haight Street entrance that leads to the Children's Playground is also always interesting. The Haight Street gate catches the earliest sun and is usually lined with hippies warming themselves after a night outdoors. One can see strange things around the Haight Street gate. In 1967, when the flower children were in blossom, the slope between the gate and Alvord Lake was a favorite gathering place for those with a message and those who would hear them. There was usually a speaker standing on a metal milk crate at the bottom shouting poetry or philosophy through a battery bullhorn to the lounging throng, who would shout back poetry, philosophy, and obscenities. Also in this area, either at the gate or on the slope, was an old gentleman, as bizarre in his neat gray suit as the hippies were in their beads and bells, who would perform on the musical saw. He was there every day from sunup to sundown. It must be admitted that he played a very bad musical saw—knee-action is vital in this instrument and when you get a little creaky, it shows—but you hear the musical saw so seldom nowadays that many made the trip to the park just to hear him.

That was a curious era, the love summer. A chapter on the Haight-Ashbury was originally planned for this book, but, alas, the Haight is no longer a place to visit. It seemed at first that the flower children could change the world through sheer numbers and moral conviction. They were believers, almost to a man. It was almost like a summer-long revival meeting, everybody children of God, and sweetness and love flowed like a stream. And it was fun; free sex, music everywhere and stoned every day on dope. It was the first time in the history of America that large numbers of our middle-class youth had ever indulged themselves in guilt-free, out-of-bounds behavior.

The golden days were doomed from the start precisely because it was a grass-roots middle-class phenomenon. There were really no goals, except the nebulous "We all *are* Children of God" assertion and the open rejection of many of the standard American middle-class goals. The thing was that since they were self-proclaimed rebels and outlaws, they clasped to their bosoms all the other outlaws of society. Since the flower children had huge amounts of money, the real outlaws swooped down upon them and gobbled them up. Thugs, deadbeats, metaphysicals, freeloaders, thieves, charlatans, hoods, and drug pushers took gross advantage of their innocence. Never, outside of war, did so many young Americans get so much experience in so short a time as did the flower children in the summer of 1967.

The spin-off of that summer can be seen in bits and pieces all around us. I'm convinced, despite objections, that the women's liberation movement grew out of the summer of love in 1967. Huge numbers of girls of middle-class background got casually knocked up that summer. All these well-educated, formerly well-off girls were suddenly faced with the problems of raising their kids with no help whatsoever from the kids' vanished fathers, little help from their parents, and only the degrading institutional help they could get from the county. And lots of them had to go seriously to do a job of work for the first time in their lives. The lower-class girls in the same predicament had faced the same problems for years without complaining because they didn't know the words. Not these middle-class girls. The American midle-class has never been silent where "conditions" were concerned, or shy about going right to the top to change them. Naturally, these girls immediately started raising hell about job discrimination, variance in pay for the same job, in a word, women's lib.

The summer ended, though, and most went, disillusioned, back to their homes or colleges. The ones who stayed, dedicated to the ideal, have organized themselves into self-protective communes; or they have gone into various aspects of the Hindu and Buddhist religions; or into radical politics;

or they scattered and set up their own little Haight Streets all through the city and countryside. What is left in the Haight is mostly hoodlums, thugs, and those screwed up by drugs. Haight Street is a ghost town, block after block of boarded-up stores, a sad victim of love and high intentions.

That summer left two legacies to Golden Gate Park that persist today—one good and one bad. As you go through the Haight Street gate, the benches along the slopes down to Alvord Lake are full of the most indolent panhandlers I have encountered on two continents. Panhandlers are common to every large city in the world. It is a unique experience, though, to be asked for cigarettes or pocket change by a person, sun-bronzed and comfortably lazing on a park bench, who is too lazy to unhook his elbows from the back of the bench. It might be historically proven that the surest sign of a civilization's decline is seen in the lack of effort put out by its beggars.

The positive legacy of that summer was the establishment of HIPPIE HILL. Take the right hand path after passing through the tunnel. On any sunny day, the hill and the meadow beneath are crowded with young people enjoying the sun and trees. There are always a group of drummers on the bench at the bottom of the hill and often several other instruments, running heavily to flutes and guitars. Sometimes one can catch something particularly curious, such as the first time in my life I ever heard an acid rock violin. I hope it is the last time—it makes your teeth ache.

It is very pleasant to visit Hippie Hill and watch the action. Kids are running around, the musicians are playing, championship Frisbee matches are in progress all over the place, and tight groups of men are huddled around three-card-monte and shell-and-pea exhibitions (though here they use three wine-bottle caps and a ball bearing).*

---

* I was surprised to discover these games here. I hadn't seen them since boyhood carnivals in Ohio. The games are sporadic and obviously prearranged. No one's there, then all of the sudden twenty or thirty dudes appear and the action starts. I have seen $50 and $100 bills flow across those blankets like nickel chips. Of course, it's fascinating to watch. The operators have hands like concert pianists.

Occasionally people will be so moved by the music, grass, trees, air, and sun that they will shed their clothes and dance naked upon the greensward. They dance until a mounted policeman shouts at them to put on their clothes, and that is usually fun to watch.

On Hippie Hill, too, are celebrated many exotic religious rites—at the solstices, or if the moon is in Scorpio, or whatever. The Hindus gather to chant and smoke marijuana and dance. There is a lot of clothes-taking-off at these gatherings too. I don't know what it is about this place that encourages so many people to take off their clothes. The trouble with Hippie Hill is that it is so pleasant to sit in the sun there, the people so interesting, and the music usually so good that before you know it you've blown the whole afternoon without planning to.

Children's Playground itself is just south of Hippie Hill. It is one of the very finest places in the park. The children, of course, are the main attraction. Kids of every size, shape, and color are all over the place. Children's Playground is one of the finest advertisements for integration to be found anywhere, because here one can see the wonderful results of race mixing. Every possible kind of race mixing—black, brown, white, yellow, and red—all jumbled up in all kinds of combinations. More damn kinds of kids than you ever dreamed of and they are all fascinating and all beautiful. Because of the kids, the playground offers one of the very few opportunities to meet those of other races on strictly common ground. The universality of the problems of parents permits a very free and unencumbered sharing of experience. Prejudices and preconceptions disappear when two mothers meet who both have two-year-olds who hit the baby. It is one of the rare places where blacks, whites, and Orientals meet on a strictly personal and social level.

The playground is large and offers many things of interest to children and adults. Besides the standard swings, slides, sand piles, and gymnastic equipment, there is an old California Street cable car to clamber around on and, in the Sharon Building, there is always something going on, a puppet show or painting, for example. The playground equipment is far enough apart and plentiful enough that the kids aren't on one another's heads—which means a minimum of fights, confusion, and broken bones. Two special features, though, "The Farm" and the merry-go-round, lift the Children's Playground from just another place to air the children to a very special place, a pleasure to visit again and again.

THE FARM is a small corral containing thirty or so guinea pigs, ten or so big rabbits, a flock of chickens, lots of ducks and geese, and goats, sheep, occasionally a llama or pig—a menagerie of tame and friendly animals that provide endless fascination. All these animals are hooked on the popcorn sold at the refreshment stand. It's a wonderful experience to watch the children feed the animals. Here stands the timorous little girl holding out a popcorn. On comes a sheep with a chicken roosting on its back keeping its feet warm in the wool. The sheep gently nibbles the popcorn from the little girl's fingers. Because the sheep has actually accepted food from her hands, she is thrilled, nearly bursting—but she never fails to count her fingers after she has made the gift.

The MERRY-GO-ROUND at Children's Playground is such an exquisite work of art that I almost included it in the section on monuments. Its evaluation deserves a worthier critic than I, because I must admit that before I saw it, I had no interest in merry-go-rounds at all. However, this is a flawed merry-go-round taken as a whole. It has no automatic orchestra (music is supplied by records)—a serious omission, I imagine, to merry-go-round experts. Also, it lacks the gilding and ornamentation found, say, in the merry-go-round at the Zoo and is not as speedy as the one that used to be at Playland-at-the-Beach. These technical shortcomings, though, are not missed. Indeed, on this merry-go-round, they would be distractions from the finest collection of pop-art statuary in San Francisco (if not the finest, certainly the most delightful). It is unfortunate that the animals on the merry-go-round must be catagorized as pop art or handicraft or folk art or whatever, because each of the animals is exquisitely sculptured and deserves serious artistic attention. The merry-go-round itself deserves attention because it is a very curious art form, both ancient as the wheel and modern as the latest exhibition at the

Museum of Modern Art—if not more modern. Even the poorest merry-go-round commands a degree of multilevel involvement that would make any modern sculptor gnash his teeth in envy. The rider not only actually becomes a part of the work of art and within it is physically and aesthetically acted upon by the motion, lights, and music, but he is almost compelled to fantasy by the beast he rides. This applies to children of a certain age, of course, but it might be speculated that the whole thrust of modern art is an attempt to create a merry-go-round for adults.

The thing that makes this merry-go-round special is that final, most important, ingredient—the magic of adventure and fantasy that these magnificent animals compel. The man who carved these beasts—and it must have been only one man because all the animals bear the stamp of a single genius— solved the very complicated aesthetic problem of creating a statue which looks perfectly right both standing still and at full gallop. Every animal here is totally alive and involved, and each has its own personality. The horses here are not your run-of-the-mill going-around-in-a-circle horses. No, each of these is off to give chase to the enemy—Indians, Saracens, or outlaws. The intense, withdrawn green frog in his red coat forever bounds off to his destiny with the witch who transformed him; the pig is not just a pig but a huge boar with a stolen stalk of corn in his mouth. You can tell by their very demeanor that the dog, the cat, and the goat are animals of very noble character engaged in some heroic deed. Even the ostrich, as impossible as it sounds, is so splendidly made that his dignified strides command respect. Each animal deserves close examination and together they comprise a unity of form not often seen. A comparison with the Zoo merry-go-round will show you why this is so fine. At the Zoo, the animals are insipid and wooden. Here they are alive and full of magic.

Within a five-minute walk of Children's Playground are three other points of interest that should be visited. Directly adjoining the playground and sharing its parking lot are the BOWLING GREENS (No. 3 on map, page 91). Lawn bowling, like polo, is a sport seldom seen by the average American.

It is a seasonal sport in most of America and the cost of maintaining a bowling green has always made it an upper-middle-class recreation (the green must be perfectly level and the grass clipped nearly as carefully as a golfing green). But it, like its rather disreputable cousin, *bocce,* would catch on like wildfire if facilities were available across the country. Although it is a sedate sport, it has all the elements of the kind of sports Americans take to. Skill is paramount. It takes a steady hand and keen eye to bowl the biased ball (flattened on two sides) in an ellipse toward the object ball, called the "jack." It has a complicated etiquette and, often, close measurement is necessary to decide the winner, which allows for polite kibitzing and disagreement. It is suspenseful and fascinating to watch, a perfect TV sport in that every bowl is a crucial one and the outcome may be totally altered by the next move. There are millions to be made in lawn bowling—and in *bocce,* which we will examine when we go to Aquatic Park.

The path over the hill from the bowling greens leads to the TENNIS COURTS (No. 4 on map, page 91). The courts are worth a short pause, if only to view one of the few discords in the whole park complex and to contemplate human foibles. It's amazing what people will put up with to play here. The tennis courts are organized athletics with a vengeance. After waiting in line for a court, you must satisfy nine separate rules concerning dress, decorum, qualification of participation, and duration of play—they shout at you through loudspeakers for the slightest deviation—and it has a pro shop. Why a public tennis court needs a pro shop is more than I can fathom. Tennis is certainly not golf, where sixteen basic pieces of equipment are required to play the game. With so much stuff to buy or replace, a shop near the links is needful. In tennis, all that is needed is one tennis racquet and three tennis balls. The rest is ornamentation.

But if the tennis courts are disturbing, following the path toward the Main (John F. Kennedy) Drive, over the hill, and through the tunnel is an interesting and worthwhile experience. The tunnel is an especial delight to the children because it echoes like crazy. A three-year-old can become a roaring dinosaur in that tunnel. From the crest of the path, one observes the CONSERVATORY (No. 5 on map, page 91). Now this is a very curious building. It is a main feature of Golden Gate Park, but the peculiar qualities of the building call for some comment. My first visit gave me the same feeling of being cut off from dimensions that one experiences on a visit to St. Peter's in Rome, but with inverse impact. At St. Peter's, the closer you get, the larger and larger it grows. Here at the Conservatory, it is the other way around. Seen from the Main Drive, the Conservatory is monumental; when you enter it, the dimensions diminish. Ceilings that seemed to be at least fifty feet tall turn out to be twenty-odd. The noble dome, which looks at least a hundred feet high, is only forty, if that. You have to go outside to reassure yourself that you're visiting the same building you've seen. But after the shock of having been deceived wears off, you can look upon it as it is; one of the most perfectly proportioned buildings that the city possesses. And perfectly proportioned, not in the cheap boxy way the new downtown office buildings are, but in keeping with the 50 yards of formal gardening and landscaping before it and the huge trees framing it from the rise behind the building. The more you contemplate it, the more it delights you, even if you can't understand it.

The Conservatory is yet another of James Lick's gifts to San Francisco.

Monastery

When you go up the little asphalt path behind the De Young Museum off Kennedy Drive opposite the Rose Garden (No. 5 on map, page 91) you will find a huge jumble of carved yellow limestone blocks that used to be a Spanish monastery. William Randolph Hearst bought it, had it dismantled, every block carrying cabalistic markings to facilitate reassembly, and shipped it to America. For some reason, the disassembled monastery wound up in Golden Gate Park and rests here yet. Apparently there were several plans underway for its reincarnation, construction either here or on one of

Hearst's estates. But it was neglected in the anxieties of the Depression, the decline of the Hearst fortune, and the war. And a vandal set fire to the straw-packed boxes of stones, so that most of the put-together marks were burned off. So what is viewed now is a great pile of cut stone which has, and has had for the last thirty years no value whatever other than promise. The money and effort needed to put it back together has posed such a problem that neither the city that owns it, nor any other interested party, has the steam really to attempt to reconstruct it. This is curious in the light of the intrinsic value of the monastery. It is priceless. Judging from the photographs, not only is the monastery lovely, it is also, certainly, the last Spanish monastery that will ever be dismantled stone by stone and shipped to America.

As the monastery stands now—rather, lies all around the place in pieces—it is of utterly no worth, except to ants and beetles and lichens. Erected, its value would be in excess of one million dollars (counting everything: history, uniqueness, art value, postcard concession). It seems to me that the easiest thing would be to offer the dismantled monastery as a project for budding archaeologists in the University of California. Potential diggers-out and putters-back-together of ancient Egyptian, Assyrian, Greek, Roman, and whatever temples and buildings could make this a summer project—worthwhile field work, getting experience in reconstructing strewn stone into a known result.

A more exciting idea, and certainly more fun, would be to open the monastery to competitive bidding from games manufacturers. The highest bidder—both in earnest money and percentage of gross—would earn the right to measure the stones and reduce them to such a size that when the monastery was completed it would occupy a 3-by-6 table. The sets could be sold for $50 apiece. And San Francisco could then offer a really fine prize—say $100,000—to the first who successfully put the monastery back together again. Every church, service group, fraternal organization, PTA, Boy Scout troop, social club, atheletic organization, and fire house in the country would buy a set for a try at the hundred grand. If it were handled well—simultaneous delivery of all the sets at the same time, for example—it could well be the damnedest competition ever seen in the history of America.

But, although eminently feasible, the suggestion is probably bureaucratically impossible to carry out. They're talking now about using some of the cut stone in the subway we're building. As America's last shipped-in monastery, it deserves better than that.

Spreckels Lake

Undoubtedly one of the most pleasant places in the park and one of the finest "civilized" lakes anywhere is SPRECKELS LAKE on the Fulton Street side off 36th Avenue (No. 9 on map, Page 89) Spreckels Lake is a manicured lake. It is ringed with a broad, well-kept walk, which in turn is surrounded by fine lawns and carefully pruned trees. It reminds you very much of European park lakes and offers the same peaceful recreations—strolling around the lake, feeding the ducks, resting on the benches, picnicking on the lawns under the trees, enjoying the children, the sun, the water, the trees. There is no finer place for a couple who has just fallen in love to visit. The formal, but not stiff, aspect of the setting calms people and there is no raucousness, no shouting, no unnecessary movement except with the children. It is a soothing place to spend an afternoon.

But as the most staid-appearing New England town sometimes harbors a secret snake-worshiping cult, the outwardly peaceful Spreckels Lake is the locus of an intense and bitter secret conflict. The use of the lake is allotted on alternate Sundays to the model sailboat enthusiasts and the model motorboat enthusiasts. Both must share the facilities of the model-yacht-club building just west of the lake. Each despises the other and his philosophy. The result provides a great deal of amusement to anyone not involved. Now, both the sail and the motor people put a horrendous amount of work into their hobbies. Those sailboats are built with such painstaking, loving craftsmanship that every plank and nailhead is exactly as it would be in an eighty-foot yacht. The motor people tinker with the lines of their craft and their motors as if they were going to compete with Miss Bardall. The competitions are as intensely fought as if the America's Cup were at stake.

The model-boat people are intense in their philosophical differences. The sailboaters keep to themselves and talk about lateens and flying jibs. The model-motor people are divided into several categories. There are the fixed-rudder people who have, say, a miniature hydroplane that goes like mad in a huge circle from the launching point and back again—bouncing like the real thing on the miniature waves of Spreckels Lake. Then there are the remote-control boats that can be in any form from a destroyer to a speedboat that cuts capers in the water. There are also the variety-boat builders who have copied every kind of motor craft on the water. One of my favorites is a model remote-controlled steam tug complete with remote-controlled steam whistle. Of a six o'clock in the morning, I watched two men anchor a hydroplane static-line to an overflow pipe near the west bank and turn it loose, checking its speed with stopwatches and chalked sighting marks on the walkway. "Eighty miles an hour!" one said, but they wouldn't tell me if they were model-boat enthusiasts, toy-motor engineers, or the CIA.

As I say, the amusement lies with the disinterested observer. It's not often that the model-motor people come to see the model-sailboat competitions because there's not enough action. But at every model-motorboat competition, there are sailboat builders who mutter on the sidelines just waiting for the many times when the motorboats poop out in the middle of the lake. These boats are retrieved in two ways; either they are cast for with a tennis ball tethered on the fish line of a surf-casting rod or someone has to row out after them. Then the sail people are instantly recognizable. They're the ones who inquire, "What's the matter. Run out of gas?" in a way that nearly always moves the motor owner to profanity. They also give the tennis-ball casters all kinds of helpful advice: "Don't throw too hard, you might hit the motor! That's it, more to the right . . . pity you have to ruin a good tennis ball for something like that . . ." I have to admit, having lived next to the lake, that my allegiance lies in the direction of the sail people. On a Sunday morning, it gets mighty rackety when twenty little boats are blatting around the lake. Even the ducks leave.

Recently, the retrieving dingy was rammed and sunk by an out-of-control hydroplane. The sail members of the model yacht club refused to contribute to a replacement.

Water-Treatment Plant

When we lived on the edge of the park, at Fulton and 32nd Avenue by Spreckels Lake, my wife and I walked nearly every day in the park. We were often puzzled by the eerie cries we heard, especially at dusk. The cries were like those of howling cats, but much more shrill, much wilder. One evening we decided to investigate, and, following the shouts, walked through the polo grounds to Metson Lake on Middle Drive. The sounds were definitely from the east. Middle Drive is a seldom-used road even on a Sunday afternoon. At dusk, during the week, it is lonely. As we drew nearer, the cries became shrieks—the trees and distance not interfering, the calls were not muted. The closer we got, the more they seemed to scrape upon our very bones. But as we continued down Middle Drive, the cries gradually stopped and we found ourselves at the water-treatment plant (No. 8 on map, page 89). The sudden silence was as unnerving as the cries had been. Then suddenly, directly over us, it shrieked! A huge beast launched itself from a branch 40 feet above our heads. Its wings seemed twenty feet wide. When the huge bird landed heavily near us, the mystery was resolved. It spread its tail and we saw that it was a peacock. As we looked around, we saw a whole flock of them roosting in the trees around the WATER-TREATMENT PLANT.

When you see the strutting peacock, on the ground, in the park or Zoo, you tend to forget that it is a bird at all, it is so ornamental. And you fully realize how huge they really are. I wasn't even aware that they could fly. After this peacock determined that we had no food, it ran a few steps and flapped ponderously back to its perch overhead. It is an interesting, but for some reason disquieting, experience to see a bird that large fly. But if you have ever wondered where the peacock goes at night, come to the water treatment plant at dusk. Listen to its cries and watch it roost. It will make you appreciate the warmth of your house, the locks on your doors.

Polo Field

Across from Spreckels Lake in the center of the park at 34th Avenue is the POLO FIELD (No. 10 on map, page 89). In the summer, it's used on alternate Sundays by two sports, polo and rugby, that are seldom seen by Americans. Admission is free. Of the two, polo is the more glamorous, but rugby is more interesting to watch. In fact, polo must be one of the dullest spectator sports in the world. It might be the perspective from lack of height of the stadium, but I don't even think that height could help it. This is because of the nature of the sport and the size of the playing field. The players are usually so bloody far away, and milling around so furiously, that you can't see a thing. All that you can catch is what looks like twenty little horses all bunched together, then there is a flash of mallets and the ball shoots out of the melee and bounces forty yards down the field, the whole bunch galloping hell-bent after it. Then there is another bunching together and the ball goes thirty yards in the other direction. It has always seemed to me that in polo you have to be playing to really see what the hell is going on. This makes the game boring to watch. What is interesting to watch, though, are the polo spectators. At every game, there is a little group who come to cheer their favorites, eat a champagne picnic lunch, and drink thermos jugs of martinis. They can't see any better than you can, even if they know the players, and the spectating—especially about halfway through the martinis —becomes a happy, tipsy gossip session spiced with a good deal of slap and tickle. The polo field is a fine place to watch the rich at play.

Rugby is another thing. I've never been able to understand it, but there's certainly a lot of action involved. There are two teams of great, monstrous guys who, with a great deal of grunting and thokking of heads, push each other from one end of the field to the other. That goes on for a good while too; then they all go, muddy and bloody, some place to drink beer together.

At the polo field, also, one can find horses for hire and obtain information about the fine bridle paths in the park.

Buffalo Paddock

I am about to divulge a secret so fine, so rewarding, that this small section will more than repay the cost of the book. It is the secret of the BUFFALO PADDOCK. The buffalo paddock is interesting enough to visit by itself, even without this knowledge, but with it, it is made even finer. The buffalo paddock is located off John F. Kennedy Drive opposite 37th Avenue (No. 12 on map, page 88). It contains a fine collection of large ungulates—buffalo (bison), of course, goats, and deer—fallow deer, whose magnificent rack of antlers, causes people to mistake them for elk or reindeer. It's worthwhile to visit here often because the cow buffalo and the goats bear young every year and you can watch their development. The goats remain more or less the same, but the buffalo calves start out much like the calves of cattle, then slowly change; growing burlier around the head and shoulders and narrowing in the flanks. The end result is a huge, shaggy beast, massive in the front and trim as a thoroughbred race horse in the back.

By constantly visiting the paddock, you may also have an opportunity to witness a buffalo roundup. No other city in the world, major or minor, offers this attraction. Every several years, some dummy knocks the locks off the paddock gates and the buffalo roam through the Richmond district. It is a hell of a job to get them back in the paddock—but on to the secret.

It was discovered by accident. The buffalo, deer, and goats

love bread, especially sourdough French bread. As I said, we lived on the edge of the park and my wife and I often fed the animals through the eastern fence in back of the model-yacht clubhouse. To attract their attention, we shouted and rattled the bread wrappers along the chain-link fence. At one period we were there so regularly that the mere sound of the rattling paper would be enough to bring them over to us. Other than the pleasure of the feeding was the convenience of not having to walk another block to where the animals usually stay, near their manger. The paddock is large and encompasses an area of about three acres.

I thought nothing of this accomplishment until a friend from the East stopped for a short visit. He was a super New Yorker—the worst kind of person outside a super Southerner. Cynical, very quick on the bad-mouth quip, always right in there with the instant put-down—especially when a comparison of the attractions of San Francisco and New York were being discussed; never, ever, impressed by anything—you know the type. Well, after giving him the grand tour of the city, we took him to the buffalo paddock. Because I was frustrated and angry, I rattled the bread wrapper on the fence and shouted. It was wonderful. The animals were all grazing in the middle of the field about fifty yards away. They lifted their heads and looked at us. "Don't just stand there," I said, *"come!"* I shouted, rattling furiously. First the goats stepped toward us, then the deer, then the buffalo. The goats walked faster, broke into a trot, then a run. The deer and the buffalo followed suit and in an instant, the whole bloody herd was thundering toward us at full gallop! My friend edged gingerly away from the fence. It scared hell out of me too to see all those animals galloping right at us and not sure if the fence would hold, but at that point, I would not have budged had they been elephants. "Come to me!" I shouted, lifting my arms like Moses parting the Red Sea. "Now, just a minute . . ." he said, and he ran and hid behind a tree.

The animals pulled up just short of the fence and milled around begging for the bread. I passed it through the fence, calling each affectionately by newly invented names and I urged my friend to join me. "Don't be frightened," I said. "They know you're with me." It was one of the most magnificent and triumphant moments of my life.

Through an experiment, using disbelieving neighbors, we found that anyone can call the animals in the same way in only one week of regular feedings. Stay on the same side of the paddock every time; be there approximately the same time each day; and rattle the bread wrapper and shout to attract the animals' attention. If you follow these simple instructions, the results are guaranteed. It is most pleasant, once in a while, to be thought a hell of a fellow. Here, at the buffalo paddock in Golden Gate Park, you can buy it with only fifteen minutes a day for a week and seven loaves of sourdough French bread. Some can't buy it with a thousand dollars.

Fly-Casting Pools and Archery Field

The ANGLER'S LODGE and FLY-CASTING POOLS lie approximately opposite the buffalo paddock on J.F.K. Drive (No. 11 on map, page 89). The ARCHERY FIELD is on the road off the Main Drive that leads to the exit at 47th Avenue (No. 13 on map, page 88). Although these recreation areas are far apart, the casting pool and the archery field have so much in common that they can be considered together. Both areas are out of the way and both are used only by members of their particular cults. Fly-plug casting and archery are both apparently fun to do, but to my mind, they are even more interesting to contemplate. This is because both sports have been so refined from their original function as to become arcane pursuits. So refined indeed that the original functions —the landing of the mighty fish in the case of the casting people, the killing of the mighty elk in the case of the arrow people—have been completely forgotten in the concentration upon technique. But for this reason, both are interesting to watch and both places interesting to visit.

The casters are intensely interested in, and put out a hell of a lot of money in buying, the very finest rods—and argue to the millimeter and milligram the proper length and weight of their various rods. They tend to be well dressed and, when casting, place two fingers on the wristwatch area of the forearm to assure themselves that the wrist is doing the casting, not the arm—incredibly necessary for control of the plug. There are three pools for the casters, a large one in the middle and two smaller ones flanking it. At various distances from poolside are varicolored plastic rings. When the caster plunks the fly or plug into the rings, he has won the game. Dedicated casters spend all their leisure at the casting pool trying to hit the rings. Some practical joker has stocked the pools and all of them are swarming with trout.

The archers are of the same sort; particularists who are involved more with the technique of the weapon than its original function. At the *archery field,* you find (and at the most peculiar times and under the most terrible weather conditions) the archers arching. As in Robin Hood's day, the archers shoot at a mark, but the bows and arrows they use today are as complex and exotic as a moon craft. For most of us who have, as children, gotten a bow and arrow set for Christmas, a visit to the archery field elicits mixed feelings of admiration, frustration, and obsolescence. The bows are incredibly beautiful triple-S curved, molded, laminated things and the arrows are of machined aluminum (if indeed they're not solid silver, they're so pretty). As I say, the feeling of obsolescence is strong. For example, the archers no longer pull the bowstring back with the fingers. Now, anyone who has gotten a Christmas bow-and-arrow set knows that as a matter of course, the real and true archer always displays a raw and bleeding forearm and fingers so chewed up that they won't bend. Between the bloody forearm and ruined fingers, no one could possibly deny that you could indeed arrow the mighty elk. They don't do that any more. The modern archer has a little hook complexly attached to his wrist that draws back the bowstring and he, while aiming at the mark, trips a *trigger!* As far as I'm concerned, that's a hell of a way to shoot a bow and arrow. The only helpful observation I can report is that they miss the target as often with their laminated bows and wrist triggers as we did with our Christmas bow-and-arrow sets. There's some comfort in that.

Beach Chalet

The end of the park by the beach offers a great many attractions. On the Fulton Street side is the archery field, which we have already visited; farther in is the DUTCH WINDMILL, then a nine-hole golf course, two SOCCER PITCHES, the SEWAGE-DISPOSAL PLANT and the MURPHY WINDMILL near Lincoln Way. At the end of the park on Great Highway is the BEACH CHALET (No. 14 on map, page 88).

All these attractions are of great interest and put to great use by San Franciscans. The two windmills were built to tap the great fresh-water sources that supplied the irrigation water for the park for many years. McLaren ordered the wells dug when he found indications of fresh water only a block from the ocean. It was pumped from there to the main reservoir on Strawberry Hill (Stow Lake) and thence throughout the park. The windmills were expensive to operate and electric pumps installed. The Boy Scouts have a money-raising project to reactivate the Dutch Windmill and it is to be hoped that in the near future the sails will be turning once again.

The *soccer pitches* are in constant use. It has always been an active underground sport in San Francisco because of the many immigrants from *futból*-happy countries. English, Irish, Central and South American, German, and Scandinavian social clubs all maintain soccer teams. It's interesting to note that in June 1972 only 3,500 baseball fans went to a night game at Candlestick to watch the Giants play and the same night 23,000 turned out at Kezar Stadium to watch Pelé play one of his last exhibition matches.

The *sewage-disposal plant* in the park is open every Saturday morning to those organic-minded residents who want the free digested sewage sludge for their gardens. The city park system (and Department of Public Works, which plants street trees) is intensely organically oriented. All the cuttings from the park (and the manure from the riding stables) is composted in a huge half-block-square, two-story-high compost heap near 25th Avenue. This compost and the sewage sludge is what makes our parks so green—chemical fertilizers might hurt park users and result in civil suits. Milwaukee sells its sludge as "Milorganite" at five bucks the fifty-pound bag (1972 prices). Here, it is free for the taking, and rich stuff indeed—I refuse to believe that Milwaukee's sludge is as rich as San Francisco's sludge and you need only look at my tomatoes and cucumbers for proof.

The *Beach Chalet* is sort of an orphan of the park system and it's a shame. Built in 1900 and put to many money-losing uses since, it is now leased as a concession to the Veterans of Foreign Wars as a meeting hall, with a bar open to the public on the first floor. It's a gracious building, the second story all glass overlooking Ocean Beach. Most interesting are the murals by Lucien Labaudt over the bar and around the room, done through a WPA grant. Unlike the workers—*über-alles* murals in Coit Tower, this deals with San Franciscans at play. The murals contain portraits of the leading figures of San Francisco at that time, including a very dapper Benny Bufano on horseback, William Randolph Hearst, and John McLaren sitting on a park bench. The elegant carved banister of intertwined sea creatures by Michael Jon Mayer is a beautiful thing. The building is now shabby and run down. I hope it will be rediscovered and put to better use.

Statuary

Golden Gate Park is a gold mine for dedicated statue-watchers. Around the Music Concourse alone, an area of about two city blocks, there are 15 fine statues and statuary groups; within a short walk there are 5 more. (There are 37 statues in the park as a whole.) Each is of aesthetic, cultural, sociological, historical, or political interest (in one case at least, the Doré vase, the work is of considerable psychological interest). The statuary in the park is made even more interesting when you learn that around each individual statue raged the conflict of two unalterably opposed forces.

On one hand were the statue donors, high-minded groups of art lovers, civic embellishers, and special pleaders who wielded their not inconsiderable political muscle upon the politicians to get their statues exhibited in the finest possible setting, which is Golden Gate Park. Opposing them was John McLaren. McLaren, the "Father of Golden Gate Park," hated statues, buildings, music concourses, stadiums, conservatories, indeed anything that detracted from the purely "natural" aspect of the park. McLaren's argument ran that since Golden Gate Park was the most painstakingly created "natural" park in the world; that since every blade of grass, every tree, every bush and flower was hand-planted and made to flourish in that former wasteland of sand dunes only through a huge amount of work, thought, time and money; then why in the world defeat the whole purpose by cluttering it up with man-made objects? The statues and buildings could just as well be erected elsewhere where no carefully nurtured trees and shrubs would have to be cut down to accommodate them.

It must be said that everybody concerned benefited by the hassle. It was a thirty-year running argument with McLaren (and the park) coming out rather on top. His opposition was so fierce that he prevented the park from being turned into a stoneyard. He permitted so few statues to be erected that in effect he acted as a one-man screening committee, guaranteeing that any statue erected would be first rate. His opposition didn't stop there, for even if a statue were erected, he would carry on a kind of botanical guerrilla warfare on it, so screening the statue with shrubbery that some still peer out through veritable tunnels of vegetation. One further word about McLaren. It might be wondered how a civil servant at the tail of city government, so to speak—the Recreation and Park Department—could wag the dog at City Hall. It was simply that he was a shining, incorruptible man in an era of grand-scale corruption. His dedication was so complete, his accomplishments so great, that he could do no wrong as far as his fellow San Franciscans were concerned. Even his hiding of the statues was not only tolerated but looked upon with a good deal of amusement. Few civil servants have earned such esteem in San Francisco or anywhere else. Anyone who has visited Golden Gate Park is indebted to this man not only for the beauty he created but for his philosophy, which has guided the whole viewpoint of this park.

WILLIAM MCKINLEY. By Robert Ingersall Aitkin. At the very beginning of the Park Panhandle at Broderick and Fell streets.

This McKinley memorial is one of the most impressive memorials I have ever seen. It has dignity, grace, and wonderful proportion. A huge, stern figure of Justice with a broken sword stands majestically on a simple but impressive pedestal. It is interesting that Robert Aitkin did both this and the Dewey memorial in Union Square. McKinley dedicated the Dewey memorial and the ground for this memorial was broken by President Theodore Roosevelt. The completed statue was dedicated by Mrs. Theodore Roosevelt.

JAMES A. GARFIELD. By F. Happersberger. Near Conservatory.

This is an elegant memorial with a heroic standing Garfield. It was done by Happersberger, who also sculptured the Lick Memorial. Seated beneath Garfield is Mourning America with wreath and broken sword (you seldom see mourning ladies on statues any more). There are two high reliefs of patriotic-military symbols and one relief of Garfield's inauguration. Happersberger liked to use this combination of statues and reliefs in his work. All in all it is a very fine memorial, even when hippies ruin the effect by going to sleep in Mourning America's lap. Curiously, the statue was sculptured in Munich and cast in Nuremberg. You wonder if Happersberger did Garfield from photographs, woodcuts, or what. Long-range portraiture is always difficult. In 1885, when the statue was erected, it must have been even more so.

GENERAL JOHN J. PERSHING. By Haig Patigian. East side of Music Concourse.

This is undoubtedly the most spit-and-polish statue in the

state of California. It must have been a real challenge to the sculptor to include all the accouterments that World War I officers wore—Sam Browne belts, riding boots and spurs, tunic and riding breeches—a very complex problem. The officers in those days were spiffy. Today, they look like businessmen wearing bus-conductor hats.

An unusual piece of information about this statue is that, according to the San Francisco Arts Commission, it is the only statue of Pershing in the United States. I find this very hard to believe, in the light of Pershing's immense popularity. But perhaps it's possible when you remember that most cities honor extraordinary men by naming schools, bridges, or streets after them. We can see this in San Francisco in the case of George Washington. Although there's a street, a park, a school, a grove (with plaque) in Golden Gate Park dedicated to Washington, to my knowledge, there is only one statue of Washington in the whole city. That's in the Veterans' War Memorial Building. Loads of Lincolns, but only one Washington.

DOUGHBOY. By Earl Cummings. Opposite 10th Avenue off John F. Kennedy Drive.

This statue was donated by the Native Sons and Daughters of the Golden West, a four-generation-ancestor organization. When you look down upon it from the drive, your first impression is that the statue is dedicated to the Boy Scouts. You see a bare-headed, very young man standing between two flagpoles. Only when you get close do you notice that the thing he is clutching to his breast is a World War I tin hat. Even when you look at him and read the inscription, you can't imagine that this boy is honoring those who marched off to the filthiest war ever fought. He obviously did not march off to war; he is all dressed up to perform in a patriotic pageant. This is a very fine example of kitsch. You wonder, when you look at this statue, what the real veterans thought when this very clean young boy was dedicated to those who were sent out to march against machine guns, burned to death with mustard gas, and suffocated with chlorine. But then again, the feeling behind the statue couldn't be better expressed, I guess. There will always be clean, very young men sent out to die, all dressed up as for a patriotic pageant.

ADMISSION DAY MONUMENT. By Douglas Tilden. Located about 100 feet from *Doughboy.*

You would swear that the same boy posed for this statue who posed for *Doughboy,* the faces are so similar, but that would be impossible. The *Doughboy* went up in 1930 and the Admission Day Monument in 1897. Another important difference is that while *Doughboy* is definitely a mamma's boy, this tad is full of ginger. He strides into the future holding aloft the new flag—with the added star of California's statehood—and totes upon his hip the biggest hog-leg pistol I have ever seen. It must be at least .55 caliber, and from the looks of him, he enjoyed shooting it just for the hell of it. It is a pleasure to be around such exuberance. When you consider that the many pioneers of that day were exactly like that, cocksure, feisty, you wonder how in the world they were stopped by something so trivial as the Pacific Ocean. It's amazing that they didn't take the whole earth.

PIONEER MOTHER MONUMENT. By Charles Grafly.

This lady with two children is found off John F. Kennedy Drive opposite 16th Avenue, near the road up to Stow Lake. Erected by the Native Daughters of the Golden West in 1940 (sculptured in 1915), this is a puzzling statue. The execution is only fair, but with curious embellishments (the device of cow skulls used as pedestal ornaments, for example). It is puzzling because the lady herself is too untrailworn to have been a pioneer mother. She obviously came to California by stagecoach and, from the sheer prettiness of her, looks as though she worked the dance halls on the way out. You can't imagine her flogging an ox. As if to prove it, the two children at her feet (presumably hers) are stark naked. I wonder about the reaction to the statue when it was first exhibited in 1915. There were plenty of real pioneer mothers around at that time, and although they might have been flattered by this very pretty, unwrinkled lady representing the idealized pioneer mother, they could only have been scandalized by her permitting her children to run around like that. The tongue-clucking must have been deafening and that is perhaps why they didn't put it up till 1940. Of course, all pioneer mother statues suffer in comparison with the fantastic Madonna of the Trail. I grew up with one copy on Route 40, outside Springfield, Ohio. That lady is a fiercely determined woman, strong as the earth, not pretty, indeed lantern-jawed; carrying one baby, with a toddler clutching at her skirts; and, as I remember it, there is a rifle involved. She wears high-top men's boots and could most definitely flog an ox. Under no circumstances would she let her children run around bare-bummed.

The Golden Gate Park Pioneer Mother is like Doughboy, so sweetened and idealized that the value as a memorial is lost in the sentimentality—a penchant often noticed in Native Sons and Daughters statues. But this statue is also of great historic interest in that it is one of the last statues erected to Womanhood. There was a last-gasp movement in the Gold Star Mothers Memorial Rock (a twenty-ton boulder with a plaque inscribed with the names of 39 mothers whose sons were killed in World War I, but nothing has been heard from it since—no monument honoring those mothers whose sons got killed in Korea or Vietnam). It is almost certain that no statue or monument will be erected ever again that honors Womanhood as an Ideal. There will be no memorials to Working Mothers or Secretaries or Clerical Workers (all deserving some statuary recognition). No, unless the militant women do it themselves, Womanhood is a dead letter as far as statuary goes.

JOHN MCLAREN. By Earl Cummings. Opposite 6th Avenue near the Conservatory on John F. Kennedy Drive.

Poor Uncle John must have voiced many ghostly mutterings and imprecations when this memorial was erected in 1944. Not only was this implacable statue-hater memorialized in bronze and planted in the park, but the statue is protected by signs telling people to keep off the grass—something he was absolutely against. Such signs are found nowhere else in the park. It's a crying shame what people will do to you when you're dead and can't fight back. Of course, there's none more deserving of a memorial statue in Golden Gate Park than John McLaren. It's a handsome, life-sized, very human statue of McLaren and his dog, but a much finer memorial was suggested by himself. When asked by the City of San Francisco what in the whole world he would like as a gift for his seventieth birthday, he replied, "Ten thousand yards of horse manure." Uncle John would have been happy and proud of a McLaren Memorial Horse Manure Grant, but, of course, a statue is easier. The only thing about his memorial he would have enjoyed is its position. His statue has been placed so far back from the Main Drive, and the bushes and trees are so crowded around, that the statue is hardly visible.

FATHER JUNIPERO SERRA. By Douglas Tilden. On the Music Concourse.

Father Serra, the founder of California's major missions (and therefore major cities—San Diego, Los Angeles, Santa Barbara, San Jose, San Rafael) is shown as a heroic monk brandishing a huge cross. It is a fierce statue and Father Serra's work in establishing pockets of Christian civilization in virgin California is considered so great that he is being promoted for sainthood by many of his admirers.

Tilden's monument reflects this heroic aspect of Serra's work, but when everything is considered, the statue makes you wonder about the man and his ultimate achievements besides leaving some very beautiful missions and, of course, place names. The problem is that when you look at the statue, a lot of things come to mind, not the least being that a huge number of California Indians he converted and civilized didn't want either Christianity or any other civilization but their own. California had the largest population of Indians in the country because the living then, as now, was easy. Fish and shellfish, game, wildfowl, fruits, grain, and vegetables were so plentiful, the climate so benign, that much of their time was spent in singing, dancing, gambling, self-adornment and taking steam baths. You can imagine what Father Serra thought about all this. He and his fellow monks made them into upstanding Christians; building missions, working in the fields of the land grantees (those *ranchos* were indeed *grande*), and generally teaching them all kinds of worthwhile trades such as plowing, woodchopping, brick-making, barge toting, and bale lifting. The monks clothed their nakedness and taught them to keep decently dirty—cutting out all that steam-bath nonsense. In retaliation, the Indians died in great numbers. No sooner would Serra civilize one than the Indian would say, "To hell with it" and lie down and die of sheer civilization. It must have been frustrating for the good fathers to have much of their labor force up and die on them, but undoubtedly they had the satisfaction that the savages passed on shriven. With so many pyrrhic victories, it is interesting to speculate how Father Serra felt about the whole thing. He was obviously an entrepreneur, a religious entrepreneur founding not just one but fourteen missions.

Cultural Memorials

Only eight creators of culture are honored with monuments in Golden Gate Park, and the breakdown, aesthetic and ethnic, is curious. Five of the eight are writers—Goethe, Schiller, Robert Burns, Shakespeare, and Cervantes. Music is represented by Beethoven and Verdi. The fine art of the Irish, politics, is represented by Robert Emmet. And that is all. The Germans come out ahead with three of the eight, and Scotland, Ireland, Spain, England, and Italy are honored by one countryman each. What is strange is that no Frenchman is honored with a bust or statue, even though there has always been a large and influential French colony in San Francisco. Poets, writers, and musicians are well represented, and the various religions are handled nicely. There are statues of Father Serra and Chaplain McKinnon (Catholic), Prayer Book Cross, which commemorates the first religious service in English by Sir Francis Drake's chaplain (Protestant), Gump's contribution of the Buddha in the Japanese Tea Garden, and an elegant Thomas Starr King (Unitarian). But there are no memorials to philosophers, artists, architects, scientists, or scholars, nor are there monuments to Americans of artistic genius.

But on to the statues. All these monuments are located around the Music Concourse.

CERVANTES. By Jo Mora. On the Music Concourse near John F. Kennedy Drive.

If there were a polling of statue-watchers to determine the most perfect and delightful monument to genius in Golden Gate Park, it is almost certain that the *Cervantes* statuary group would win hands down. The monument is a tableau depicting Don Quixote and Sancho Panza kneeling in homage before the bust of Cervantes perched above them on a pedestal. The bust of Cervantes is a copy of a long-lost portrait bust that was rediscovered just before the turn of this century. Cervantes and his two heroes are a perfect blend of truth, madness, and humor. Only rarely does a monument thrill the viewer by saying it all. You can't help acknowledge, "That is right, that is exactly right!"

Cervantes looks as if he must have been a hell of a fellow, strong and proud, dignified, but infused with humanity. Don Quixote and Sancho are depicted just as you imagine they must have looked. Sancho is humble and reverent without being carried away with it. Quixote projects *so much* self-possession, dignity, heartfelt respect, and above all virtue, that you have to smile because he is obviously crazy—humorously crazy in a very personal, nonsick way, like a rampant vegetarian. But while you smile at virtue carried to the point of caricature, it makes you sad that all heroes are not so fine. You know that only the mad can be so pure in heart and intention. This statuary group is so fine you find yourself showing it to your friends, as if you had sculptured it yourself.

It might be said that Jo Mora had an easy subject in Cervantes, in that, of his writings, only one book and two characters epitomize his work. With any other author of Cervantes' stature, it would be difficult to select let us say even three characters who, together with the bust of the author would give the whole message. It might make an interesting parlor game to try to make things fit. Lear, Iago, and Falstaff honoring Shakespeare? Or would it be Hamlet, Lady Macbeth, and Bottom? Who would delineate Joseph Conrad, Charles Dickens, Ibsen, Steinbeck, Hemingway, Dostoevski, Gide, Camus, Faulkner? And in what attitudes would the characters pose? At any rate, Jo Mora was perfect in capturing the essence of Cervantes. Another interesting feature of the sculpture is the steps leading up either side of the characters, so that one may examine them from above as well as from below. It is worth a special trip to view it.

BEETHOVEN. This was donated by the Beethoven Männerchor of New York to be exhibited in the 1915 Exposition. This exposition was one of the proudest moments of San Francisco history. Four-fifths of the city had been utterly destroyed by the 1906 earthquake-fire, but the rebuilding was carried on at such a furious rate that only nine years later the city was not only rebuilt but had within itself generated enough capital to mount a world's fair, an amazing accomplishment. (Think of it, the whole system of utilities, water, gas, electricity, streetcar lines re-established; the city rebuilt all with hand labor; no cement trucks, prefabricated paneling, or things like that— we're talking about a city of 200,000 souls.) The monument is a heroic bust of Beethoven upon a two-stepped pedestal. Although Beethoven is properly fierce and hugely withdrawn within himself, it is a rather prosaic monument, too full of dignity and austerity to really grab you—even if it weren't hidden fairly effectively by bushes, probably planted by John McLaren.

VERDI. By Ettore Patrizzi. A few dozen yards from Beethoven, toward the road behind the band shell, Verdi is another thing entirely. It was donated by the Italian citizens of San Francisco in 1915 and is a marvel. You see a huge bust of Verdi. If there were a statue proportionate to the bust, it would be at least twenty feet tall. Although it is not fair to compare the monuments of Beethoven and Verdi, it is interesting to do so. Beethoven is clean-shaven, bushy-haired, and wearing a Nehru jacket. Verdi is sparse of hair, but with a full beard and naked from the shoulders up (as in the busts of Roman patricians). Both are fierce geniuses, but Verdi comes out the fiercer. This is probably because of his apparent nudity. The reason is lost, but I'm sure that everybody has noticed that as far as fierceness goes, a fierce naked bearded man has it all over a fierce, clean-shaven man who's wearing a Nehru jacket. It may be simply that, since the bust of Verdi is larger than the bust of Beethoven, Verdi is fierce closer at hand while Beethoven is remotely fierce. But then again, Verdi's fierceness is enhanced by props. Beethoven's bust is lonely-fierce upon his pedestal. Verdi's pedestal, on the other hand, is embellished with two overwrought Italians with flags who appear to be trying to get at him for some reason.

ROBERT EMMET. By Gerome Conner. Donated by former Mayor James Phelan.

The uniqueness of this statue is more interesting than the statue itself. The statue depicts Emmet making his final impassioned speech before the English hanged him for his revolutionary activities in 1803. Since his face and personality are so little known to the average American, there's not much on which to base an opinion of the statue (as to whether it's a good Emmet or a bad Emmet). It depicts a man in Colonial-times dress—knee breeches, hose—of the kind that might be found in front of any New England courthouse honoring a local hero of the Revolution. The interesting thing about this statue is that De Valera himself spoke at the dedication in 1919—something that makes it much closer to us. It is also one of the very few memorials in this country raised to Irishmen of cultural or historical moment; indeed it is one of the few raised outside Ireland itself (not including saints). There have been loads of hyphenated Irishmen honored; Irish-Americans like Phelan, who donated this statue—he has a bust in City Hall; Irish-Englishmen like George Bernard Shaw and Oscar Wilde; Irish-expatriate like James Joyce, but damn few Irish-Irish. It's time that the Irish promoted their own. I'm sure that San Francisco could find a place for a heroic statue of Brendan Behan or De Valera himself. All they have to do is find an Irish sculptor. They are all overseas.

SHAKESPEARE. In the Shakespeare Garden opposite the Arboretum.

This bust is of great intrinsic as well as cultural value in that it is one of the two castings in the world of Garrett Jansen's *Shakespeare,* sculptured in 1616 shortly after Shakespeare's death. It is a little hard to find and even harder to view. The bust is located in one of the secret pockets of Golden Gate Park, the Shakespeare Garden which lies tucked way off a footpath approximately opposite the Arboretum. The garden itself, a project of the California Spring Wildflower Association, is delightful. Enclosed by huge screening hedges is a wide lawn ringed by benches. It's quiet there. The garden contains every flower mentioned by Shakespeare in all his works. At McLaren Lodge you can get a list of these flowers that gives their names in Shakespeare's time; the common name for them today, when it differs; and the Latin botanical designation. This pamphlet lists, as well, all the vegetables and trees mentioned in Shakespeare's works (340 plants; flowers, trees, weeds, shrubs, vegetables, and fruits). Flowers, of course, can be used as lyric metaphors, and were. Common then was a whole language of flowers, as subtle but precise as the wording of an inner-office memo. It was a mark of Shakespeare's genius to introduce the common turnip and onion, the leek and the radish, the cabbage and the parsnip into the dialogue of a dramatic performance and make their mention equally meaningful. No other playwright has ever accomplished this. The vegetables, unfortunately, were not thought worthy enough by the California Wildflower Association to honor by planting in this garden. It's a pity because if anything could deculturize Shakespeare, it would be a planting of the turnip along with the rose. It's really a double pity, brought about by the Association's ignorance of the flowers of vegetables permitted to go to seed. They are often as lovely as the plants grown for the flower alone. Anyone who has admired the delicate yellow blossoms of the lettuce can attest to it. Indeed, I understand that it is usual for the families working on the Ferry-Morse seed farms to make holiday to the fields when the radish comes to bloom.

At any rate, the bust is hard to view because at this writing, and for the last six months, it has been hidden behind iron shutters because of fear of vandalism. It is probable that if a plot of leek were planted here or a patch of cabbage, the vandals would rip them up and eat them, get rid of their aggressiveness, and do no harm to Shakespeare.

Most of the fine-art sculpture in Golden Gate Park is located on or near the Music Concourse. The majority of it is of interest in a historic sense only—looking at what our grandparents thought to be beautiful. There are a few, though, that still grab you and are worth a special trip to view.

Two of the grandest sculptures adorn the spandrels of the band shell—officially, the Spreckels Temple of Music. Robert Ingersall Aitken's two middle-relief nudes are certainly the most gorgeous, voluptuous, sexy, and *saftig* nudes to be seen in the city. Undoubtedly, when they were dedicated in 1899, they came complete with high-blown allegory, paeans to their purity of form, and raptures about their appeal to one's artistic sensibilities. Doubtless, too, they appeared just as sexy to our grandparents as they do to us today, if not sexier. Grandfather, especially, must have been overjoyed. In those days, as today, a man is suspect if he too obviously loiters around naked statues, gawking and ogling. These huge reliefs so conspicuously adorn the spandrels that they permitted Grandfather to appear perfectly upright, indeed enlightened and instructive when he brought grandmother and the children to be edified by the band concert.

The whole approach to the naked body in Victorian and Edwardian times, as compared to our own, is extremely interesting. The three major naked statuary works in the park, *Roman Gladiator,* the *Apple Press,* and those delectable ladies on the band shell, were dedicated in 1893, 1894, and 1899 respectively. The only other nude in the park is the statue of a little girl with a squirrel (now in ruin) near Children's Playground, which was erected in 1928. Contemplation of the impact of the nude upon Victorian thought patterns provides considerable amusement. Here are a lady and gentleman out for a stroll in the park. She is wearing perhaps thirty-five pounds of clothing which covers her from wrist to neck to below the shoe. He calls his legs "lower members." They approach *Roman Gladiator* opposite De Young Museum. *Roman Gladiator,* except for a helmet, is as bare as a turnip. Some comment must be uttered because, as a recognized work of art, it perforce twangs the aesthetic strings of everybody's cultural sensibilities. By a process of doublethink, *Roman Gladiator* ceases to be naked and becomes an allegory. The gentleman spouts Virgil, the lady babbles about lines and planes and each tries not to be caught looking at *Roman Gladiator's* genitals. Repeat this thousands of times and you have a very funny era. Certainly in no other period in man's history have so many bald lies been nobly spoken, so many euphemisms and circumlocutions invented, so much claptrap, conversational and cultural, been blathered to justify the viewing of a work of art (unless it is in our own time since abstract-expressionism).

The need for nudes, though, would not be gainsaid in those days. American Heritage's *American Album,* a collection of antique American photographs, points this up very nicely. On page 212 we see a typical middle-class Victorian lady knitting in her parlor. She is garbed to the eyeballs—almost literally since the only flesh showing is her hands and face. On the mantlepiece, however, even more prominent than the pieces of cut glass and porcelain figurines, are an alabaster *Aphrodite,* naked as a jaybird, on one side, and *Roman Gladiator,* figleaved but otherwise bare on the other.

It is curious how far the pendulum has swung. The nude body in our time has lost considerable favor as a fit subject for a work of art. In most instances it has become lines, planes, and masses. With the exhibition of the human body all about us—on the streets and in movies and advertisements—we have lost the need to keep an alabaster *Aphrodite* around to remind us what the human body looks like under all our clothes. This might seem to be enlightenment, but it's not that simple. It could also be argued that the viewing of so much public semi-nudity has jaded us to the point where the human form is no longer artistically interesting—and that is decadence.

Since we've brought up *Roman Gladiator* and the *Apple Press,* we might as well describe them here. ROMAN GLADI-ATOR, by Guillaume Geefs, was a gift to the city for the 1893

Midwinter Exposition. He stands a little under life-sized (probably life-sized for Romans) and although he doesn't make you fall on your head in sheer wonder, he is a fine example of a lost tradition. I speak of groups, organizations, or communities that donate statues to a city for a fair or exposition. Many of the statues we now enjoy in Golden Gate Park, especially the cultural ones, were given by organizations who wanted a finger in the pie. This was usually done for a combination of status and promotional reasons. Expositions then, as now, were grand things, and if an outside city or association could include itself in this grandness, it was thought very worthwhile indeed. It certainly kept the sculptors busy. Fresno, for example, sent to the Midwinter Exposition a fine statuary group entitled *An Allegory of the Raisin,* depicting a gorgeous nude picking grapes from an overburdened vine while a stalwart farmer looked gratefully at the sun and a pioneer-type mother made rice pudding. Petaluma, the egg and poultry capital of northern California, donated a ten-foot granite sculpture of a noble chicken entitled *Hymn to the Hen.* Both these works are unfortunately lost (although it is rumored that the chicken is still around somewhere in somebody's barn).

It nicely points up an interesting difference between then and now. Photographers and architects now dominate the exposition field and sculptors are out in the cold (photographers and architects do not have the direct physical involvement with their arts that sculptors have).

APPLE PRESS, by Thomas Shield-Clarke, was also purchased for the Midwinter Exposition. Although it is a handsome and ingenious work—a naked, well-muscled man turns the screw of the press while a naked boy watches the action—with a clever built-in gimmick—the spout of the press runs into a sculptured bucket in which is concealed a drinking fountain—its choice is a little baffling. As far as I know, California was never famous for its fabulous apple juice, or cider, or applejack for that matter, while the wine industry has been celebrated here since Mission days. The only thing I can think of is that the Prohibitionists got to the statue commission and shouted down the alternate submission, *The Wine Press*. Naked apple-squeezers *Si,* naked grape-trompers, *No!* Although why an apple-presser would be naked in the first place is more than I can fathom—at least grape treaders are functionally naked from the knees down to save their pants and boots.

THE BALL PLAYER. By Douglas Tilden. Acrosss from the Conservatory on John F. Kennedy Drive.

This is one of my favorite statues and depicts a baseball player dressed in the uniform of the 1890s winding up to pitch a ball. With the sole exception of the new statue of Stan Musial recently erected at Busch Stadium in St. Louis, this is, to my knowledge the only life-sized statue of a baseball player in the United States (excluding the Baseball Hall of Fame in Cooperstown, N.Y.). It was erected in 1892 and it seems incredible that, in spite of our passion for this sport—indeed, all sports—we have handled our baseball players and other athletes so shabbily—as far as statues are concerned, even though we hold high the qualities that make them household words. Willy Mays, falling back for an imposssible catch, would make a wonderful statue. *The Ball Player* does something to balance the scale, but it was created nearly seventy years ago. It is time to honor an athlete again.

BRONZE LION AND THE BROWN GATE. These two animal sculptures are considered together because they are unique pieces and have a lot in common. Bronze Lion, near Cervantes, is perhaps the most powerful sculpture of a lion in San Francisco. This lion, by R. Hinton Perry, is a hungry, snarling, out-of-sorts lion, skinny, with his backbone showing. This lion is not a noble beast, as most of them are, but a ferocious beast. The noble lion is a terrific subject for a sculptor. Aloof, dignified, handsome, the lion has adorned more public and private buildings than any other animal in the whole earthly zoology. For whatever reason, we have many approaches to the lion in San Francisco. We have the truly noble lions of the Palace of the Legion of Honor; we have the croquignoled Lions guarding the gates of San Francisco College of Women—probably the only lions with permanent waves in the world; we have the lipsticked and fruity lions in front of the Sutro Mansion on Twin Peaks; we have Oriental lions in Chinatown; we have great roaring lions on the façade of the Superba Market on Haight Streeet, whose gaping maws once held light bulbs; and we have probably the most foolish lions ever created, the marble lions who sit in front of the big apartment house at Washington and Laguna with ribbons in their mouths.

Bronze Lion in Golden Gate Park, though, is in a class of its own. I have seen little children scream in terror when their parents wanted to put them on his back for a cute photo. *Bronze Lion* is one hell of a lion.

The Brown Gate. At 8th Avenue and Fulton. Perched on two pillars flanking the 8th Avenue entrance are a mountain lion and a bear. They are very fine in several aspects. First, they are snarling, ferocious, dangerous-looking animals. You can almost see the saliva drip from their snapping jaws. Second, they are so placed on either side of the roadway that they vent their rage upon the automobiles going to and from the park. The people walking along the path are not growled at, only the cars. It would be interesting to learn whether Earl Cummings, the sculptor, plannned it this way or whether it just happened. Although The Brown Gate was erected in 1908, it is very comforting to realize that there are indeed eternal verities and that this protest against nonpedestrian traffic in public parks goes back sixty years.

GODDESS OF THE FOREST. By Dudley C. Carter. This huge (26-foot) statue was carved from a single redwood log. It depicts a very large seated lady holding a bear in her lap. The size of the thing really grabs you. It must be at least seven feet in diameter. Any monolithic-type statue seven feet thick and nearly as tall as a three-story building cannot fail to be impressive. It's located on the Lindley Meadow off John F. Kennedy Drive around 30th Avenue. I imagine that such a huge piece of material to work with would drive any sculptor a little mad. The posssibilities of hacking and chopping to your heart's content would indeed be heady—balanced only by the depressing knowledge that if you failed, you'd be stuck with a huge lump of ruined wood three stories high and seven feet thick. Dudley C. Carter must be commended in that he accepted the challenge and succeeded. Many have failed with lesser opportunities.

POOL OF ENCHANTMENT. By Earl Cummings. Located at the entrance of the De Young Museum, this is Earl Cummings' finest work—of all his work in the city. It is a curious statuary group. At first you are disposed to put it down merely as a blatant attempt to work on your sentiment. Two mountain lions perched on one rock in the middle of the pool listen raptly to a little Indian boy who is playing the flute to them on another island about eight feet away. The message comes across pretty strong at first—"Music hath charm . . ." but then something intrudes. You look at the lions. They are not charmed—they are not relaxed as if they were attending a recital. They are eying that little Indian boy with a mixture of curiosity about what he is doing there on that island and what is making all that noise? You look back at the Indian boy and notice that it might not be a flute at all, it might a whistle and he is deliberately blowing it to annoy hell out of the mountain lions. You look back at the lions and discover that their rapt attention is not directed as much to the music as to eighty pounds of juicy little Indian boy and they are measuring the distance between the islands. You look back in fear at the Indian and see that he is not as charmed with his own music as he thinks the mountain lions are; in fact, he has a very calculating look on his face. You immediately search his island for a hidden Sharps repeater and have bad feelings about sneaky, underhanded Indian boy-flautists—indeed all flautists. But there is not a gun, not even a penknife. You search the pool. There are no other islands upon which mighty hunters, who are using little-Indian-boy whistle blowers as bait, might be concealed, but there are several suspicious-looking reeds through which they might be breathing while hiding in the water. The whole aspect gets very spooky after a while. Here is something that could be resolved, but isn't. The lions could jump across and eat up the kid; the little fakir could call in the troops and skag the lions; both the lions and the kid could quietly go away and leave you in peace. But as it is, looking at the *Pool of Enchantment* is like reading about the moves and countermoves of politicians—a very unrestful situation. I am not at all enchanted with the *Pool of Enchantment*. I don't look at it any more.

DORÉ VASE. There was a lot of soul-searching before including the Doré vase with the other Golden Gate statuary. In the first place, it's located within the De Young Museum itself, which takes it out of the category of public statuary. My first excuse is that it used to be outside until just two years ago. The second is that vase is undoubtedly one of the most bizarre and unusual pieces of sculpture in the world, ranking in quality and uniqueness with the grotesqueries of Messerschmidt. The Doré vase boggles the mind. At far glimpse it is merely a very beautiful and elegant embellished vase. A huge vase, to be sure, ten feet tall, but so perfectly proportioned that it doesn't look ungainly or outsized from any distance. Gustave Doré, of course, is noted for his etchings, especially his dark and terror-filled illustrations of Dante's *Inferno*. His sculpture is less well known, but, as you can see from the vase, it is also full of darkness; it is also a terrifying piece of work.

The terror of the vase builds slowly. When you first see it, you are delighted by its sheer exuberance. Here is one hell of a big vase covered from lip to base with charming cherubs, cute Cupids, naughty Pans, satyrs and nymphs, tipsy Bacchuses, and a host of little animals and insects enjoying themselves immensely. All these demigods (there are 88 separate figures) cavort amidst a veritable jungle of grapevines and other foliage. You are full of admiration of Doré's handling of the strictly technical problem of incorporating this army of flora and fauna on the vase without detracting at all from the graceful lines of the vase itself. And you smile to yourself as the naïveté of an age that would go to much frou-frou to make a work of Art.

The superior smile gradually fades as you notice details in the vase. The cute little Cupids and cherubs are the first to make you lose your innocence. They are shown at play, for example, with one of the drunken Bacchuses. Their play, which at first seemed innocent teasing, appears on closer examination not innocent at all but the working of gross indignities upon the sot. Then you notice the Cupids playing with the rat. This is no cute little mouse but a snarling sewer rat. He looks dirty and dangerous. He is not playing with the Cupids, he has been cornered by them and you are aware that this is a prelude to torture. The same is true with the Cupids and the fly, the lizard, and the butterfly. The portrayal of lower animals and insects in a major work is extremely rare in Western sculpture, therefore these examples are unique. You don't realize it until you see these beasts and think about it. Sculptors usually use only animals that can be raised to allegory: bulls, lions, or dragons. Like the rat, the fly here is not glorified but is the common, disease-carrying housefly sculptured about four inches long. He is waiting to have his six-inch wings torn off. The tormented lizard is also a common garden lizard. The tone of the work is probably best seen in the butterfly. The butterfly, which usually connotes beauty and pleasant, warm summer days is shown here with grotesquely swollen wings. Wings like tumors. At first you think that it is because of the difficulty in casting the bronze, but each piece on the vase was cast separately and attached individually. The grape leaves are thinner than the butterfly's wings, so it must have been deliberately done.

These details throw a chill over the whole vase and force you to examine it all. The terror deepens. The cherubs and Cupids, as you look at them, become vicious, deliberate juvenile delinquents, reveling in their delinquency. The Bacchuses, who at first glance were antique celebrants in Dionysian ecstasy, become death-wishers of alcoholic oblivion. The nymphs and satyrs, who at first glance glorified life through exultant orgy, become de Sade creatures who glorify deliberate perversion. The vase, which appeared at first to be a quaint Victorian expression of Elysium, becomes a terror-filled Hades; the demigods, demons; the host of creatures, a mob! And disconcertingly showing through it all and keeping its purity is the shape of the vase itself. There is probably no other piece of sculpture in the world so surrealistic. The vase is worth a special trip to the De Young Museum.

5
Bars and Bookstores

It is not for nothing that San Francisco has the reputation of being a convivial and literate town. The ratio of our bars to bookstores to people is probably unique in America. There are (in September 1972) 1,760 establishments in San Francisco where a thirsty man can get something to drink. With a population that hovers around 700,000 this gives one bar for every 400 citizens. At the same time, there are 207 bookstores within the city limits, listed in the telephone book. This gives a ratio of one bookstore for every eight drinking places in town. These figures are startling. When I discovered them, I attempted to establish a grand conviviality-literacy schema for the major cities of America. I thought it would be interesting to match this ratio to that of other major cities and see how the results jibed with what one knows and feels about the city —its reputation. What is the bar-bookstore-population index for Cleveland, for example, and for New Orleans, Boston, Kansas City, or Salt Lake City?

The research promptly fell to pieces because of the variables and the difficulty of research. The number of bookstores was easy to count because they're listed in the yellow pages of the various phone books. Bars are something else. Resort towns will be somewhat loaded in favor of bars because drinking places are also restaurants, night clubs, and hotels. College towns will be heavy on bookstores because textbooks are sold and most states forbid selling drink to those under twenty-one. Again, when is a bar a bar? It's imposssible to find out unless you write the state or local licensing agencies. One of the most famous bars in town, the Top of the Mark, is not listed as a tavern, a cocktail lounge, or a restaurant in the Yellow Pages.

The research wasn't altogether lost, though, for I did learn two interesting pieces of information. The first was that Boston, generally thought of as a literate city, has only sixty bookstores listed as being in Boston itself. That struck me as odd, and odder still was the fact that only 180 bookstores are listed in the Greater Boston area—Brookline, Cambridge, Dedham, Natick, Lexington, etcetera. Compared to San Francisco, which has 207 bookstores, Boston seems to be a bit on the short side. The same is true of Philadelphia, a much larger town than either San Francisco or Boston, where only 118 bookstores are listed as being in the city. There must be some significance here, if only that San Franciscans buy their books in bookstores and people in these other two cities join the bookclubs. Someone should investigate this in depth.

Bars

> "There is nothing which has yet been contrived by man, by which so much happiness is produced as by a good tavern or inn."
> —Samuel Johnson

The great number of drinking places in San Francisco can be explained in two ways. First, it is a tourist city—many of the drinking places are also restaurants or night clubs. Second, the density of population shows that many San Franciscans live in apartment houses and hotels, especially in the downtown area that runs roughly from Divisidero to the Bay. Bars are important social gathering places, almost like clubs or churches. They are easy places to meet people, without the bother of formally joining groups. For the young unmarried, there's no better place to meet members of the opposite sex for social intercourse or whatever. Indeed, the most popular gathering places are referred to locally as "Body Exchanges."

With the great diversity of people in the city, it is to be expected that there are to be found some great bars—people make the bars. The list that follows is a parochial one in that these are the bars that I have enjoyed. Now, there are bars and there are bars. I am no great bar-goer—I don't drink regularly in any given bar. The places listed, though, have great character, and characters; you can loaf in these bars without feeling as though you're merely loafing. There are some similarities in the bars on this list. Nearly all of them are well lighted, none of them blast a perpetual jukebox—you can converse in them without shouting—and each maintains its own integrity; none is like any other bar in the city. They are scattered so as to give a haven in nearly any part of the city in which you might find yourself. We might well start at Harrington's.

HARRINGTON'S. 9 Jones Street. Harry Harrington's bar is next door to St. Anthony's Kitchen on Jones Street. The bar is also next to the main office of the Hibernia Bank on the corner where the poor waiting for lunch used to lounge in the marble recesses of the ground-floor windows of the bank. Often they panhandled the bank's customers. The bank, chagrined and embarrassed by this blatant exhibition of insolvency, finally put metal spikes on the window sills. The bankers thought this a master stroke, for, at one blow, they discouraged the bums from sitting on their property and turned the bums into upstanding citizens. It was, of course, foolishness on the bank's part because the bums still hang around and panhandle the customers. Much more could have been accomplished by putting up a sign reading:

LOOK AROUND YOU!
These people are bums because they didn't open a savings account at
HIBERNIA BANK

But bankers are notoriously shortsighted and their minds are closed to ideas such as this.

The type of bar Harrington's is can be illustrated by an event that happened at one of its fabulous St. Patrick's Day parties. Now, most of Harrington's customers are Irishmen— no, super-Irishmen, almost professional Irishmen. For St.

Patrick's Day, Harry Harrington usually hires four Irish piper bands that play from 6 AM when the bar opens till 2 AM when it closes. Often the line of people waiting to get into Harrington's on St. Patrick's Day stretches halfway round the block.

Well, it seems that one St. Patrick's Day, a blowsy Irishwoman with typical Irish wit came in with a little snake, which she brandished in the faces of the patrons shrieking, "Here's one snake Blessed Saint Pat didn't drive from Ireland!" This was greeted with much good humor and many free drinks until the joke wore thin. One patron, who had been brandished at once too often, asked the lady to remove the snake from his face as it was getting into his drink. With a whoop and giggle, she persisted. He then used stronger language, requesting her to take the snake and . . . The lady grew surly and thrust the snake again in his face, whereupon he grabbed the snake and bit off its head. The ensuing brouhaha is still remembered by the patrons and the police, who had to be called, and philosophical discussions about the morality of the act go on yet today.

TOMMY'S JOYNT. Van Ness and Geary. Tommy's Joynt is a long-time San Francisco landmark. As seen from the outside, with huge new garish decorations (except for the ratty old buffalo head mounted above the sign), it looks like a genuine, phony-baloney tourist trap. Once inside, you are positive it is a genuine, phony-baloney tourist trap. The walls and ceilings are decorated with the damnedest collection of awful trash you have ever seen. It is not until you begin to examine the "decorations" at close range that you begin to appreciate it. Tommy Harris (billed outside as the proprietor and founder) is a collector and Tommy's Joynt is his gallery. Hanging over your table might be a unique collection of bootleggers' business cards, or brass chits from houses of ill repute. It is a house of outrageous and bizarre ephemera. After it dawns on you that he is serious—that everything inside is "good stuff" to this crazy collector, you know that this is a very special place. Every time you go, you find something that you missed before. Tommy serves an excellent *hofbrau*—one of the few places where "sliced before your eyes" sandwiches of roast beef and turkey can be told apart by flavor, not texture alone. Buffalo stew is a specialty and the bar serves a collection of beers from twenty countries.

EDINBURGH CASTLE. 950 Geary (Geary between Larkin and Polk). This is a huge, barnlike place. A grand bar, tables along the walls and on the balcony. A home away from home for English, Scots, and Scots-Irish and their friends, it is as fiercely British-Isles-once-removed as the Frankfort Hilton is a bastion of America in Germany. There are bagpipers on weekends, pints of English beer, furious dart games, nostalgic bursting into English song by the nationals sitting at the tables. Around the corner on Larkin is the Old Chelsea Fish and Chip House that was the original and is still the best fish and chip house in San Francisco. Edinburgh Castle will let you eat it there, while drinking their beer, as a matter of course—something rare in a bar.

It's a happy and serious place with a clientele of talkers. With no effort on your part, you can get into fifteen discussions in the same number of minutes. In the Men's Room of Edinburgh Castle, I saw the most malicious, gleefully grating graffiti I've ever come across. Some joker wrote, " 'Tis a pity that you can't trust an Englishman's word, the Scots are such cowards and the Irish tend to homosexuality." I saw it early in the evening and, later in the evening, saw that someone had put his fist through it, plywood and all.

THE RATHSKELLER. 600 Turk (Turk and Polk). This is a very comfortable German bar-restaurant in the basement of California Hall, the center of German-American activities since after the earthquake-fire. The bar is a gracious place, the back bar hand-carved Bavarian with cut flowers in vases. There is a warmth about this bar, afternoons or evenings, that makes you feel relaxed even before any drinking is done. The restaurant connected with the bar serves excellent *hasenpfeffer* and *sauerbraten* (it's a favorite lunch spot of those who work in City Hall and the State and Federal buildings). On weekends there is usually a singer–accordion player in lederhosen.

THE PUB. Geary and Masonic—opposite Sears. The Pub has been around since 1926 but has recently acquired a new popularity. A couple of years ago it was just another neighborhood bar, but, after a change of decor, it turned into a very nice drinking place, often visited by local radio and TV personalities. It's an open and airy place with hanging plants, but what makes it special, although you don't catch it right off the bat, is that there are no booths or little tables. There are overstuffed couches and chairs around coffee tables, dining-room tables seating six or eight. It's like drinking at home, with lots of company, a comfortable and relaxed kind of place. The great option is that if the company bores you, you can walk out—something you can't do at home.

ABBEY TAVERN. Geary at 5th Avenue. As Edinburgh Castle is English-Scots, the Abbey Tavern is Irish. The talk is mostly of sports (soccer) and politics. I wouldn't be a bit surprised if this were a hotbed of IRA activity. This is a great sitting-around and talking place. Entertainment on weekends.

2901 CLUB. 2901 San Bruno (San Bruno and Woolsey near McLaren Park). This is a neighborhood bar, but San Bruno Avenue being what it is, it's not what you think when you hear the term. A bastion of working-class conservatism (there's a sign over the bar, "Support your local police"), it is labor radical, most of the patrons being union members. I was a little wary my first visit because I have a beard, but I didn't even get a glance from the patrons, in fact, was almost immediately included in an argument about freeway building that had been going on for some time before I came and was still raging when I left. Adjoining the bar is a *bocce* court. The players will tell you how to play the game, and if a court's open, you can play yourself. This is a great neighborhood with fine bars. Down the street is a place called the "Club Firefly." Until it was torn down for a supermarket there was another grand bar called "Forty Shades of Green."

OLD CLAM HOUSE. Oakdale and Bay Shore. Near the produce market, on the way to Candlestick Park, is this surprising bar-restaurant apparently stuck out in the middle of nowhere. It's an old joint that serves the best clam chowder in town (and great other seafood). One of the nice customs here is to serve a demitasse of hot, spicy clam juice with your first drink. The walls here are decorated with San Francisco memorabilia. At lunch- and dinner-times, it's crowded with workers from the nearby industries and the executives from those places as well. A comfortable place.

RIBELTAD VORDEN. 3200 Folsom (Precita and Folsom—Bernal Heights). The name comes from the silk embroidered banner behind the bar. The original owner was a merchant seaman from Costa Rica. When he was in Japan, he thought it would be nice to have the Costa Rican seal embroidered as a souvenir. He gave a copy to the embroiderer and the man did a first-rate job, except that the country's motto "Libertad y Orden" came out as "Ribeltad Vorden"—as good a name for a bar as any.

This section of Bernal Heights became fairly well populated with refugees of the love generation who fled the Haight when it turned sour. Most of them are working artists or craftsmen, and so, interesting. The bar itself is a large, high-ceilinged room with hanging plants and interesting prints. The clientele is probably the most mixed of any bar in town. One afternoon, I saw three Hell's Angels with their girls, two insurance salesmen, assorted workingmen and hippies, an old lady beer drinker from the neighborhood, and two Air Force chaplains (there are few bars in the neighborhood, so this one catches them all).

It's a beer-wine bar where one may linger or read a newspaper. They have just introduced lunches and live entertainment on weekends.

COOKIE'S STAR BUFFET. 708 Kearny (Clay and Kearny, across from Portsmouth Square.) From the exterior, you'd never mark this as a bar of any interest. It looks drab, even seedy—inside, the impression lingers. But Cookie Pucetti's is the haunt of all kinds of interesting people. Cookie seems to know everybody in town, politicians, boxers, baseball and football players, lawyers and stockbrokers, merchant seamen, gamblers, hookers, union leaders—you name it. You can overhear the damnedest conversations here, and arguments and bets. A fascinating bar.

It adjoins the Star Cafeteria, a place where one can buy two eggs, toast, potatoes, and coffee for 63 cents.

ENRICO'S COFFEE HOUSE. 504 Broadway. Enrico Banducci is the former owner of the Hungry I, where he launched the careers of, or gave a big boost upward to, the likes of Mort Sahl, Bill Cosby, Phyllis Diller, Irwin Corey. The night club is no more, but his present establishment, though not more than ten years old, is a solid San Francisco landmark. It's a bar-restaurant, sidewalk café, basically, but much more. It's a gathering place of visiting celebrities (and local ones), running heavily to the arts and show business. Actors, singers, comedians, writers, and celebrities of all description meet at Enrico's. It's a casual place and no one cares if you're not a celebrity.

RENO'S. 123 Post (and Kearny). TEMPLEBAR. 1 Tillman Place (off Grant Avenue, between Sutter and Post Streets). These two downtown bars are listed together as good drinking places because they both have much in common. Both are good luncheon spots and the clientele of both are lively and exciting. Reno's runs heavily to sporting types, Templebar runs to Montgomery Street entrepreneurs. It is at this point that I might give some information about two San Franciscan phenomena, dice and dominoes.

The rattle of the dice cup is a strange sound to most visitors from the Middle West. Stranger yet is the click of the domino tiles. Both are bar passions in San Francisco. While all other kinds of open gaming is forbidden under California law, the dice cup is a standard bar fixture—in San Francisco domino sets are also available. Shaking dice is certainly an easy way to resolve the old argument, "This is on me", "No, this is *my* round!" and all that foolishness. Liars Dice, Bull Dice, the games are as numerous as the bars and in each bar there are experts. One of the recent local best sellers was a book explaining the games and strategies involved in each. Most bartenders will roll for your drinks—double or nothing—and will explain the games if they're not rushed. Dominoes has become a local sport (a sport is a fad that lasts longer than five years). It's a complicated simple little game that has reached such popularity that an annual Domino Championship is held by the *Chronicle* (the teams are sponsored by bars and social clubs at a stiff entrance fee), the proceeds going to charity. This is another facet of San Francisco bar life and these two bars are good places to witness it.

BUENA VISTA. 2765 Hyde Street (Near Ghirardelli Square). HENRY AFRICA'S. 2260 Van Ness Avenue (Van Ness and Broadway). PERRY'S. 1944 Union Street (Union and Laguna). These three are also listed together because they have much in common. Foremost is that all three are very nice bars. Buena Vista offers a beautiful view of the Bay; Henry Africa's is a bright, comfortable place, and Perry's is usually full of interesting people. The second thing these bars have in common is that they are all resorts for the single and searching, great places to meet people. Perry's and Henry Africa's are relatively new to the city, but the Buena Vista has been around for forty years. All are good places to go.

MOONEY'S IRISH PUB. 1525 Grant Avenue (Grant and Union). Upper Grant Avenue has a wealth of great bars, but Mooney's Irish Pub is one of the finest. In the heart of Bohemian North Beach, it is an attractive place to drink and draws all kinds of colorful people—artists, writers, and talkers—especially talkers.

VESUVIO CAFÉ. 225 Columbus (near Broadway). The slogan around the top of the façade, "I am itching to get away from Portland, Oregon," might put you off as hoky tourist, but the bar is genuine. The caption is from the 1890s postcard of a couple being eaten up by bedbugs—a collection of these cards is flash-projected onto a screen above the bar. The clientele is youngish, the drinks cheap, and the atmosphere pleasant.

RIORDEN'S. Embarcadero and Mission (Ferry Building). Once the Embarcadero was a very rough place with a plethora of colorful (and dangerous) waterfront bars. What with the freeway, the tearing down of the old Produce Market, and the new construction around the foot of Mission Street, there are just two old-fashioned waterfront bars left. *Riorden's,* at the foot of Mission, is the more colorful of the two remaining. It is visited mostly by merchant seamen and longshoremen, and it's a rough and raucous but pleasant place to drink. Clean and well lit, it has ships' models decorating the bar and merchant nautical stuff on the walls. The last time I was there, a miserable-looking gent in a neat gray suit came in and sat a couple of stools down. His face was a mess, nose bruised, one eye closed, the other cut. "Where are you from?" the bartender asked. "Sweden," the guy said and the bartender burst into laughter. "Had to come all the way from Sweden to get your head punched in, that's a hell of a note!" The people at the bar roared and the bartender gave him the first drink on the house. It's that kind of place.

THE EAGLE CAFÉ. Embarcadero and Jefferson (Fisherman's Wharf). The Eagle Café is longshoremen, fishermen, and Muni. Right at the fringe of Fisherman's Wharf (the Municipal RY bus barns are nearby, the Longshoreman's Hall is a block away), it opens about 5:30–6 AM—when the crabbing boats begin to come in—and closes at 4 PM. The breakfasts and lunches are excellent and inexpensive, the bar usually packed all day. This is a place where you could fool away the whole day listening to the bar conversation and consider it a day well spent.

BEACH CHALET. End of Golden Gate Park on the Great Highway. The bar at the Beach Chalet, indeed the whole building, is run by the Joseph P. McQuaide post of the Veterans of Foreign Wars. During the week, it's open from 4 PM to midnight, on weekends from noon to 2 AM. Built by the WPA, it's one of the most gracious drinking places in town. On the walls over the bar and around the room are the excellent murals by Lucien Labaudt. They are rather a tour de force of 1937 local comment. John McLaren sits on a park bench, William Randolph Hearst is shown as a press photographer, an elegant Benny Bufano is riding a polo pony, Lucius Beebe leads one of his St. Bernards, Harry Bridges pushes a hand truck in a waterfront scene, and on and on. It's almost a secret bar, gone rather seedy because of the restrictions placed upon it by the Rec and Park Dept. (no advertising, for example). If you're on Ocean Beach of an afternoon, be sure to visit it.

This by no means a comprehensive listing of San Francisco bars. It is rather a sketch. There are 1,760 drinking places in town. This list doesn't even include the most famous, the Top of the Mark and the Crown Room of the Fairmont—the most popular view bars in town, or the new bars in the Cannery or Ghirardelli Square. These bars, though, are attractions in themselves, good places to go, and relax and enjoy yourself.

Bookstores

With 207 bookstores in San Francisco, any presentation of the best or finest is even harder than a selection of good bars. Space prohibits listing them all; each one is different; to a bookstore freak, there is a special quality to each of them. With bars, great discoveries can be made by the average visitor walking down any given street. Bookstores are spread more thinly. Since there is considerable opinion in this book anyway, I will list those I think best and make apologies to those not listed here. The ever-loving yellow pages will direct you to them all.

Two of the best bookstores are not listed as bookstores. One is specialized, the other so general it boggles the mind. We will start with them.

RAND McNALLY & Co. 206 Sansome (corner of Sansome and Pine near the Stock Exchange). It's a store of books of maps, atlases, globes, and the Rand McNally guides and geographies. It is one of the few Rand McNally outlets and a handy store to know about. You know how frustrating it is to try to find current geographies when you're planning a trip or looking something up. Most bookstores (even libraries) do not have the information you're looking for. Rand McNally's store has it all. It's also one of the few places you can find those wonderful topographical plastic three-dimensional maps.

GOVERNMENT PRINTING OFFICE BOOK STORE. Federal Building. Golden Gate between Larkin and Polk. This is another unique outlet. The Government Printing Office publishes a stupendous number of publications on every subject under the sun and in outer space. In most cities, the publications are available only through ordering by mail. Here, there is available a huge assortment of GPO material, the most popular publications. The scope is so broad that it's hard to give a fair impression of what you will find here. We'll go around the racks. At the door are piled the latest releases of consumer interest, government reports on pollution, water-quality control reports, detailed automobile-tire-performance data, etcetera. These are next to the rack of space exploration publications and military-service-school texts. There are gorgeous photos and books of photos of the moon and the Gemini and Apollo missions (the best-quality photos and reproductions suitable for framing). Complete courses on electricity and electronics, celestial navigation, how to fly a helicopter, lead to a rack on the nitty-gritty of how to operate a barber shop, small manufacturing company, or dry goods store. That sort of swings into books and pamphlets on the national parks and reports on the state of the nation's wildlife; statistical analyses of every aspect of America there are figures for. Near the cashier's desk is a rack devoted to nutrition and cooking. How to can and freeze meat, poultry, fish, and vegetables; how to cook them; a great book on the nutritional value of everything from artichokes to zucchini; lots of menu books. Along the wall on that side are the handsomely bound copies of the presidential papers of the last several presidents. Moving to the right you'll find Department of Agriculture publications on everything from how to slaughter pigs and beef on the old homestead to the raising of catfish and roses. There are also publications telling you how to build a chimney, how to wire

and plumb your house, how to *build* your house. A separate
Department of Agriculture booklet gives the room plans of
elegant pine and plywood homes that you can put up yourself
(the frame at least) for $5,000 (developers would charge
$10,000 for the shell, and another $10,000 for the electricity
and plumbing). You can send away for the complete plans
and instructions. For some reason, as we move around to the
right, the bound copies of the special Congressional committee reports are mixed or are close to historical and sociological booklets. *The Child from One to Six* is not far from
an investigation into the violence of the late '60s (where the
completeness of the report includes the radical sabotage information on how to construct a pipe bomb in your own
home).

I've dwelt so long on this bookstore because it is ours, and
we taxpayers paid for the writing of these books. Because it
is nonprofit, the bookbuyer will go crazy here—everything is
so cheap. Most of the books and booklets are staff-written and
concern a single subject. If you want to know how to raise
strawberries, here is a booklet covering strawberry-growing
in the whole country—no frills, no fancy binding, no glossy
cover, and it costs 30 cents. I can't recommend the government bookstore too highly.

One of the marvelous things about San Francisco bookstores
is diversity. The buyers of books here support a good number
of foreign-language and special-interest bookstores that are a
delight to the visitor who usually has to send away for anything out of the ordinary. The following will show you where
to go to find these stores.

Foreign-Language Bookstores

Russian

The AMERICAN RUSSIAN INSTITUTE, 90 McAllister (near
St. Boniface Church), handles books, pamphlets, posters, and
craft items imported from Russia. The Russian-English, En-
glish-Russian dictionaries are a good buy.

ZNANIA BOOKSTORE, 5237 Geary (around 16th Avenue),

is a White Russian bookstore offering classical Russian literature, antique Russian books, and craft items.

French

The FRENCH BOOKSTORE, 1111 Polk Street (at Post), is the most complete French bookstore in town and carries books and magazines.

Italian

CAVALLI ITALIAN BOOKSTORE, 1441 Stockton (at Vallejo), has Italian books, records, and magazines.

LIBRERIA DEL MAESTRO, 522 Columbus. Italian paperbacks and magazines.

German

HANS SPECKMAN'S books, magazines, confections, and lederhosen across from his restaurant at Church Street and Duncan.

Spanish

LIBRERIO MEXICO, 2631 Mission (22nd Street), with a branch store at 2915 16th Street (16th and South Van Ness).

SANCHEZ SPANISH BOOKS AND MUSIC STORE, 2130 Mission (at 17th).

SPANISH LANGUAGE BOOKS, 300 Pennsylvania (Potrero Hill).

Chinese

TOM'S BOOKSTORE, 861 Clay.

WAH KUE BOOKSTORE, 11 St. Louis Alley.

SING SANG BOOK CO., 40 Waverly Place.

JULAN CO., 918 Clay.

ORE HING BOOKSTORE, 725 Clay.

All these are in Chinatown and sell not only books but art prints and stationery.

Irish

IRISH IMPORT SHOP, 2123 Market Street (at Church).

Japanese

GO SHA-DO CO. BOOKS AND STATIONERY, 1680 Post.
HONNAMI TAIEIDO, 1722 Buchanan.
JAPAN PUBLICATIONS AND TRADING CO., 1255 Howard Street.
KINOKONIYA BOOKSTORES OF AMERICA LTD., 1581 Webster (Japanese Cultural Center–West Building).
Most of these are also craft stores.

European

The bookstore at 925 Larkin has a grand collection of books in French, German, and Spanish.

Hebrew

LIEBER'S HEBREW AND ENGLISH BOOK AND CRAFT STORE, 5445 Geary Boulevard.
THE BOOK SHOOK, Noriega and 31st Avenue.

In keeping with specialized bookstores, the following is a list of the kinds of bookstores one only finds in a big city.

Science-Medical-Technical

STACEY'S, 581 Market (Market at Battery, near the financial district). Stacey's is a great store for books of a technical nature, both in hardcover and paperback. Great browsing place for those interested in nonfiction—especially hard-to-find nonfiction.
ROBERT EUSTACE, 218 23rd Avenue.

Cinema

THE CINEMA SHOP, 522 O'Farrell. Sells only books, posters (playbills of old movies), and photos for the movie-freak trade (hang a Hopalong Cassidy on your wall).

Comic Books

COMIC BOOK NEWS, 3339 23rd Street (23rd and Mission). This is an underground collector's center recently made respectable (before, one didn't brag that he read comic books, no less collected them). On your walk through the Mission, stop in here. You'll be surprised at the depth of the items offered for sale. You'll be aghast at the prices the fans of Captain Marvel (*Shazam!*) will pay for an original.

Martial Arts

MUTUAL SUPPLY CO., 1090 Sansome (at Vallejo). Specializes in defend-yourself books—Judo, Karate, Kendo, etcetera.

Photography

FOCUS GALLERY, 2146 Union Street. Specializes in photography books and books on the art.

Law

HASTING'S BOOKSTORE, 198 McAllister.
HENRY BLAKE, 138 McAllister.

Aeronautica

For the airplane freak, Edward L. Sterne specializes in out-of-print aeronautica. He has no store. Only a phone number and post office box is given in the yellow pages (that *is* a specialized audience). Consult the phone book.

Black Interest

MARCUS BOOKS, 540 McAllister (across from the Veterans' Memorial, Civic Center).
MORE BOOKSTORE, 855 Divisadero (and Fulton).
Both specialize in writings, crafts, and art of black writers, craftsmen, and artists.

Radical

BAY AREA RADICAL EDUCATION PROJECT, 647 Valencia.
THE UNDERGROUND, 1588 Market. (Paperbacks and Comics.)

**STATUES AT THE STOCK EXCHANGE, BY
RALPH STACKPOLE**

Chazz Sutphen

THE PALACE OF FINE ARTS

THE MARINA YACHT HARBOR, LOOKING NORTHWEST TOWARD THE GOLDEN GATE BRIDGE AND MARIN COUNTY

Chazz Sutphen

Chazz Sutphen

SOUTHEASTWARD VIEW OF SAN FRANCISCO FROM THE FIRE DEPARTMENT RESERVOIRS

UNION STREET

THE HIGH ALTAR OF ST. MARY'S CATHEDRAL

Chazz Sutphen

RUSSIAN HOLY VIRGIN CATHEDRAL
OF THE CHURCH IN EXILE

Chazz Sutphen

THE CONSERVATORY, GOLDEN GATE PARK Chazz
Sutphen

CHINA BOOKS AND PERIODICALS, 2929 24th Street. Selling books and magazines long before President Nixon's trip, this outlet of mainland China propaganda is well worth the visit. Like other propaganda efforts, this place sells excellently printed cultural material (on the arts or archeology, for example) as loss leaders to entice you to look at their political stuff. Great buys here in art books and the like. The propaganda is the same as any other propaganda—"We're divinely *right!* You're devilishly *wrong!*"

MODERN TIMES BOOKSTORE, 3800 17th Street (at Sanchez). Predominantly women's liberation, it has a perpetual coffee pot for the browsers.

Astrological-Metaphysical-Religious

Everyone is intensely serious about the development of the metaphysical aspect of his life on earth and I have no inclination to sort it all out. These are the bookstores selling aids to spiritual development—the esoteric on the left, the established religions on the right.

LA SCALA VARIETORIUM, 1605 Polk Street.

METAPHYSICAL ASTROLOGICAL TOWN HALL BOOK SHOP, 345 Mason Street.

METAPHYSICAL CENTER AND BOOK STORE, 420 Sutter.

THE ORACLE, 396 Broadway.

SOLUNAR, 1805 Polk.

THE SOURCE, 388 22nd Avenue.

BUDDHIST BOOK STORE, 1710 Octavia Street.

CATHOLIC GUILD, 706 Market Street.

GIFT OF GOD RELIGIOUS BOOKS, 304 Plymouth.

GRACE CATHEDRAL GIFT SHOP, California and Taylor.

MCCOY RELIGIOUS BOOKS, 111 Golden Gate.

METHODIST PUBLISHING HOUSE, 85 McAllister.

That, I believe, covers it. There are more in the phone book.

Now comes the hard part. Aside from the specialized stores, there are a good hundred and fifty general bookstores in town, paperback, hardcover, and valuable-used-antique stores. The following is a list of my favorites. I only wish I could list them all. It will be a general guide. By all means, consult the telephone book and look at the others.

Paperback

The places you will get the best selections of paperbacks are:

ALBERT HENRY'S, 524 Geary (three blocks up from Union Square). Also specialized and foreign-language newspapers and periodicals.

CANTERBURY CORNER, 5301 Geary Boulevard (near 17th Avenue).

CITY LIGHTS, 261 Columbus (at Pacific). Three floors of paperbacks running heavily to avant-garde radical. This was the bookshop that made the landmark in pornography for having sold to the public Alan Ginsberg's *Howl* in the 1950s—those many years ago.

BOOKS, INC., 156 Geary, Paperbacks and hardcover.

TRO HARPER'S, 140 Powell. Paperbacks and posters and remainders, and patented aluminum egg slicers (the Market Street store deals more with remainders (hardcover books that are new, selling at $1.98 when people stopped buying them at $7.00—the stuff remaining in the publisher's warehouse after the book has gone into paperback).

GALLERY BOOK SHOP, 1922 Clement (at 20th Avenue). They buy used paperbacks and have a huge collection.

General

The bookstores that carry *mostly* hard cover and new books are listed here with some reservation. Every bookstore is unique and all these sell other things, but quality new books is the criterion.

B. DALTON BOOKSELLER, 149 Stonestown Mall.

BONANZA INN BOOK SHOP, 650 Market.

BOOKS, INC., 156 Geary.

BRENTANO'S, 256 Sutter, 228 Montgomery.

BRUNO'S BOOK SHOP, 1220 Polk.

DOUBLEDAY BOOKSHOP, 190 Post.

ELDORADO BOOKS, 1020 Clement Street.

MINERVA'S OWL BOOKSHOP, 2181 Union.

TILLMAN PLACE BOOK SHOP (Newbegins), 8 Tillman Place.

SCOTT MARTIN, 527 Sutter.

UPSTART CROW, in the Cannery, 2801 Leavenworth.

EMPORIUM and MACY'S bookstores—in the respective department stores.

Twelve general bookstores are given here. There are 26 more.

Antique, Valuable, and Used Books

San Francisco is a town that loves books and is a clearinghouse for valuable books. There are 31 bookstores that will buy single books or whole libraries (not counting the salvage shops that sell donated books). They run from John Howell, who specializes in Western Americana, and John Scopazzi, who deals in rare maps and first editions, to McDonald's, who sells collector's magazines and complete sets of *National Geographic*, as well as stacks of used books. If you, like me, are a bookstore freak, these are the places to go. There's something fascinating about these places. Rich store or moderately priced, they have treasures, hidden on the racks, overlooked, that you can acquire as your own and keep or sell—but especially brag about. The classic case was in Tro Harper's on Powell Street. Tro went to England and bought leather-bound books by the pound—mostly collections of no-longer-read English authors, handsomely bound—something that would look good in any bookcase. Tipped into one book on painting was an original Rembrandt etching. Tro sold the book for $3 and the buyer sold the etching for $2,000.

In the bookstores specializing in antique and valuable books, that kind of fluke never happens, because they are specialists. They do sell books, prints, and maps that are fine to own and better to give. If you're going to spend a few bucks on a present, a rare book, an antique print or map is a good investment. It can only appreciate in value.

Listed with the bookstores specializing in valuable stuff are the bookstores selling used books. These are good places to shop because you can finally buy books you've always wanted to own at prices you can afford. These are sometimes the most treasured things in your library.

It's impossible really to sort them all out, but I'll put an asterisk before those that sell used books but specialize in antique, out-of-print, or valuable books. One might find all of these in unasterisked stores, but these are the major shops for the rare.

*ALBATROSS BOOK CO., 166 Eddy.

*ARGONAUT BOOKSHOP, 792 Sutter.

*BRICK ROW BOOK SHOP, 251 Post Street.

*HOLMES BOOK CO., 22 3rd Street.

*JOHN HOWELL, 434 Post Street.

*ROBERTS BOOK SHOP, 47 Golden Gate.

*BERNARD M. ROSENTHAL, 251 Post Street.

*DAVID MCGEE BOOKSHOP (appointment only, number in phone book).

*JOHN SCOPAZZI, 384 Post Street.

*R. DECKER, 1525 Irving Street.

*JOSEPH THE PROVIDER (appointment only, number in phone book).

KENNETH REXROTH BOOKS, 2038 Union Street (the poet Rexroth).

*ROBERT KUHN, 720 Geary (a peripheral bookstore—few books, but valuable autographs and signed photos, a museum of collectables).

THE LION BOOK SHOP, 1415 Polk.

MCDONALD'S BOOKSHOP, 48 Turk. A magnificent jumble of old books and magazines. You could lose yourself here for hours. If you want a copy of *Flying Aces* pulp, a 1952 copy of *Modern Screen*, a book of George Price's cartoons, a set of a turn-of-the-century encyclopedia, you can find it here, after you sift through privately printed volumes of poetry, American Legion magazines, and ten thousand unwanted, unread novels. It's one of my favorite used-bookstores.

*SUNSHINE ALLEY BOOKS, 926 Irving (out-of-print children's books).

*TUMBLEWEED, 165 Jefferson.

6
Museums

"Museum," unfortunately, is a word so full of heavy connotations that its very mention evokes feelings of solemnity, culture, and tired feet. Somehow, the idea of a museum has become very closely tied to uplifting fine art. And that's a pity, because museums are not so serious. In San Francisco especially, they're not that serious.

Since the Gold Rush, San Francisco has always been a historic town, rich in the comings and goings and doings of man, and extraordinary men. It is no wonder that, in a city full of abstract money and raw gold and silver, a minting city, we find two small (but rich) museums—both run by banks—devoted to the display of rare currency, gold bars, nuggets, dust that originated here and along the western slope. San Francisco was, and is, the American focus on the West Coast for cultural and commercial intercourse with the East (one of the reasons our consular corps is way out of proportion to the size of the city). Avery Brundage located his magnificent collection of Asian art here because in any other city it would have been unnecessarily exotic (like the Rosicrucian Egyptian museum in San Jose). The Center of Asian Art and Culture in Golden Gate Park, which displays priceless art objects, is balanced by the Chinese Historical Society's museum in Chinatown, which displays exhibits of the working papers required of coolies imported in the last century.

There are 23 such "institutions devoted to the procurement and display of objects of lasting value" in San Francisco, aside from the five major ones. Among them are two houses, five ships, and a fort. The exhibits include riveted buffalo-hide fire hoses, diamonds from the Feather River, mint-condition Graham Paige autos, scimitars from the pirates of Tripoli, talking birds, and devices for levitating entranced young ladies.

Most of these museums are free; those that charge admission are well worth the tariff and, all in all, there are no finer places in the city to take the children.

San Francisco's Major Museums

For the tourist who has time only to hit the high points of the city, these five museums should be on the list of the things he must see. All of them are conveniently near other major attractions. Three are in Golden Gate Park around the Music Concourse; the Palace of the Legion of Honor is on the 49 Mile Drive, and the San Francisco Museum of Art is next to the Opera House right across the street from City Hall in the Civic Center.

THE DE YOUNG MEMORIAL MUSEUM. Golden Gate Park Music Concourse. Daily, 10 AM–5 PM. Free (admission charges for special exhibits).

The De Young offers old masters, antiquities, and fine art in general. It's San Francisco's "official" museum, and whatever famous or popular exhibition is touring will be shown here. These can be fine indeed; the complete Van Gogh and the Tutankhamen treasures were shown here—these special exhibitions are available only in a few cities in the country, so watch for them.

San Francisco is not particularly rich in old masters. It's a common put-down to say, "Put the three fine arts museums in San Francisco together and you'll get a minor fine arts museum." This might be so, but still here you'll find works by Rubens, El Greco, and Cellini. Of special interest are several paneled rooms from famous eighteenth-century French homes, imported as a piece furnished with appropriate antique furniture (one with a Poussin *Madonna and Child* hung casually on the wall). There are also an Elizabethan bedroom, and Italian and German antique rooms set up here. As a balance, there used to be four early California rooms on display, but they lost space to the museum adjoining.

SAN FRANCISCO CITY AND COUNTY CENTER OF ASIAN ART AND CULTURE. Avery Brundage Wing, De Young Museum. Although it is connected to the De Young and keeps the same hours, this is a separate museum. It houses the $30-million Avery Brundage collection of Asian art, a collection so vast that it can be shown only in segments. We've heard a lot about Brundage as the pernickety (some say hard-headed) overseer of the Olympic Games—the chucker-out of professional athletes. But all that is in this museum in his, given to the public.

The closest most Americans get to Asian art is Asian craftsmanship—Chinese porcelain, Indian carvings, Indonesian intaglio and filigree, Japanese lacquer ware. Here, one gets a fuller appreciation of the whole sweep of the finest Asian artistic development—pottery, carving, statuary, metalwork. At first hand are the Asian art objects usually seen by Americans only in fine-arts books.

ACADEMY OF ARTS AND SCIENCES. Civic Center next to the Opera House, opposite City Hall. Daily 10 AM–5 PM, 9 PM in summer. Admission: adults, 50 cents; children 12–18, 25 cents; under 12, free. No charge the first Saturday of every month.

This building complex is a complex of museums. It used to be three separate buildings around the beautiful, intertwined whale sculpture-fountain in the middle. The new Cowell Hall joined it all together. Historically, the Academy has two firsts to its credit. The Morrison Planetarium was the first such facility in America. More important, the Academy was the first to display animal specimens in a setting of their natural habitat, native grasses, trees, and appropriate background. This museum changed the whole way of museums around the world.

To the right, as you enter, is *North American Hall*, displaying the major mammals of the continent. Especially interesting to those who don't live on the Pacific Coast are the displays of sea mammals, including sea lions. To the extreme right is a small entomological room, the chief display of which is an incredible butterfly collection. Continue through and you'll find Mineral Hall, full of museum specimens of the riches of California geology. Here are two nice things for kids—the black light display of fluorescent minerals and the push button earthquake-explainer machine (backed up by a working seismograph that shows if you're being caught in an earthquake at the very minute).

The *Bird Hall* is next and is the closest to rare and disappearing bird life you'll ever get.

There is a small paleontological display in the next room with dinosaur and extinct mammal fossils. The most interesting thing in the room is a view through a hole in the floor of the bones of an ancient reptile *in situ*, as a paleontologist would see it, half freed from the rocks. This room leads to the west end of the Aquarium.

The *Steinhart Aquarium* is one of the most frequently visited features in the park; it is always full of people. And no wonder. I've seen Marineland in Miami and the Marineworld in San Mateo (not yet the Marineland in San Diego), and they do not compare with the Steinhart Aquarium. It's the intimacy of the place that makes it so special. Here, you're nose to nose with an incredible variety of fresh and salt water fish. The other places have dolphin displays and performances you watch from bleachers. Here, the huge dolphin tank (white-sided dolphins and harbor seals) has its water level near the ceiling of the wall of glass. One is almost in the tank with the dolphins themselves. Other rare mammals on display are a manatee and a rare Amazon dolphin. At the entrance to the Aquarium is an alligator swamp that includes members of the crocodilian family and turtles large and small. For some reason, probably rooted deep within the human psyche, this seems to be a favorite place for visitors to chuck coins. The floor of the pool is littered with nickels, dimes, and quarters. I've heard of chucking a coin in a well or fountain and making a wish, but it amazes me that people would want to wish upon an alligator. Surrounding the swamp are herpetological displays, with a nice collection of the snakes that most fascinate people; the poisonous ones and the large and dangerous varieties. Rare frogs and lizards are seen also.

The *Morrison Planetarium* and related out-of-this-world displays adjoin the Aquarium. You may see how much you weigh on the moon, and there are many meteorites. An excellent exhibit of time-measurers, candles, water clocks, mechanical clocks, and watches is here, as well as a display of the lamps that man has used over the centuries to light his way. Morrison Planetarium is a must for the visitor—there are few cities that boast a star projector, so take advantage of it while you are here. It's especially enthralling to kids. It's daylight outside, and suddenly it's night with millions of stars. Near the Planetarium is a hall used for changing exhibits. In the last year, there have been well-planned exhibitions of life (with a gigantic representation of the living cell), ecology, and, at this writing, the artifacts of the American Indian. In the hallway to the Planetarium a display is usually in progress concerning expeditions underway or completed by scientists associated with the Academy. In a darkened room near-by is an eight-foot illuminated globe of the moon. Farther on is the African Hall, with preserved specimens of that continent in natural-habitat display cases.

CALIFORNIA PALACE OF THE LEGION OF HONOR. 34th and Clement. Daily 10 AM–5 PM. Free.

One of the most elegant buildings in the city, it houses a good fine-arts collection. (Mrs. Spreckels, the donor of the building, was a friend of Rodin and here you'll see many examples of his work.) It also contains the Achenbach Foundation for Graphic Arts, one of the very finest graphic arts collections in America. It should be visited both for the art and for the view from the grounds.

SAN FRANCISCO MUSEUM OF ART. Veterans Memorial Building, Van Ness and McAllister. Tuesday–Friday 10 AM–

10 PM; Saturday, 10 AM–5 PM; Sunday, 1 PM–5 PM. Free (admission charge for special exhibits).

This museum specializes in modern art and contemporary trends in paintings and sculpture. There is a fine collection of the old "modern" artists, such as Cezanne and Matisse. But the main interest is in what's happening now. Here, you're able to see the huge new things created for museums only (few homes, no matter how large, could contain these works of art) and exhibitions of long-lost antique photographs, great floating plastic sausages and artfully arranged boulders. Whatever your feelings about new art, you'll find it here and it is fascinating.

Specialized Collections

The following are specialized collections of things of lasting value and, taken as a whole, are at least as interesting and exciting as the major museums.

CALIFORNIA GEOLOGY MUSEUM. Ferry Building. Monday–Friday, 8 AM–5 PM; first Saturday every month, 10 AM–noon. Free.

The first wealth of California was derived from its mineral riches, so it's fitting we start here. Maintained by the California Division of Mines and Geology, this museum-library offers a threefold look at the mineral resources of California not seen elsewhere. At the entrance are the grand exhibits of such precious things as gem stones, native gold and silver nuggets, diamonds from the Feather River, and four-foot-high quartz crystals. In the cases along the inner wall are spectacular specimens of mineral formations (more complete than the showcase specimens in the Mineral Hall of the Academy of Arts and Sciences). In the cases in the main hall are neatly catalogued examples of the major minerals, ores, and rocks found in each county of the state. These hold some surprises, such as the gold ore and black sands found within the city limits of San Francisco (as well as semiprecious stones). On the walls of the hall are seen examples of the products manufactured from these basic minerals. Geological maps and specialized books are available at the desk.

WELLS FARGO HISTORY ROOM. 420 Montgomery. Monday–Friday, 10 AM–3 PM. Free.

Here is the Gold Rush re-created. Wells Fargo was one of the first banking, express, bullion-handling companies in California and its name is romantic indeed. The History Room brings an era to life. Through prints, antique pistols, Pony Express saddles, gold watches given to the capturers of stage robbers—and especially gold, gold, gold specimens from every mining area in the state, you get the feel of the excitement of that time. It's on the ground floor of a modern bank building, and smack in the middle of the room is a huge Concord Stagecoach. How they ever got it inside is a mystery. With Black Bart memorabilia and a one-pound silver watch for his captor, it's one of the most exciting museums in town.

BANK OF CALIFORNIA GOLD AND COIN MUSEUM. 400 California. Monday–Friday, 10 AM–3 PM. Free.

A more scholarly approach to the money side of the Gold Rush, this exhibit is downstairs near the safe deposit vaults. There is a fine collection of U.S. gold coins, but more interesting is the private coinage and currency from Alaska, British Columbia, Oregon Territory, California, Colorado Territory, and the State of Deseret (Utah) all of which filled the currency voids found in these remote areas. Utah, for example, issued its own currency, for lack of available ready cash, and here you'll see one-dollar, two-dollar, and three-dollar notes signed by Brigham Young and countersigned by three bishops of the church (a sure way to defeat inflation—you can only write money until your hand wears out). Because of the shortage of coins, many assaying and banking companies minted their own coins, which differed slightly in intrinsic value (weight and fineness of gold). There are at least fifteen such coins represented. They must have made for some interesting poker dialogue . . . "I'll bet a Conroy and a Blake and Agnell." "I'll see you with a Clark-Gruber and raise you a Baldwin, a Kellog and a Bowie . . ." You'll see all these coins here.

SOCIETY OF CALIFORNIA PIONEERS. 465 McAllister Street. Monday–Friday, 10 AM–4 PM. Free.

Across from City Hall is this small but elegant museum run by one of the most exclusive pioneer historical societies in America. Membership is limited to the male descendants of those resident in California prior to January 1, 1850. The museum-library has a constantly changing exhibition of Californiana that always seems to capture the essence of our history. Spanish cutlasses and bronze draft-beer taps of memorable pre-Prohibition saloons; the silver service of a Mexican governor and California election ephemera; Indian acorn grinders and fused coins from the 1906 quake-fire are all shown with the same importance. Try to visit when the Highlights of the 1915 Panama-Pacific Exposition slide show is being presented.

FIREMAN'S PIONEER MUSEUM. Presidio at Pine (Pine Street is one-way out and ends at Presidio Avenue). Monday–Friday, 1 PM–4 PM. Free. Group tours on weekends by special arrangement.

San Francisco is a fire-conscious town and its firemen very highly regarded. This collection of fire equipment and memorabilia is a jewel of a museum. The large pieces on exhibit include two hand-drawn manual pumpers dating from the 1850s (the days of the volunteer fire brigades); a horse-drawn steam pumper; a 1908 Ahrens-Fox piston pumper, and a 1908 high-pressure battery and hose tender. Some of the fascination of the equipment (like railroad equipment) is that it is monumental and lovingly crafted. Cabinets around the walls display leather hoses and buckets, water grenades, antique pieces of uniform, relics from the earthquake-fire, excellent photographs, and the box planted in the cornerstone of the old City Hall. That City Hall, built by friends of grafting politicians, literally shook to pieces in the first sixty seconds of the quake (while warehouses and office buildings rode it out)—a huge scandal. The box, a kind of time capsule, contained a whole raft of stuff—the list is with it—including a chip from Solomon's temple and two bottles of California wine. The firemen let you ring the bells on the engines, but upon entering, you must sign a waiver absolving the department from fault in case of accident.

SAN FRANCISCO CABLE CAR MUSEUM. Washington and Mason streets. Monday–Thursday, 10 AM–6 PM; Friday–Sunday, 10 AM–10 PM. Free.

Unique to San Francisco, this museum is also the working center of the San Francisco cable car system—a museum piece in itself. One may think that the retention of the cable cars is merely a Chamber of Commerce gimmick, or results from nostalgia of the citizenry. Not so. The cable cars are still an efficient, clean, and quiet means of moving people over the hills—as many citizens utilize the cable cars as tourists. At the museum here, one can see the magnificent machinery used to drive the cables (and realize how the Victorians became so enthralled by monumental machinery). On the gallery is the first cable car (from 1873). The car barns are also open to the public and here are displayed cable cars from a discontinued lines (one can't say *antique* cars, because the ones running are only a few years younger—each car is now handmade). Photographs and pieces of equipment are to be seen, a fascinating place.

OCTAGON HOUSE. 2645 Gough Street. First Sunday and second and fourth Thursday of every month, 1 PM–4 PM. Free.

The hours are so cockeyed because the Octagon House is run by volunteers. Built in 1861, this eight-sided house is an architectural curiosity as well as an interesting museum filled with Colonial furnishings. Here one may see many fine examples of Chippendale, Hepplewhite, Sheraton, Queen Anne furniture as well as a Trumbull portrait of George Washington. The anomaly of a West Coast Civil War house furnished with Colonial pieces is the result of the Octagon House ownership. It's the headquarters of the California branch of the Colonial Dames of America—a Revolutionaryancestor organization. The Dames cheerfully answer any questions about the house and furnishings.

THE CALIFORNIA HISTORICAL SOCIETY. 2090 Jackson Street. Tuesday–Saturday, 10 AM–4 PM. Free.

The administrative headquarters of the California Historical Society usually has an exhibit of Western genre paintings or paintings by Western artists. The main reason to visit the museum is the mansion itself. The Whittier mansion is one of the very few places in the city where the public can get a hint of the elegant life the rich enjoyed at the turn of the century. It was a fine life indeed, as seen in the beautiful parquetry flooring; wide, handsome fireplaces; carved wainscoting—all the little things that go into making a home a mansion. Enough period furniture is retained to preserve the essence of posh, but not enough to detract from the exquisite work of the expert joiners, cabinetmakers, stonecutters, plasterers— indeed, all the fine hand craftsmen who put the thing together. In the bathrooms on the second floor, you may show your children how toilets got the name "water closets" or W.C. (a little lead-lined closet of water near the ceiling contains the flush).

CHINESE HISTORICAL SOCIETY OF AMERICA. 17 Adler Street. Tuesday–Sunday, 1 PM–5 PM. Free (Special tours arranged by writing in advance.)

Adler Street is a short alley between Grant and Columbus, a few steps south of Broadway. Here one finds examples of pioneer Chinese-American life collected from the whole of Western America. There are exotic items on display—antique Mandarin robes, lily-foot slippers, opium-smoking paraphernalia—but the mundane items are much more exciting. Household articles; the contents of an unclaimed immigrant's trunk (which shows what was thought to be important to bring to America); a sampan—strictly Chinese, but built in Marin County; a cook's spoon from a lumber camp, so valuable that when it cracked, it was welded with the most available metal, gold; a doweled wheelbarrow from the gold mines of the Sierra; a blue denim coolie's jacket; baskets, pots, china; temple and religious items. Most interesting are the antique photographs of pioneer Chinese-American life and private and official printed ephemera—passports, working papers, invitations to social functions, and appeals for aid to the Chinese victims of the earthquake-fire.

SAN FRANCISCO MARITIME MUSEUM. Foot of Polk at Aquatic Park near Ghirandelli Square. Daily, 10 AM–5 PM. Free.

It's to be expected that such a fine port would have a fine museum devoted to maritime matters. Here, you'll find an excellent collection of every aspect of man's life on the sea; antique navigational aids, ship models, scrimshaw, evolution of ships' gear. It's both a scholarly place, with technical displays, and a romantic one. If you visit here first before you go aboard the five museum ships on the Embarcadero, you'll appreciate them ten times more.

SAN FRANCISCO MARITIME STATE HISTORIC PARK. Foot of Hyde Street at Fisherman's Wharf. Daily 10 AM–8 PM summer; 10 AM–6 PM winter. Admission: adults, 75 cents; children, 6–17, 25 cents; under 6 free.

These four floating museums are of special interest. Restoration of these antique ships is an on-going process and you can watch shipwrights, seamen, and rigging experts at work. All were gathered to the Hyde Street Pier to form a unique collection of working ships of the Pacific Coast.

Eureka: The last paddle-wheel walking-beam passenger-auto ferry to operate on San Francisco Bay, it is one of the finest arguments for the restoration of Ferry Boats on the Bay to be seen. One side of the auto deck is loaded with beautifully restored antique autos and trucks—Model T's, Packards, Nashes, a Graham Paige among others. The passenger section has very nice touches, such as the old cigar stand displaying antique periodicals and a coin-operated mechanical piano.

C. A. Thayer: This three-masted sailing ship was originally a coastal lumber schooner. No glamour here, but it gives an excellent idea of the life aboard a workhorse of a ship. There were hundreds of Thayer-type ships at the turn of the century. When I visited, Sea Scouts were taking snapshots of each other against the complicated rigging.

Wapama: a steam schooler built in 1915, it carried cargo (mostly lumber) and passengers between California ports and the Pacific Northwest. A walk through the passenger section, salon, dining room, smoking room, shows that traveling by steam schooner must have been an exciting adventure. The whole passenger section is not yet open to the public, but a peek through the curtains of the cabins shows a meticulous restoration job in process (here an antique toiletries set, there a huge old wireless receiver). The state is doing an excellent job and when the restoration is completed it will be even more fascinating.

Alma: A "hay scow," this is the only remaining example of the once-most-numerous vessels on the Bay. Its shallow draft and wide beam let it carry all kinds of common freight to the most remote areas in the Bay–Delta North–Central river complex of California.

THE BALCLUTHA. Pier 43 (Fisherman's Wharf). Daily, 9 AM–10:30 PM. Admission: adults, $1.25; children 12–18, 65 cents; under 12, 35 cents. Two or more children under 12 admitted free with parents. Price includes 45-minute hand-carried, tape-recorded tour of the ship.

Built in 1866, this three-masted deepwaterman was restored by the San Francisco Maritime Museum. It is one of the last of the Cape Horner sailing ships left in the world. With its banners and canvas signs, unfortunately, the *Balclutha* looks like a hoky money-grabber from shore, a Fisherman's Wharf attraction. Once on board, though, this feeling abruptly passes. When you look up through the rigging, you can understand John Masefield's poems. And when you go into the bow of the ship, "before the mast," and see where twenty full-grown men were crowded into a space a little larger than the average living room, you can understand the statement of the "Emancipator of Seamen," Andrew Furuseth, "You can put me in jail, but you cannot give me narrower quarters than as a seaman I have always had." In the two holds of the *Balclutha* is a museum of deepwater gear, equipment, and photographs—one especially interesting showing how many black deepwater sailors manned ships like *Balclutha*. Again, these are the officers' quarters. From reading books, especially books by disgruntled seamen, you get the idea that the officers lived in sultanic opulence. Here you'll see the true dimensions. The admission price is high, but the experience of walking the ship is well worth it.

SAN FRANCISCO AFRICAN-AMERICAN HISTORICAL AND CULTURAL SOCIETY. 680 McAllister Street. Monday–Friday, 12 noon–5 PM. Free.

A new museum in San Francisco, this small but growing collection exhibits artifacts from the whole of Africa as well as memorabilia of black America. Antique African carvings and pottery are balanced by modern African cotton prints and styles of dress. An exhibit of Dr. George Washington Carver's fantastic utilization of the peanut is followed by photographs delineating the wide range of achievement by black athletes and military heroes, and the black rich—made in a society that has always put blacks down. It's likely to become a major museum someday.

FT. POINT. In the Presidio beneath the Golden Gate Bridge Toll Plaza. 10 AM–5 PM every day. Free.

For a century the thick brick and granite walls of Ft. Point have guarded the entrance to the Golden Gate. From the Civil War to now, it has never had to defend itself or the city from attack, but its very stance, I believe, like the cast-iron righteousness of an angry mamma, has deterred Confederates, Spanish, Germans, and Japanese from trying to invade San Francisco. To say that the fort is a monumental building might seem redundant, but that's the only way to describe it. Within it, you may wander through the officer's and men's quarters and look through the gun ports where cannons once stood. The Fort has recently been declared a national monument, which means a little more money for its restoration, but even now, it's a fine place to visit. The small museum (off the guard room of the three-cell stockade) is very worthwhile.

AMERICAN LEGION TROPHY ROOM. Veterans Memorial Building; McAllister and Van Ness across from City Hall. Left of entrance. Free.

A secret, small museum in a public building. There are no regular visiting hours. It used to be open from 6 PM to 10 PM, but vandalism closed it. From 8 AM to 5 PM, ask in the office immediately to the left for a janitor to lock you in and out.

Items on display include Crusaders' swords; Henry Morgan's pirate cutlass; a French officer's sword from the *Bonhomme Richard*, 1799; World War I carbines; General Pershing's West Point shako; British and Hessian flintlocks; Tripoli pirate's cutlass; Hotchkiss, Krag, Ward, Burton and Lebel World War I infantry arms; a French wall gun from the French-English War of 1758—a hodepodge of arms and decorations heroically gotten and proudly displayed.

PALACE OF ARTS AND SCIENCE (EXPLORATORIUM). Old Palace of Fine Arts. Baker and Beach. Wednesday–Sunday, 1 PM–5 PM. Free.

The *Palace of Fine Arts* is the last remnant of the 1915 Panama-Pacific Exposition. If this is any indication of what the rest of the buildings were like, it must have been a glorious thing indeed. Ostensibly, the Exposition was to celebrate the opening of the Panama Canal, but really it was a showcase for the city itself. Nine years earlier, four-fifths of the city had been burned right down to the ground in the quake-fire. In those nine years, the city had not only been rebuilt but was wealthy enough to sponsor a World's Fair.

The original Palace of Fine Arts was a lathe–chicken wire–plaster temporary building to house the fine-arts exhibit of the Fair. It was so lovely, though, that when the other Fair buildings were torn down, it was left standing to fall into ruin. The thing is, it didn't. It somehow kept standing, growing even more lovely as the years went by. It wasn't perfect, though; through the action of weather and vandals (one dummy got on top and knocked off all the heads of the lady statutes with a baseball bat), the place was getting dangerous. There was some agitation to tear it down, but even stronger public pressure to save it. Walter Johnson, a rare millionaire, gave $2 million toward the restoration and the rest was raised through state money and a city bond issue. Miraculously, most of the old molds for the sculptured works were discovered in a warehouse, and the Palace of Fine Arts was reconstructed in steel and reinforced concrete, exactly as it was. And, the interior now usable, it's one of the very finest places in the city to take the kids. The *Exploratorium* has the broadest collection of completely delightful exotic visual-aural-olfactory exhibits. It's a technology museum that shows that machines and unnatural things are not always to be deplored. A beautiful collection of holographs (two-dimensional pictures that seem three-dimensional), laser tricks, a musical instrument that is played by the sun's light, a continuous movie that shows how a computer becomes an artist, exhibits of how artists use electronics, and visual tricks beyond description—put your hand through a solid object. Outside is the magic of a brand-new reinforced-concrete reconstruction of a 1915 re-creation of a Roman ruin (swans and rare ducks swim placidly upon the lagoon that mirrors the Palace); inside is a copy of Alan Shepard's Freedom-7 space capsule and an aluminum-foil-walled strobe-light room that changes your perception about the movement of your body.

WORLD OF OIL. Standard Oil Building, 555 Market Street. Monday–Friday, 10 AM–4 PM. Free.

No matter what your feelings are about the petroleum industry in general, there is no better place to get an education about oil than in this museum. At the entrance is a continuous movie showing the history of the earth and formation of oil deposits. Then there are the exhibits of oil—the complicated processes of finding it, the drilling for it (huge drill bits are on display), then the even more complicated processes of cracking crude oil into its various components. There are three dioramas—one illustrating the use of oil in the home (circa 1910), an antique service station and a bulk oil plant. The museum is educational and worth visiting, but the presentation comes across as a little too slick: as if they were propagandizing oil, not proudly displaying the achievements of a historic and vital industry. Nowhere, for example, is money mentioned and God knows that is a fascinating part of the oil game.

McGoon's Magic Cellar Saloon. 630 Clay Street (financial district). Tuesday–Saturday, 8 PM–2 AM. Admission $1, 2-drink minimum ($1.50 the drink). Children admitted.

A curious museum in that it's a bar, a nightclub, the home base of Turk Murphy's Dixieland Jazz Band. The cellar holds one of the most incredible collections of stage magicians' tricks and effects to be seen anywhere in the country. They were the property of Carter the Great, a famous illusionist who circled the world eight times with a magic show (a huge thing—sixteen in the company, thirty tons of equipment and costumes). At one time he was in partnership with Houdini. On view are fourteen major production effects—vanishing elephant; levitation stuff; having a lady put her head, hands, and feet through holes in a cabinet, and having the head go down to the floor while the hands and feet stayed where they were. Showcases holding smaller "hand magic" items and memorabilia line the room. The tariff might seem high, but the Cellar is connected with Turk Murphy above so you get dancing and Dixieland above and magic below at the same price. There is always one magician performing during weekdays and several on Friday and Saturday. The bartenders are happy to explain everything except how the tricks are worked.

Josephine D. Randall Junior Museum. Museum Way (off Roosevelt Way—halfway up Corona Heights Park). Tuesday–Saturday, 10 AM–5 PM; Sunday, 12 noon–4:30 PM. Free.

School children know this fine place through school field trips, but many adults have never been there and that's a pity. It's almost too good for children. There are excellent small displays of paleontology, geology, and Indian artifacts. Best, though, is the collection of small animals which one can touch and hold; foxes, raccoons, coatis, skunks, opossums. Reptiles ranging from tortoises to iguanas to boas are on exhibit, as well as birds—owls, hawks, crows, eagles. When my son was one and a half years old, he was taught how to say "hello" (instead of "hi") by one of the myna birds here. Don't miss it. There are fine places on the adjacent Corona Heights to picnic.

MISSION DOLORES. 16th and Dolores. Daily, 10 AM–4 PM. Admission: 25 cents.

The proper name is the Mission San Francisco De Asis—and from this the city derived its name. It was founded in 1776, an imposing structure to be built in such a remote area at that time. This is the sixth of the missions established under Junipero Serra that has given California Spanish names for its coastal cities (San Diego, Santa Barbara, Los Angeles, San Luis Obispo, San Jose, San Francisco, San Rafael, Santa Rosa, et cetera).

Upon entering, you are given a little broadside giving the statistics—that the walls are four-foot-thick adobe brick; the redwood roof timbers and tiles still the original ones put up by the Indians. It doesn't mention the fact that this building rode out the 1906 earthquake while many more modern ones were shaken apart.

Of unusual interest in the museum is the ceiling, painted by the Indians in vegetable colors. The pattern is of bisected rectangles and sort of zigzag chevrons along the beams, all in red, while, yellow, and gray-blue—a remarkably modern pattern and very pleasing.

Along the north wall are several glass cases with parts of the old vestments worn by the priests and various artifacts. You'll see some rawhide lashings used in the construction as well as some of the manzanita-wood pegs. Part of the old church records are on display, as well as some of the books from the old library, and small found stuff—a Spanish spur, a copper spoon, a razor.

Both in the Mission and in the graveyard outside, you'll see the burying places of some of the early pioneers, governors, and explorers and understand the naming of San Francisco streets. There lies here Noe, Arguello, Palou, de

Haro, Moraga, and others. In the church lies William Alexander Leidesdorff, a prominent early businessman. His resting place within the Mission shows his prestige. There is a short street named after him in the heart of the financial district. He was black.

7
Salvage Shops

It's easier to describe what a salvage shop isn't than what it is. It's not *quite* a secondhand store or thrift shop, but it's both. It's not *quite* an outlet for goods donated to charity to enable the poor to furnish and clothe themselves cheaply—but it does that too. The San Francisco salvage shop is a unique institution in our mercantile spectrum, a curiosity.

The name itself is promising in an ecologically motivated era. In other cities, the unwanted, the castoff, the outgrown (unless it's antique), is generally catagorized as "secondhand," and generally held in low esteem—something to be sold to the poor. The term "secondhand" has no good connotations—as seen in the recent move by real estate sellers to term *houses* as "used" or "secondhand" in order to push newly built houses in a development. *Salvage,* though, means stuff rescued from destruction, a nautical term that this port city uses as a generic term to cover these shops.

While middle-class citizens in other cities usually don't want things bought in a secondhand store, there is no reluctance or embarrassment on the part of San Franciscans to exult over a great item bought for next to nothing in a salvage shop.

Salvage means exotic plunder. San Francisco has always been a pack-rat city. For many years, most stuff had to be shipped in from the East Coast, Europe, or the Orient (lack of local hardwood prevented a thriving furniture industry and lack of suitable clay precluded a porcelain-dishware industry).

Since San Francisco is a port city, many items of exotica passed through, and citizens picked them up. Since everything cost so much, San Francisco was a saving city, hoarding everything of any possible use. Today the city abounds with discoveries.

The salvage-shop phenomenon began about twenty-five years ago with the opening of what is now the Patrons of Arts and Music Salvage Shop at 1967 Jackson Street. Others claim to be older, but this salvage shop that Alma Spreckels opened in her carriage house must be the beginning. It remains the most elegant secondhand store in the world. The property itself is worth at least a cool million. Originally, the thrust of her charity through this shop was directed to the Maritime Museum in Aquatic Park, and through it the reconstruction of the museum ship the *Balclutha*. She was a great social power and had no trouble in getting donations in goods from her friends, especially when it was found (the second boost to the growth of salvage shops) that donations in goods are as tax deductible as donations in cash. People who would hesitate to give $20 to a charitable enterprise were happy to get rid of a piece of "lumber"—an old couch, for example—that was worth $200 if they could write it off on taxes.

With Alma Spreckels, salvage shops became respectable— not only respectable but social. In the '50s we saw the great breaking up of family houses. Married children no longer lived at home, an eight-room Victorian house was too much work for a couple on the verge of retirement. Salvage goods were available to charitable organizations. And salvage shops were discovered to be a gold mine for charitable organizations—a continuous rummage sale in which the goods were free, the help volunteer, and the only cost the renting of a storefront.

Another boost came from the love generation of the middle '60s. Antique clothing, ratty old fur coats, old furniture were bought by the hippies, first for practicality and pleasure, then as the "in" thing to do. *Funk* shops and boutiques developed and spread everywhere, another example of San Francisco leading the way—but a curious way indeed. A whole new merchandising approach grew out of the salvage shops. The hippie entrepreneur would buy a 1920s ball dress for $2.50 at a salvage shop and feature it as "camp" to be sold for $30 in his funk shop.

Over the years, the salvage shop has become more savvy, and huge bargains are not to be picked up when you walk through the door; but the bargains are still there. Today in San Francisco there are some 37 salvage outlets run by some 22 charities. Each charity demands a regular donation from each of its members for the shop, which means a steady inflow of goods. There's a lot of junk, but also very fine things that even the sellers don't know the real value of. Recently I bought a Peerless Quartet recording of "Just Like Washington Crossed the Delaware, General Pershing Will Cross the Rhine" for 25 cents, and a mint condition pair of World War I army cavalry officer's riding breeches for 75 cents, and that's a hell of a buy.

It's curious that near most of the salvage shops in the city you'll find antique shops as well. In San Francisco it follows that if you're interested in one, you'll be interested in the other. The Salvage Shops listed here are run by charities. (There are others, of course, and some of great interest. Along 6th Street between Market and Howard are salvage shops that sell stolen goods and the remnants of lives destroyed by drink.) The list is in no particular order. Consult your street map for the location of individual stores. Nor can one vouch for quality, because it's impossible to say from one month to the next what will be on sale. All of these, though, are long-established salvage shops and should still be there when you go.

PATRONS OF ARTS AND MUSIC SALVAGE SHOP. 1967 Jackson Street. Monday–Saturday, 10 AM–4:30 PM.

There are 1,500 to 2,000 rich members of this organization, all of whom contribute to the salvage shop. It's a mixed bag of offerings. The clothing is interesting. My wife once bought a rhinestone-studded black chiffon long dress (with a train) for $1.20 that immediately transformed her into Vampira for several Halloween parties. The last time I was there, antique lace, still in its paper, was selling for $7 a yard, which is a bargain, a Spanish horn comb for $8. You will find furniture, prints, records, sheet music—a whole spectrum of merchandise. This is the original salvage shop in San Francisco and the lady on duty at the time of my visit said that they have had inquiries from all over the country from charitable groups wanting to set up a similar operation, indeed some who came to study it.

SALVATION ARMY. Monday–Thursday, 9:30 AM–6 PM; Friday, 9:30 AM–9 PM; Saturday 9:30 AM–5 PM.

No explanation necessary. The Salvation Army thrift shops have furnished many a home, if only in "Salvation Army Modern." They get a lot of good stuff from people who know their donations are going to direct relief and rehabilitation. The Salvation Army pricers are knowledgeable about the going prices for antique furniture and clothing, but bargains slip through. I saw a high-wheeled, lacquered English baby carriage, an elegant thing in perfect condition with a price tag of $45 that would have sold at any antique store for $200.

There's an awful lot of junk on sale at Salvation Army and all the other salvage stores, but look through it. Hidden beneath a ton of five-and-dime dishes is a piece of antique porcelain; with the cast-off cooking stuff might be a silver tray, all tarnished and mungy-looking, that needs only cleaning, or a piece of pewter; in the glassware might be hidden a jewel of cut crystal.

There are six Salvation Army stores:

26th and Valencia—the main store.

1833 Fillmore.

1085 Mission Street.

4735 Mission Street.

1173 Sutter (the corner of Sutter and Polk, where they send their most expensive and rare stuff).

2149 Taraval Street.

ST. VINCENT DE PAUL. Monday–Saturday, 9 AM–4:45 PM.

Also a direct rehabilitation charity. Their main store is at 1745 Folsom (13th and Folsom).

Whenever I visit there, I always kick myself for not having

bought the two croquignole machines I first saw in their old Mission Street store. These were the Frankenstein-monster 1920s permanent wave machines—a pole on a wide base, four thousand (it seemed) electric wires from the top with curling irons on the tips, that the ladies to be beautified plugged into. I saw it just at the height of pop art. With a little paint and by stiffening the wires so that they all stood out like a dandelion gone to seed, I could have made a pot of money and a reputation as an artist, with no effort on my part. The management, though, is ultra conservative and still thought of them as utilitarian devices, something that a budding hairdresser might use to set up shop, and priced them accordingly, something like $80 per croquignole, and it was beyond my means.

I did find great 78-r.p.m. records there, and the store seems to be the repository of defunct church embellishments. If you want a good, weeping St. Anne for your garden or genuine church pews, this is the place to go.

GOODWILL INDUSTRIES. Monday–Saturday, 9:30 AM–5 PM.

Goodwill is almost as famous as Salvation Army and St. Vincent de Paul. This organization also deals with the handicapped. They claim to be the first thrift shop in San Francisco, opening their shop of donated goods just after the earthquake in 1906. Goodwill has three stores:

986 Howard Street.
2279 Mission.
2042 Fillmore.

They refinish their goods (especially furniture) in their shops, and thus aim to supply the poor with good, inexpensive household items. At their main store at 986 Howard (between 4th & 5th streets), though, you'll see some extraordinary things, from beautiful antique clothing and musical instruments on the second floor to a grab-bag in the basement. It was in the basement that I found a powder-blue, plastic, three-bosomed mannequin (small, medium, and large) used to display brassieres in shop windows. For two dollars, it was the perfect Christmas gift for a bachelor friend who was slightly nutty on the subject.

BARGAIN MART. 1815 Divisadero. Tuesday–Saturday, 10 AM–4 PM.

At Divisadero and Post streets. There are several salvage shops operating along the next several blocks. This is sponsored by the National Council of Jewish Women.

ORT, 2028 Fillmore (Pine and Fillmore). Monday–Saturday, 10 AM–4 PM.

The Organization through Rehabilitation and Training is a Jewish women's organization that sponsors vocational schools in twenty-three countries. The organization is ninety-one years old, and the shop is interesting to visit.

VOLUNTEERS OF AMERICA. Monday–Saturday, 9:30 AM–5:30 PM.

This has three shops in San Francisco:
2904 Mission.
1529 Polk.
524 Valencia.

THE ATTIC SHOP. 1040 Hyde Street. Monday–Saturday, 10 AM–5 PM.

Run by the St. Francis Memorial Hospital Auxiliary (wives of the doctors at St. Francis Hospital). You'll find some curious stuff here—Persian lamb coats, silver, and crystal—along with a lot of junk. In one of my visits to this shop, I saw in the books section a beautiful leather-bound, superbly illustrated (all the color prints looked hand-tinted) medical tome, *Diseases of the Anus and Rectum*. It was going for $15, which I didn't have at the time for frivolities, but I have enjoyed this book a thousand times—thinking of personal enemies, political opponents and TV personalities to whom this would have made a perfect gift.

NEW TO YOU SHOP. 1036 Hyde (Hyde and California). Tuesday–Saturday, 11 AM–4 PM.

Operated by the Cathedral School (Grace Cathedral) ladies, it's next door to the Attic Shop and has about the same kind of stuff, but not so literary. The Cathedral School is a rich school and castoffs from the rich can be rich indeed.

BLIND BABIES BAZAAR. 1219 Polk Street (Polk and Sutter). Monday–Friday, 10:30 AM–5 PM.

Operated by the Variety Club of Northern California Tent 32 Auxiliary. You can find some surprising things there, especially in women's clothing. It's a show biz place and the last time I was there, they featured an original Jean-Louis Scherrer gown designed for Elizabeth Arden for $395 that was selling for $40.

CLOTHES CLOSET. 3585 Sacramento Street (Sacramento and Laurel). Tuesday–Friday, 10 AM–4 PM; Saturday 10 AM–1 PM.

Run by the Town School ladies (Town School is a school for boys). You can find some great buys in quality kids' clothing. The line runs heavily to the special and dress-up clothing that the kids outgrow.

PURPLE HEART THRIFT SHOP. 1855 Mission. Monday–Saturday, 9 AM–9 PM; Sunday, 10 AM–5 PM.

The Military Order of the Purple Heart, Wilson Chapter No. 15, sponsors this outlet. Although you will find mostly utilitarian clothing and furnishings, there are some surprising buys there. I once found an authentic Henry Poole (of Saville Row, London, England) tailored suit hanging among the others; it was selling for $7 and looked perfectly respectable. I bought a lot of good flowerpots for 5 cents each that were selling for 30 cents at Cost Plus.

TREASURES UNLIMITED. 917 Clement Street. Monday–Friday, 11 AM–5:30 PM.

This is the Hadassah Ladies thrift shop, the proceeds going to Hadassah hospitals in Israel. A small shop, but full of interesting things.

STILL STYLISH SHOP. 2404 California (California and Fillmore). Monday–Friday, 11 AM–4 PM.

Proceeds to the Florence Crittenden Home. A small shop with many things for women.

NEXT TO NEW SHOP. 2226 Fillmore. Monday, 10 AM–4 PM; Tuesday, 10 AM–6 PM; Wednesday–Saturday, 10 AM–4 PM.

Run by the Junior League. Next to the Patrons of Arts and Music Salvage Shop (Alma Spreckels place on Jackson), this has to be the most aggressive and money-making and *social* salvage shop in San Francisco. The Junior League is actively engaged in at least nine community efforts from the Hunter's Point Girls' Club to money into Sesame Street; from the drug-abuse education program to the Audubon Canyon Ranch; from the Exploratorium to the Chinatown after-school program. This store is a significant source of money for the programs because it's run in a fairly heavy-handed way. Each member of the Junior League *must* donate one item of clothing each month for sale in this shop—a fairly stringent commitment. It's a great place for good buys, especially in women's clothing of the best quality, often never worn. This shop supplies several other salvage shops with clothing when it gets overstocked.

THE TREASURE TROVE, 1033 Irving (10th Avenue and Irving). Tuesday–Saturday, 10 AM–4 PM.

This small shop that sells for the Diabetic Youth Group is a specialized charity, the proceeds of which go into the operation of a summer camp for diabetic children. (The special dietary requirements of diabetic kids automatically excludes them from most organized camps.) There are good things to be found here.

ONCE REMOVED, 1000 Irving Street. Tuesday–Saturday, 10 AM–3 PM.

The outlet for the Mills College Alumnae has a good collection of clothing, small furnishings, and toys donated by the members. The help is all volunteer and you may find something sold cheap that is worth more than the ticket price.

PRESBYTERIAN HOSPITAL THRIFT (GARDEN) SHOP, 2020

Webster. Monday–Friday, 11 AM–4 PM; Saturday, noon–4 PM.

This three-story shop, with an elevator, is the most lavish of the hospital charities as far as space goes. It is run by doctors' wives. Paintings and small appliances are on the first floor, a book nook in the lower level, and larger pieces on the third floor. With the development of the hospital, I don't know how much longer this will last, but go and see it. There's a lot of junk, but there are a few treasures too.

I've emphasized the small stuff, because that's what you can carry away as a tourist. In all these places, though, there are good solid bargains to be had in things that have to be shipped. Look for them. A plain, modern mass-produced love seat in the discount houses costs at least $150–$225. There are old, broken-down love seats, beautifully carved, in these shops that can be shipped home and worked on. The same is true of the china, crystal, pewter, and silver. You have to look. Good hunting!

8
Viewing the Rich in San Francisco

San Francisco is a rich town, full of rich people. In most large cities, the rich are either invisible or inaccessible. They live in exclusive suburban enclaves or keep expensive apartments in blank apartment houses; you don't see them. In San Francisco, they are both visible and accessible. Because of topography, more than anything else I can think of, once-fashionable neighborhoods have remained fashionable for an unusually long time. A view of or proximity to the Bay has enduring monetary value. Any kind of property in San Francisco is valuable and the choicer spots, for the last fifty years anyway, have increased in choiceness. With few exceptions, where the rich once lighted in San Francisco, they stayed.

I didn't realize how interesting the viewing of the rich was until my sister and her husband came to the city for a convention. With them was another couple from Ohio. Giving the standard tour, I took them along Marina Boulevard. I was pointing to the yacht harbor, Golden Gate Bridge, and the Bay Islands to the right, but the women were enthralled by the living-room windows to the left. I was a little miffed that my spiel was being ignored until I realized that while looking at the Golden Gate Bridge in the flesh merely confirms ten thousand travelogues, the free glimpse of the up-to-the-fashionable-minute wallpaper, decor, coffee-table accouterments, was a rare treat. Looking at the homes of St. Francis Wood gave them ideas of fine points they could apply to their own homes. It was all out of *House Beautiful* (in which many of the homes they saw and you'll be seeing have appeared as features).

There are about nine wealthy neighborhoods in San Francisco now. The first posh neighborhood was South Park, an elegant residential oval built in imitation of the malls of Bath and London. Mark Twain wrote of making holiday calls in the 1860s at the fine homes on this short street off 2nd Street between Brannan and Bryant. It is one of the few rich neighborhoods in San Francisco that has declined into a slum. The street is still there, but the rich abandoned the finest climate in San Francisco for the elegance of the hills above the financial district. Nob Hill was first favored for mansion building, then the other heights—Russian Hill, Pacific Heights, and Telegraph Hill. After the earthquake-fire, several rich-in-the-city communities began to be built—St. Francis Wood, Forest Hill, Seacliff. These are semi-autonomous neighborhoods providing their own street repair, irrigation of their special landscaping, and upkeep. In return, they got permission to abandon the grid street plan that covered most of the city and plan their houses around the natural contours of the hills. The people in St. Francis Wood pay $100 a month per house for this amenity, the people of Forest Hill probably a little less, those of Seacliff more. Curiously, while the rich are fleeing other large cities, there seem to be other affluent neighborhoods abuilding here. Award-winning homes now stand on the flanks of Twin Peaks and more are going up. Even in Bernal Heights, there are showplace homes. But let us go look at them.

Of necessity, this is a driving tour. I noticed in my research that some sightseeing buses cover the Pacific Heights–Seacliff area on their way to the Palace of the Legion of Honor, but city buses only touch the edges of the fine houses. Three tours are here offered: Marina-Seacliff, Pacific Heights, and the rich in the Sunset. Nob, Russian and Telegraph Hills are mostly the blank rich apartment houses mentioned earlier. One gets only a fleeting glimpse. These are the best shots at the rich and all are guided from Union Square.

MARINA-SEACLIFF

From Union Square, go out Geary (it's one way) to Van Ness Avenue. Turn right on Van Ness and thence to Bay Street. Turn left on Bay (almost at the end of Van Ness)— farther down is Aquatic Park. The parklike facility on your right is Ft. Mason, one of the major troop debarcation points of World War II and still the headquarters of the military transports to the Far East. Turn right on Laguna (the signs say Golden Gate Bridge) and you are on Marina Boulevard. From here to the yacht harbor, you will find showcase homes, in a literal sense. These are rich places with huge picture windows where the curtains are never drawn. In the daytime, the interiors are open, at night, the interiors are well lighted. One seldom sees the inhabitants in their living rooms day or night, and I have the feeling that, like the poor, they spend most of their time in the kitchen. The rooms are vacant but beautiful and well worth taking in.

Stay in the right lane and, at Baker, turn into the yacht harbor. This is a haven for deep-water sailing boats, cruisers, and the motor yachts, manned by a crew, that fall into the super-rich category. They take your breath away—the big ones do. They are toys of the rich, but fantastic.

From the yacht harbor, continue out the highway toward the bridge, stay in the right lane, and just before the toll plaza of the bridge, turn right to the viewing area, left under the tunnel and right again to Merchant, which will lead you to Lincoln Boulevard down and out of the Presidio. Follow El Camino del Mar. Now you are in Seacliff.

The houses are magnificent and historic. Those of you who listened to radio might remember the foghorns and tense narration in the old *One Man's Family* series. In Ohio we worried about that Barbour family. This is where the Barbour family lived, in Seacliff. After you see the magnificent homes of Seacliff you won't worry about the Barbour family any more. Follow El Camino del Mar and you're back to Geary Street and on your way to the ocean or back downtown.

PACIFIC HEIGHTS

This is a nebulous area running from Van Ness to the

Presidio along four streets. The moneyed crest of Pacific Heights follows Washington, Jackson, Pacific, and Broadway. You'll see fine houses all along this stretch of streets.

Follow Geary out to Van Ness and turn right. Turn left on Jackson and two blocks up; the opulent homes start to appear. Between Washington and Broadway to Fillmore, there are nothing but mansions and high-rise apartment houses. This is the oldest section of Pacific Heights and from Lafayette Park you can look down into the Spreckels mansion. The California Historical Society museum, listed before, shows how the old mansions look inside. Fillmore to the Presidio along these four streets (and down to Green Street) is all prosperous. The homes are impressive, the streets are charming, and in this area you'll find most of the consular residences in San Francisco. Follow your own route here and meander through the streets. You can't get lost. Down the hill is Lombard, which will take you back to Van Ness and Geary. Up the hill is California Street, which will take you back to Powell Street and down to Geary. Follow these streets out to Arguello. At Arguello and Washington you will come upon Presidio Terrace, a privately owned property that boasts the most architecturally varied housing in the city—a stone house with gargoyle rain spouts is next to a modern redwood structure, and half-timbered Elizabethan homes rear next to California Spanish. Our mayor lives in this amazing and variegated quarter.

TWIN PEAKS, FOREST HILL, ST. FRANCIS WOOD

This is a nice ride through many interesting neighborhoods. Here you can combine a visit to two of the best views in the city with a tour of the wealthy neighborhoods.

Drive out Geary to Masonic (the big Sears store is on the corner, the sign reads University of San Francisco) and turn left. Drive past the Golden Gate Park Panhandle and turn right on Haight Street. Here is the heart of what is left of the Haight-Ashbury. Turn left on Clayton and drive up to Clarendon and Twin Peaks Boulevard. Follow the signs as if you were going to Twin Peaks (or go to Twin Peaks) and turn right at Mountain Spring Road and bear left up to Palo

Alto. On this street you will see some superb homes, all prize winners. Retrace back to Clarendon and turn left. Follow Clarendon to 7th Avenue, and turn left at the lake (a standby fire reservoir). Bear to your right onto Dewey Boulevard and turn right on Pacheco. You will see by the elegant street furniture that you're in Forest Hill. A good circular drive in Marcela to Magellan to Castenada to Montalvo to Dewey and Claremont Boulevard. A street map of the city is handy for this area because the streets are contour and confusing.

Follow Claremont to Portola Drive and turn right. At the intersection of Portola Drive, Junipera Serra, Sloat, and St. Francis, make a sharp left through the gates of St. Francis Wood. This is a most pleasant drive.

To return to town, retrace St. Francis to Portola Drive and follow it back into the downtown area (it becomes Market Street at the foot of Twin Peaks). There is a pullout vista area on your way back which has a fine East Bay view.

In these days of homogenized houses, ticky-tacky and cheapjack, it is grand to see what man can do with his dwelling places—if he has money.

9
Fine Streets to Walk Upon

I believe that one of the primary elements of San Francisco's appeal, the reason so many first-time visitors feel a rush of sudden affection for San Francisco, lies in the streets of the city. The European visitors feel at home and the Americans experience a combination of excitement and nostalgia. Americans are not and have never been great pedestrians—strollers for pleasure. American cities are not built that way. In Europe, land is expensive, cities are built up instead of out, strolling or walking is a normal exercise. In America, exercise has always meant an active sport—basketball, football, baseball. Distances were too great between home and work, home and marketplaces to make walking a pleasure. Probably for this reason, we are premiere in the world for inventing ways around the healthy but tedious covering of ground from here to there by foot. Even thirty years ago, perishable market stuff was brought to the door: there were the milkman, baker, fishmonger, iceman, vegetable cart, ice-cream vendor plying the city streets of even a small town like Springfield, Ohio. The only streets where the citizens strolled for pleasure were "downtown."

Going "downtown" was never a casual undertaking, but an exciting one. You dressed up to go "downtown." There were things to see, the latest goods to inspect, exciting people. It was the center for serious shopping, the focus of civic life, the heart of the city. Most cities have lost their *downtown*. For shopping, people now largely go to shopping centers. "Downtown" used to mean a place where there were people selling and working and, in the bars, loafing. Going "downtown" was a multisided experience. Downtown wasn't specific. You checked the action on foot.

This is one of the reasons San Francisco is so loved. There are few American cities that offer so many streets that evoke the nostalgia of interest, excitement, and sheer pleasure once felt in going "downtown." To older people from all over the country, there is the unbegruging envy of, "We once had something like this back home." To the young who have known only shopping centers and the ruined centers of cities, it is a revelation of how civilizing a city can be.

The appeal of the streets of San Francisco doesn't stop there, of course. This city is like no other and the streets are as wildly unordinary as is the city. Take the cultural shock of the mish-mash of converging streets in North Beach. The most Chinese part of Chinatown runs into the topless section of Broadway.

Across Broadway, Grant turns from Chinese to Bohemian-Italian; Stockton and Columbus is Chinese-Italian, shading more Italian the farther away from Broadway. On Jackson and Pacific streets, across from mostly Philippino Kearny Street, is an enclave of invitation-only fine-furniture and decorator shops—and around the corner from that are bean-sprout farms, pasta factories, and strictly commercial concerns.

The only problem with the fine San Francisco streets to walk upon is finding a parking place to put your car while you do it. Fortunately, most of the best streets have public parking lots or parking garages nearby.

North Beach, Grant, and Columbus.

As Grant Avenue between Bush and Broadway (and the peripheral streets) is of a piece, and that means Chinatown in San Francisco, so NORTH BEACH is of a piece. This is part of the oldest settled section of San Francisco, the district with the most romance, and color. The Barbary Coast, with its shanghaiing, deadfalls, and bawdy entertainments was located here; the center of the Italian community of San Francisco was and still is in North Beach, and the center of San Francisco arts and writing (working artists and writers) is still found here.

North Beach offers fine streets to walk upon and the only problem is where to begin. Since the parking garage under old Portsmouth Square is handy for cars (at Kearny and Clay), we might as well begin here to walk the streets of North Beach. If you're using public transportation from Union Square, take the No. 30 Stockton Street trolley bus and get off at Broadway and Stockton—follow the guides backward.

If you park at Portsmouth Square, go out the Kearny Street exit and you're in the heart of Little Manila. A block up and to your right are Jackson and Pacific streets, the old Barbary Coast of infamy. The 1880s buildings have been sandblasted, renovated inside, and are now the most chic fine-furniture and decorator shops in the city. When I was here in 1955, it was called the "International Settlement," a semibawdy street where most of the establishments had lost their liquor licenses because of malpractice and were selling soft drinks for a dollar apiece, with dancers on the stages wearing gauze bras and G-strings.

During the Prohibition days, this was just as rough an area as in the Barbary Coast days fifty years earlier. This was the era of crime organizing, with terrible examples from Chicago and New York. San Francisco had only local hoodlums, hometown bootleggers. The threat of organized crime invading San Francisco was experienced in the shotgunning of one bootlegger by another, Chicago-style, in 1932 on the corner of Broadway and Columbus. This triggered the most massive attack against organized crime ever seen in the country, before or since. Thousands of people were arrested in the period of two weeks. Known hoodlums, patrons of the illegal bars, bums, drunks, people who looked evil were dragged into jail and put on trial. All the five local newspapers printed box scores on their front pages as to how many criminals were caught, how many were convicted, how many were set free, and named the judges (elective then as now) who were most lenient and most stern. The innocent drinker was set free, but it was too much heat for the organized-crime characters and they left town in droves. Organized crime in San Francisco never really recovered after that (except possibly in narcotics during the last ten years). For this reason, when you walk past the topless joints along Broadway, you don't get the same feeling of menace that you do in similar nightclub areas of most large cities. There is the relaxed feeling of good times along here.

BROADWAY is an interesting thoroughfare. Referred to locally as "Bawdway," it offers a plethora of salacious entertainments for the tourists. It is more than that, though. There are fine restaurants, some of the best jazz nightclubs on the West Coast, cultural entertainments, like the Bocce Ball, a nightclub which offers operatic entertainment—arias by opera students and semiprofessionals—and some excellent restaurants—not to speak of the very fine bars in the neighborhood.

After you explore Broadway, turn up GRANT AVENUE. This is always referred to as Upper Grant—to differentiate it from the Grant Avenue which is Chinatown. This section of North Beach has for many years been the closest to a bohemian section that San Francisco can offer. Poor artists and writers have gravitated to this Chinese-Italian neighborhood for many reasons. The rents are reasonable, the neighborhood is tolerant of eccentric behavior, and it was always full of great restaurants that served a lot of good food cheaply. The San Francisco Art Institute is in the neighborhood. Upper Grant got its greatest reputation during the late '50s and early '60s when the beatniks made it their own. The beats were a curious group, a kind of early bellwether of where the youth of the nation was headed (which was *away* from the establishment). A lot of comparisons have been made between the beats and the hippies, but there really were none. Whatever else they were, they were producers of art, literate and cynical. Their spokesmen were Kerouac, Ferlinghetti, Ginsberg, Rexroth, McClure—an impressive list. The hippies have produced no art (as a culture) except the excellent posters advertising the early rock concerts and the teen-age super-movie-star kind of foolishness of the rock bands. It is no wonder that the Haight became their stomping ground instead of Upper Grant. On Upper Grant, they would have had to read a book to talk to people—or if they were "into" art, they would have to do more than "their thing" of painting toenails.

Upper Grant is a great browsing street for antiques, hand-made jewelry, fine hand-woven cloth, clothing, and small accessories. Here are at least two coffee houses left over from the beatnik days, and still as interesting. Fine bars abound and the many restaurants that made the place a mecca for the hungry but poor. At the Green Valley Restaurant, the menu for dinner reads: soup (always enough for a meal in itself), salad (tossed greens, with salami, olives, and spicy little green peppers on the side), ravioli or spaghetti (another meal), the entree (which is always hearty and delicious), coffee, cheese and fruit or ice cream, and a carafe of wine with the dinner. The price is $3.25.

Upper Grant becomes residential at about Filbert, so turn down the hill to the heart of Italian North Beach, Washington Square, dominated by the magnificent church of the Sts. Peter and Paul. Across Columbus are some great delicatessens. You can get cheese, meat, bread, and wine, and sit, as others do in the sunny square, relax, and refresh yourself. Washington Square is a great place to loaf. It's always full of fascinating people, old Italian men, gossiping ladies, denizens of Upper Grant, and footsore visitors.

From Washington Square, walk back *Columbus* toward Broadway. On Columbus and Stockton streets, along Green Street and Vallejo, you are unmistakably in Little Italy. Groceries, delicatessens, restaurants, bars, bookstores, bakeries, law offices, and tourist agencies—all are Italian. It might seem foolish and guidebookish to say that these few blocks have a special feeling about them—an Italian lightheartedness —but you'll feel it just walking the streets. The pace is different, the expression, the tone. It's a great place to explore, so I won't spoil it for you.

At Broadway and Stockton, you are approaching Chinatown again. To reach your car, turn left on Broadway and right on Kearny.

Union Street

UNION STREET, from Steiner to Gough, is a rather recent and developing attraction of San Francisco. It's developing so rapidly that in a few years, it will doubtless achieve a name as solid and well-known as Grant Avenue, Haight-Ashbury, or North Beach.

At the foot of Pacific Heights, just above the Marina district, it has always had a charm of its own. In the huge Victorian homes converted to flats on the slopes of Pacific Heights, and the smaller places from Union to Lombard, there were always lots of single young working people (pre-executives, Montgomery Street secretaries) that guaranteed some lively bars, good restaurants, first-run and art movie houses in the vicinity. They had money and had to dress well, so there were always some shops—specialty shops. The moneyed people from Pacific Heights patronized the grocery stores, bookstores, etcetera, so there were always some very fine places.

Around the nucleus of the young and the rich, Union Street has become a wonderful street to walk on. It's mainly a shopping street, but unlike any other in town for the sheer number of shops, their variety, and their own special flavor. In the 6 blocks of Union Street between Steiner and Gough, I counted 196 separate business establishments. Most are shops and this is the most curious aspect of the street. All the myriad shops—the 26 antique shops, the 28 men's and women's clothing stores, the 15 art galleries, the 6 furniture stores, the 7 imported handicrafts stores, 9 boutiques, 4 jewelers, and on and on—each one is different and distinct, each was one person's idea of how to most handsomely sell his own specialty (there are a few quality chain stores moving in, but they are so obviously plastic that the individual shop is enhanced by the contrast).

But it's not only a shopping street. There are 12 bars, 14 restaurants, 5 coffee shops, and 2 movie houses, which makes it a gathering place for people. And it's not only a new tourist attraction, it's a living neighborhood, as is proved by the 7 florists (tourists don't usually buy cut flowers), 3 drugstores,

2 laundromats, 7 grocery stores, 2 bakeries, 3 dry-cleaning shops, 10 barber and beauty shops, 6 banks, 3 plumbers, and one optometrist (plus real estate offices).

The sheer statistics of Union Street cannot describe the pleasure you'll find in walking down it, but perhaps they will give you some idea of what is to be found. One of my favorite shops is the Museum Shop on Fillmore, a block from Union toward Lombard. It sells a variety of small antique craft items—Pre-Columbian or early Colonial Central and South American pottery items, Peruvian woven mummy wrappings, tinware from early United States, antique small things from the Middle East and Asia—nice little things that you can afford, as well as exotic apparel from Morocco and India, and handicraft from all over. Another good shop is the gourmet cooking-utensils shop on Union—you can find it—that carries all the specialized cooking gear required for French and other cuisines.

Chinatown

Along Grant Avenue and peripheral streets from Bush to Broadway.

Before we walk along Grant Avenue through the heart of CHINATOWN, we must first look at the phenomenon of Chinatown itself. San Francisco's Chinatown is the most curious ghetto in America. It is the largest enclave of Chinese outside the Orient—and so a visit to Chinatown is a very realistic introduction to the real Orient—and it is also American. Chinatown is a dictionary-definition ghetto—a place set aside for the enclosure of a race (also with the evil connotations of *ghetto*—vast overcrowding, high incidence of ghetto diseases, and poverty). But it is also an *exclusive* ghetto. A friend once tried to rent an apartment in Chinatown for the sheer romance of it. He visited three Chinese rental agencies. The first agent, although he had a diploma from the University of San Francisco hanging behind his desk, all of a sudden didn't understand a word of English. The second saw his cigarette and said that they didn't rent to smokers because of the danger of fire. The third said, with a straight face, that because he was Caucasian, he would want to keep a pet and no pets were allowed. Chinatown is as tight as a Chinese drum.

San Francisco has always had a peculiar attitude toward the Chinese and Chinatown. In the gold-digging, railroad-building days, the inexpensive talents of the Chinese were utilized to their fullest extent. When the railroads were built and the mines had passed their peak productivity, the surviving Chinese were feared for their numbers, and their effect upon the employment situation. They became a fit target for hoodlums and racist rabble-rousers. Regarded as a threat, they were disenfranchised, ghettoized, and legislatively denied many avenues of livelihood. But an Oriental colony in the midst of the city was exotic. The tabloids were full of breathless stories of Tong wars, opium dens, enslaved prostitutes. Chinatown was full of mystery—and a place for every tourist to visit.

It was more. It was the repository of a culture older, and mysteriously richer, than the Caucasian. The stubbornness of these people in the midst of obviously superior civilization clinging to their heathen and pagan religions made an impression. Even more impressive was the fact that the Chinese embodied all the *super*-virtues to which Americans paid tribute. The Chinese, though sneaky, treacherous, and evil, were industrious to a fault, thrifty beyond belief, and so cagey in economic matters they put Sam Slick in the shade. They took care of their own and educated their children to a love of culture, desire for education, and respect for their elders that Americans found only in sentimental novels. The Chinese of Chinatown were something special. The bigotry against the Chinese didn't lessen, but a mystique and respect colored the thinking of San Franciscans about Chinatown.

Today, there is hardly a neighborhood in the city without a Chinese family, or several, but they are different. They are fellow grass-cutters and PTA members and victims of high property taxes. Chinatown transcends race. It is a place, and in this day and age, it is still tinged with magic. A few years ago, there was great hand-wringing in San Francisco when it was announced that the rate of juvenile crime had increased in Chinatown. You knew that the Chinese in your neighborhood had just as much trouble controlling their kids as you did, but when the *real* Chinese in Chinatown couldn't control *their* kids, there was little hope for anyone.

No doubt about it, Chinatown is a foreign place. The first time I ventured into the depths of Chinatown, I felt like Marco Polo. As a Water Department meter reader, you literally go into the depths because most of the water meters are in the basements (rather, Chinatown cellars). My first stop was a grocery store on the corner of Clay and Grant. The grocery seemed to have too many clerks above for the size of the store. In the basement, there were even more men working around huge, steaming caldrons on brick ranges. A freshly slaughtered hog hung from the ceiling by a hook in its jaw; a pan beneath caught the juices. A clerk followed me down the steps and pointed to the meters in a small room off to the side. There was a double sink in this room in which yet another man was preparing vegetables. In the narrow, steaming basement, I thought, "This is it! I am in the real Chinatown, witnessing, in this cramped cellar, a swarming hive of typical Chinese industriousness!" It wasn't until I got on the street again that I felt disappointment that the cellar was cleaner and more brightly lighted than an authentic Chinatown cellar is reputed to be.

My next basement was beneath one of the tourist shops on Grant. Again, a Chinese clerk followed me to the stairs that led to the cellar. At the top of the steps, thumbtacked next to a time clock, was a counterfeit ten-dollar bill—so phony it looked Xeroxed with a sign above it: THERE IS NO EXCUSE FOR THIS! The basement was divided by a brick wall down the middle. One side was full of shelves holding the kimonos, boxed tea sets, and bamboo pop guns. A glimpse through an open door showed a modern kitchen, dinette set, and couch. A three-year-old was racing a tricycle around the linoleum. When he saw us, he grabbed the teen-aged clerk and said, "I'm playing astronaut!" and followed us to the meters above the mailing table asking questions all the way.

I thought that it was one of the illegal apartments made so much of in the poverty reports, but it wasn't. It was the typical kitchen set-up found in most Chinese businesses from grocery stores to dry-goods stores. As part of wages, one or more meals are served to the employees. There's one butcher shop in Stockton whose mouth-watering cooking odors nearly drove me crazy every time I read the meters (I always seemed to hit it about noontime). The same guy was at the pots every time I was there. He wore a stained butcher's apron but was the oldest man there, frail and snippish. I'm sure they kept him as a fellow worker because he was such a good cook.

There are many illegal apartments in the basements of Chinatown, and they all seem to follow along the same line. A basement is transformed into a kind of railroad flat with hung curtains instead of partitions. There is usually a middle-aged Chinese woman and four or five little kids—none of whom speak English and who seem to shrink from intruders as a threat. Although they didn't follow the housing codes (no windows, for example), the apartments are invariably clean, and the kids well dressed and well fed. It is a marked contrast to the illegal apartments found in the Fillmore, the Tenderloin, and south of Market.

The basements of Chinatown have always been a source of mystery. Before the earthquake-fire (in which Chinatown was burned to the ground), the cellars of Chinatown were thought to be a warren of secret tunnels and passageways, whole complexes of ornate, exotic, hiding places where sinister goings-on were sinisterly going on. When the fire leveled the buildings, it was found, with some disappointment, that this wasn't so. It's no wonder that such speculation arose, though, because fascinating things do go on in Chinatown cellars. There is a photography studio on the ground level, with apartments above, that has a bean-curd factory working under the floor. A barber shop has its cellar stuffed with the stored trunks of immigrants (who have no space in their hotel rooms). A dry-goods store leases its basement to a classical Chinese music society. Chinatown is terrifically crowded and no space is wasted—indeed, city planners might study Chinatown for efficient use of space. And not only are the basements fully utilized but the ground floors as well. There is one Chinese grocery store that comes to mind especially. Outside are the piles of ginger root, *bok choy*, snow peas. Inside is a small cubicle behind the glass cases of candied winter melon and coconut candies. Downstairs is a processing plant for goods sold above and a butcher shop specializing in preparing meats for restaurants. From the cubicle in the grocery, the owner runs an import agency, a real estate business, and a small-scale employment agency. The grocery store is a dynamo of entrepreneurship, a small-scale conglomerate invisible to the tourists passing by, but certainly illustrating the industriousness of the Chinese.

It was in the basements of Chinatown, also, that the myth of Chinese industriousness was dispelled for me. Beneath a tourist agency, I entered a clubroom. I can't give the name of the society, but can say that it implied cultural, political, and benevolent pursuits. The basement was full of card tables on which were overflowing ashtrays, decks of cards, empty beer cans, and mah jong sets. On the walls were photographs of flowers, sunsets, Hong Kong scenes—and naked women! The nudes outnumbered sunsets and flowers three to one. The overwhelming impression was that this was a den for loafers, pure and simple. I was stunned. You don't think of Chinese men as loafers: they're either working or home with their families. As the day progressed, I passed through at least six more fraternal organizations, some occupied with genuine Chinese loafers, sitting around, telling dirty jokes and playing cards at 10 o'clock in the morning. With more experience, it came to me that, as in Caucasian fraternal organizations, the more high-flown the name, the idler the membership. This doesn't, certainly, apply to all clubs, but as in all ghettos, the neighborhood social club is the center of social life— politics, arranging picnics or outings to the casinos of Reno, choosing Miss Chinatown, organizing neighborhood charity— and loafing.

It was at a martial arts club that I saw the first of the vaunted Chinatown rats. The club was in a basement and along the walls were ranged antique swords, spears, and pikes—head-choppers right out of *Terry and the Pirates*. In the meter book was a notation, "Rats!" I saw none in the clubroom itself, but when I opened the door that led under the sidewalk where the meters were, there was the largest rat I have ever seen in my life, as big as a growing kitten. He was eating a popular rat bait as though it was popcorn. When I opened the door, he scurried away. It scared the hell out of me and I have to admit that it was the quickest water meter ever read in the history of man.

I saw no other rats anywhere else and that surprised me. Chinese cuisine demands fresh food and there are a lot of people employed in the food-processing industry. A broker in snow peas on Washington Street sells crates to a wholesaler on Waverly Place. There three women sort and clean the peas, which are then sold to restaurants in which a kitchen helper washes and chops them for the chef. The resulting food scraps and peelings *should* attract rats, but I didn't see as many there as in other sections of town. The basements of Chinatown are an amazing clean contrast to the streets outside. But there are at least 30,000 people living in about a 14-square-block area—plus the thousands of tourists who throw their litter in the streets; the debris is understandable. Inside the doors, though, it is another world.

It is not for nothing, I guess, that Chinatown begins at Grant and Bush with a lovely Chinese gate flanked on either side by two Chinese-decor hamburger joints. It is American and Oriental; Chinese-American. ST. MARY'S CHINESE SCHOOL on the corner of Clay and Stockton somehow epitomizes Chinatown. It is the home of the famous St. Mary's Drum and Glockenspiel Band that represented San Francisco in John F. Kennedy's inaugural parade, when sixty little girls in silken Chinese jackets and pantaloons swung into "When Irish Eyes Are Smiling" as they passed the reviewing stand. I went to one of St. Mary's school carnivals once. Among the money-raising games like fish pond, bingo, and cookie booth, was a contest put on by fourth graders. If you picked up so many marbles with chopsticks, you won a prize.

In pre-earthquake days, Chinatown was a sinister place. The Tong wars were real; hatchet men were paid murderers; opium dens and women enslaved for prostitution were facts of China-town life. Today, again, there is a sinister side of Chinatown. Native-born hoodlums and immigrant gangs from Hong Kong terrorize the local businessmen—there have been ten unsolved gangland slayings in the last eight months. The Tongs (fraternal, family, and business organizations) recently published in the Chinese newspapers a warning to the hoodlums, threatening reprisals against the new gangs. If you see half the people on the street watching the movements of a group of arrogant Chinese dudes who are going in the other direction, you're watching the new development in Chinatown.

In pre-earthquake days, Chinatown was an exotic place. It was China in America. It is no less exotic today. Every tourist who has been anywhere has seen the phony Indian villages, Little Mexicos, antique American establishments, cowboy ghost towns—and so forth. Each offers a hope for magic and in the end it is make believe. In Chinatown, though, when you walk down Spofford Lane and hear a radio blaring a Chinese soprano; the chatter and laughter from a sweatshop sewing factory and, under this, the complicated mechanical rhythm of a fortune-cookie factory; when you watch an old Chinese lady in a Grant Avenue delicatessen upbraid the clerk because he hasn't scraped *all* the duck fat from the butcher's block into her take-out box; when you walk through the Portsmouth Square Park and see an intense group of men kibitzing around a complicated board game while next to them a serene old gent goes through the complicated exercises of "shadow boxing," you almost glow with the knowledge that you're experiencing something special. You're experiencing Chinatown.

Take an afternoon to walk through Chinatown from Bush to Broadway along Grant. It is only eight blocks long, a nice walk, and mostly shops, but all is lost if you stride through it and back in twenty minutes. I suggest the afternoon because most of the shops in Chinatown open at 10 or 11 A.M. and close around midnight; if you go in the morning, you'll miss some good shopping. There are great buys along Grant even if it is a tourist spot. Raw silk in bolts or made into dresses or clothing is available here in an infinite variety of color and patterns. Fine porcelain tea sets and dishes aren't always displayed so go inside the stores. The Grant Avenue Chinatown is divided into roughly three parts. From Bush to Sacramento you'll find more expensive items. It's interesting to watch the average tourist with one or two children go into the Canton Bazaar around California Street. There are smaller pieces all around and at modest prices, but of a sudden there is a cloisonné vase plainly marked $2,500, perched on a pedestal. At this point, the parent begins to gather his children and tightly hold their hands as they wander through the porcelain. As the exquisite porcelain on the display cases holding $750 silk lace tablecloths come round the parent becomes more and more anxious. All is beautiful and around him are people discussing the merits of one or more pieces of teakwood furniture—one nick and he's out his whole vacation. One stroll through that shop and he's full of anecdotes to last a year . . . "We saw these dishes and Johnny was just climbing up on an elephant—a $350 *elephant,* I thought I'd die!"

For the next three blocks, from Sacramento to Washington, Grant Street Chinatown is the souvenir-hunter's delight. For a gift from San Francisco, unique, individual, and interesting, there's no better place to shop. From Washington to Broadway you will see the most Chinese part of Chinatown.

If you go through Chinatown at all, if only along Grant Avenue, it will be an unique experience and make your visit to San Francisco memorable. Here are some special places to look at.

1. The Chinese grocery stores, especially the Chinese stores from Washington Street to Broadway. The reason that there are so many delicatessens selling prepared food is that many Chinese live in rooms without cooking facilities. Here you'll see live chickens and ducks for sale. They put its head in a funnel and chop it off—saving the head, of course, because it can be used. In Chinese cooking, everything is eaten or used for flavoring, so you will see the bills and brains of the ginger ducks chopped up like the rest of the meat. You'll also see tanks of live fish for sale (in the basements of the finer restaurants, batteries of aerated bathtubs are used to hold the fish and insure the freshest fish available in any restaurants in America).

2. Along Jackson Street and along either side of Grant are

the jewelry stores. They seem to display the same goods—rather hokey Chinese good-luck signs, in chains, bracelets, or necklaces. These pieces of gold jewelry are all fine gold, 24 carat. It's unlawful in America to trade in gold coins, but it's nice in an inflationary economy to know that the Chinese good-luck sign you bought for $40.00 the ounce last year—aesthetic value notwithstanding—is now selling for $48.00 on the world market.

3. Go to a Chinese movie. There are three in Chinatown—one on Grant, one on Washington, and one on Jackson. For a non-Chinese, a Chinese movie is the most mystifying experience you can ever enjoy for $1.50. You won't understand a word, the action is wild, the audience is apparently unmoved, with much coming and going. All the talking during the dramatic parts and the constant movement in the theater is reminiscent of a Saturday matinee at a horse opera.

4. The best place to park in Chinatown is the Portsmouth Square Garage off Kearny Street. You come up the elevator to Portsmouth Square. It's a heavily used park, full of people from the neighborhood. In that particular neighborhood, that means a preponderance of Chinese, but also Filippinos and others from the hotels on Kearny Street. Most interesting are the games played on the card tables. Cards are played, of course, but there is an infinite variety of Chinese board games that resemble checkers, chess, backgammon and mah jong.

Chinese grocery stores are an exotic world in themselves, as are the shops that sell not only groceries but Chinese cooking implements. Around each corner is something to surprise or educate you. Chinatown is a city within a city. It is one of the few tourist attractions anywhere where you find more than you expected.

Clement Street

Clement lies between California and Geary Streets. Take the No. 2 Clement trolley bus on Sutter or drive out Geary and turn left a block.

I've tried to analyze just what makes CLEMENT STREET such

a fine street to walk upon. It is a shopping street—but not a great one like Union or Post. There are an interesting mixtures of cultures here—Russian, Jewish, Chinese, middle-class American—but certainly nothing like the streets of North Beach. There are entertainments and attractions, but they don't dominate. But when you begin at Clement and Arguello and walk to Park Presidio and back (about 10 blocks each way), you feel that you've been somewhere and wouldn't mind at all living near this street so you could visit it often.

Maybe that's the answer. It has great charm, but it doesn't wear you out.

Of course, people are the charm of any street, and Clement has more than its share of interesting people and shops that cater to them. The Russians are the most evident and you'll find Russian restaurants (not grand things with costumed waiters and balalaika bands, but small eating shops). It was in one of these restaurants that I saw four young workingmen come in one Saturday noon, order, then plunk a fifth of vodka on the table. The four ate huge quantities of food and finished the fifth with no effort. They left still looking thirsty. The Russian restaurants are excellent, the bakeries great enough to drive across town for. These Russians are part of the large White Russian émigré colony in San Francisco and in nearly every store—Chinese restaurant, drugstore, dress shop, or whatever—you'll see displayed posters announcing one or another of the many Russian events being held at the Russian Center.

Clement has more than a normal share of bookstores and antique shops. This always speaks of culture. It has more than its share of health-food shops and restaurants, which speaks of youth. It has more florist shops than you normally find on a residential shopping street, which speaks of graciousness. It has many great neighborhood bars, which speaks of gregariousness.

Clement Street is like Union Street before it became a major shopping street. All indications point to its becoming another Union Street. A sidewalk café has just opened, small specialty dry-goods stores are opening, it is being mentioned with more frequency by the newspaper columnists. Let us hope it will not be spoiled.

Post Street

POST STREET from Mason to Kearny is one of the most fascinating shopping streets in the city. There's something very special about the individual shops that line these three blocks that makes any walk along the street a stroll, a browse. I believe that GUMP'S has a good deal to do with it. Gump's window displays are so consistently excellent that the stores around it must exert themselves not to look dowdy by comparison. Gump's is unlike any other emporium in town. Everything in the store, from a package of paper napkins to the $6,000 jade antiques, is chosen for quality alone. You'll never find one piece of shoddy or unimaginative merchandise in the whole store. Getting back to Gump's windows, though, Gump's Christmas windows are a San Francisco tradition. People come downtown to admire them; they are written about in the newspapers. Gump's sets the tone and you'll find no better window shopping along any other street in town.

Begin at Mason Street, a block up from Union Square. There's a visitor's bureau for the redwood empire here where you can get free brochures of points of interest in northern California. Next fine shop is John Howell's Bookstore. John Howell specializes in Western Americana books and prints, but also sells valuable books, prints, and maps from all over the world. His windows are always as interesting as a visit to a museum.

Opposite Union Square, Post Street is torn up, with two new buildings under construction, the Qantas office building and the Hyatt House hotel. There are two fine men's shops here, though, Roos Atkins and Bullock and Jones.

Across Stockton you'll find Dunhill's on the corner, a place full of tobacco and elegant men's gadgets. Next is a jewelry store specializing in huge diamonds, emeralds, rubies gleaned from estate sales. Then Gump's, Abercrombie & Fitch (that's a great place to browse—the finest in sporting goods), Brooks

Brothers men's clothing and, finally, Shreve & Co., a most expensive jewelry store. On the other side of the street are Ransonhof, Schneider Brothers, Barra of Italy (all fine women's shops) and Christians of Copenhagen, fine furniture and appointments for the home.

The northeast corner of Post and Grant is a favorite stage for street musicians and entertainers. The last time I passed, it was three belly dancers (one would dance, the other two would sing and drum). Doubleday Bookstore is on this corner and upstairs you will find F.A.O. Schwarz, the best toy shop in San Francisco. Farther down is Mark Cross luggage, and Robert Kirk and Pond's men's stores. On the other side is Sidney Mobell, an excellent jeweler; Mobilia, fine appointments for the home; and David Stephen, and Hastings, both fine men's shops.

Now this whole area, from Powell Street down to Kearny, from Post to Market, and across Market, is a shopping center. There are elegant shops, from Saks Fifth Avenue to I. & J. Magnin, Macy's to the Emporium. Between Post and Geary for two blocks runs Maiden Lane, a charming shopping street. These blocks of Post Street, though, are the best stretch of shops in the city for the delight it gives the walker.

Mission Street

The heart of the Mission district lies on either side of MISSION STREET between 14th Street and Army. This is what the books of San Francisco history refer to as South of the Slot—the *slot* being Market Street. To the north and west of Market are most of the tourist attractions and white collar —South of the Slot is workingman.

Irish was the predominant culture in the Inner Mission and the peculiar inflection—the closest San Francisco can boast to a city dialect—can be heard here in the shops, especially the bars. Big-city Irish immigrants, whether in Brooklyn, New Orleans, or San Francisco, have a lot in common in the transmuting of the American English language. Here, as in the other cities, the *r* is dropped in some words, turning *four* into *faw:* the voiced *th* as in *these, them, those* tends to become *dese, dem, dose.* There are a few South of the Slot usages unique to San Francisco. Any swimming pool is a "tank," as in "He built a *huge* joint in Marin—tennis court, swimming tank, everythin'!" Nowhere else have I heard someone refer to the size of a boat and get off a perfectly succinct statement of a common condition: "He got himself a big boat, really big, eight people could sit on it, and took us out on it and in an hour I was bored stupid!" There is a great pride in the Mission and great nostalgia among former Missionites.

There was a great decay of the Mission district after the war, especially after the freeway went in along Duboce. Working-class areas turned to slum. The area from Duboce to about 20th Street is still slummy and getting worse. Many of the skid-row alcoholics, bums, and crazies, kicked out of the old Third and Howard section because of redevelopment, have settled here. A cash-for-your-blood station shifted from Mission and 5th to Mission and 17th (there's nothing that so indicates the decline of a neighborhood as a newly set-up cash-for-your-blood place). The BART station at 16th, and the beautification of the street around that area with palm trees, tiled sidewalks, benches, and kiosks, hasn't changed the situation; it's a bad and dangerous area.

From 20th on, though, Mission Street is a great street to walk upon. There is excitement, interesting things to look at, and a fine collection of various kinds of people. This is a thriving area and the BART station at 24th Street, with palm trees, benches, and kiosks, have made it even more lively. This section of Mission is becoming more and more the center of the Spanish-speaking Pan-American. Spanish spoken in California used to imply immigrants from Mexico or descendants from Mexico forebears who had been here since the early days of California. As the Irish moved out, though, the new immigrants from Honduras, Costa Rica, the Dominican Republic, Nicaragua, and elsewhere moved in, and this is probably the most cosmopolitan area of folk from Central and South America to be found anywhere. The Mexican residents still predominate and control most of the food-importing and -processing industries, the real estate handling, and the larger mercantile outlets, and they dominate the social scene, but the Central and South Americans are rising fast, as seen in the successes of the various-nationality restaurants that earn the capital that their owners expand into beauty shops and income-producing rental property.

Start at 20th and Mission at Granat Brothers manufacturing jewelers. In this rare place one may watch working jewelers fit diamonds into rings and other settings. (The jewelers work in the windows on the Mission Street side.) Across 20th, Mission Street becomes as difficult to describe as Columbus Avenue. There are shops of all descriptions: the handsome Bayview Federal Savings wrought-iron façade: restaurants, bars, cantinas. A bustle and pace prevail on Mission Street that makes it a joy to mingle with the people. There is also something subtly exotic about this end of Mission, not only in the various dialects of Spanish heard all around you, but in the grocery stores that sell colorful varieties of chili peppers; what looks like green bananas but is really plantain (a staple starchy vegetable in the tropics); long one- and two-pound white radishes; *jicoma,* a vegetable root, yucca— all kinds of things.

Turn to your left on 24th Street and you can walk through the heart of Spanish San Francisco. From Mission to Potrero, these blocks are almost exclusively Spanish. The restaurants are excellent and imports from Mexico fill the shops. After completion of this section of BART, I have a feeling that 24th Street will boom.

Other Streets to Explore

Some other fine streets you might want to explore are the following:

MARKET STREET. From the Powell cable-car turntable to the Ferry Building. This is part of the new San Francisco and the walk is full of interesting places and people.

CASTRO STREET. The neighborhood around Castro and Market is blossoming into an art, antique, handicraft area. The bars are mostly geared to the gay.

POLK STREET. From Geary to Union Street, Polk is an interesting shopping street. Many fine shops, many characters. The warning regarding the bars of Castro Street applies here.

24TH STREET. On the slopes of Twin Peaks, 24th Street from Diamond to Church is becoming more interesting. Art, handicraft, and bookstores are developing the street into an artistic enclave in the Inner Mission. Annually, the bars along here stage a boozing marathon. Some twelve bars participate about a mile from start to finish. Two drinks in each, and whoever can stagger all the way through is the winner and prizes are given. That's the kind of bars these are.

9TH AVENUE AND IRVING. The headquarters of organic food marketing in San Francisco and Northern California. The people and shops are worth a visit.

SAN BRUNO. Between Silver and Paul; this is perhaps our most polyglot neighborhood.

BATTERY. Between Filbert and Vallejo near the Embarcadero; a brand-new collection of antique and fine-arts shops selling out of renovated warehouses.

Of course, everyone who visits San Francisco finds his own favorite streets to walk upon. This, I hope, will give you some idea of where to start.

10
Transportation

For a small city, San Francisco offers a huge variety of modes of transport. For the resident, they are vitally important. To the visitor, they offer one of the last chances in the country to experience an amenity that was once common everywhere before the auto began its deadly work. The Municipal Railway System operates street cars, cable cars, and three kinds of buses. Private transport lets one experience ferry boats, trains, and the jitney. BART will soon give you the opportunity to ride one of the most advanced interurban transit systems in the world.

The Muni is one of the finest urban transportation systems in America, and it has to be. San Francisco is already strangled with the highest car-per-person ratio of any city in America. Without the Muni, the situation would be desperate. The Muni will take you anywhere you want to go in San Francisco, cheaply and quickly. The standard fare is 25 cents, which includes transfer privileges to any bus or streetcar not going back the same way you came (one must pay an extra nickel to transfer to a cable car).

Streetcars are lettered, bus lines are numbered, and cable-car lines are named.

The routes and bus numbers are found at the beginning of the Yellow Pages in the phone book. A street map is especially handy for the visitor and maps are available at every gas station, hotel, and motel (the banks and Chamber of Commerce distribute them free). The telephone-book map is very fine, labeling the main areas of the city and most of the major points of interest. If you can't find a carry-along map anywhere else, consult this one.

Cable Cars

One of the dominating symbols of San Francisco, the cable car must be the most exciting and enjoyable methods of transportation ever devised by man—especially to get over the hills of San Francisco. Introduced in 1873 (visit the Cable Car Museum at Mason and Washington), from then to now, it has never lost its practicality or charm. In the interest of efficiency, there was an attempt in the middle 1950s to do away with the cable cars and establish bus service in their place. Many lines were discontinued, but public outcry stopped the move before all were destroyed. Today three lines remain, the Hyde Street, the Powell Street, and the California Street systems. The reason for the efficiency move was the cost of the cable cars (each unit is built by hand from scratch); the salaries of two operators—the gripman and the conductor; and the carrying capacity. The test of time shows no terrific savings. The buses are nearly as expensive to buy; the breakdown of motors, transmissions, and brakes are horrendous on the streets the cable cars used to serve; and they don't carry all that many more people—to say nothing about the excitement and adventure lost when you ride a bus instead of a cable car.

In the hundred years they have been in operation, traditions have grown up about the use of cable cars. In the older days, for example, women were not permitted to stand on the outside step (the most exciting place to ride). It was too dangerous and . . . *unseemly.* Defiant liberationists put this tradition to the test, so now you see women riding on the outside step—in danger of falling to their death in the streets if their grasp fails on an abrupt turn (it hasn't happened yet, but when it does, old San Franciscans will offer no sympathy). Some traditions are still maintained, however—when Johnson was president, one of his daughters was kicked off a cable car because she brought an ice-cream cone abroad (there's so much shaking, your ice cream can soon mean another's cleaning bill).

Both the Hyde and Powell lines begin at Powell and Market and end at the Bay in the Fisherman's Wharf area. The California Street line runs from California and Market to California and Van Ness. Here is where you can go on the cable cars.

POWELL-HYDE LINE. Begins at Powell and Market. Runs out Powell to Jackson, up to Hyde to Aquatic Park at Beach. It returns up Hyde to Washington, to Powell to Market.

Nob Hill, the Mark Hopkins and Fairmont hotels. Transfer to the California Street cable car at California going up.

Chinatown. Leave the cable car on any street from California to Jackson (before it turns left) and walk down two blocks.

Russian Hill. You will know when you're at the top of Russian Hill when you fear for your life, convinced you'll never make it down Hyde Street Hill in one piece. The line ends within a block of *Ghirardelli Square, the Maritime Museum, the Cannery, Aquatic Park, Maritime Park* (the four museum ships), with *Fisherman's Wharf* a few blocks to your right.

POWELL STREET LINE. Begins at Powell and Market. Runs out Powell to Jackson, then Mason down to Columbus to Taylor Street and ends at Bay. It returns the same way to Washington to Powell to Market.

Nob Hill. Same as above.

Chinatown. Same as above.

North Beach. At Mason and Columbus, you're at the northwest end of North Beach; the Italian section is to your right.

The line ends at *Cost Plus, Fisherman's Wharf, Akron*. The *Balclutha* is a few blocks down to the Bay and right, the *Cannery* is a few blocks to the left.

CALIFORNIA STREET LINE. Begins at California and Market and runs to California and Van Ness. To reach it, from Union Square, board either the Powell-Hyde or the Powell Street lines on Powell.

At California, if you transfer *up,* you will reach *Nob Hill* (Fairmont, Mark Hopkins hotels) and *Polk Street*—a good street to walk on.

If you transfer *down, Chinatown* is at Grant and *Montgomery Street,* the financial district, is on the line. The *Wells Fargo History Room Museum* and the *California Bank Money Room* are along this route (*see* Chapter 6).

The most elegant thing about the cable cars is not where they take you but how you get there. It may seem dumb and romantic and tourist-bureau to say that a ride on a cable car is an exhilarating experience, but that's it in a nutshell. Because the cable cars run bang up and down very steep hills, they rattle over the tracks laid in cobbles a hundred years ago, and turn right angles at the same speed they run a level stretch, you are forced to participate in their getting you from here to there. You have to hang on—there's nothing passive about riding a cable car—and trust in the equipment, as in riding a roller coaster. There is no other public transportation anywhere in the world that is as thrilling as a ride on the cable car.

Streetcars

San Francisco is one of the few cities in the nation that still has streetcars, but we won't have them long, it appears. They are economical, swift, and carry a huge number of people in each unit, but, unfortunately, they lack the flexibility of a bus system. As the pattern of urban density changes, streetcars are being phased out. In a bus system, you can change the routes according to the growth or decline of population areas. With streetcars, it's not at all easy to rip out the tracks and build new ones. By a recent Board of Supervisors' ruling, San Francisco streetcars will be viable until 1975, so ride them while you can.

For the visitor, there are two notable streetcar lines. All streetcars run along Market Street from First Street to Duboce, then they branch out.

N JUDAH LINE. Board at Powell and Market on the Woolworth side of the street. The *N Judah* will take you out Market and angle right at Duboce. The fortlike building on your right perched on a bleak hill is the San Francisco (U.S.) Mint. You'll go through the half-mile tunnel under Buena Vista Heights and emerge on the fringe of the Haight-Ashbury. The line jogs left to Irving Street, where you'll see the imposing buildings of the University of California Medical Center up the hill to your left. At 9th you're in the center of the organic foods business—the biggest complex in the city. Thence you'll go out Judah, through the northern part of the Sunset district, and end one block from Ocean Beach, two blocks from the western end of Golden Gate Park.

L TARAVAL—ZOO. Board at Powell and Market on the Woolworth side of the street. The *L Taraval* streetcar is another glorious ride that takes you to the Zoo. You'll go out Market even farther, to the Twin Peaks tunnel. This is a 'very fine tunnel, about two miles long, with underground stations. If your kids have never seen streetcars and underground stations, by all means let them see this—a 45-minute ride for 25 cents. The *L Taraval* emerges at the juncture of two posh neighborhoods, Forest Hill and St. Francis Wood, then goes through the southern edge of the Sunset district and ends about a block and a half from the Zoo, three blocks from the ocean.

Buses

There are several guided commercial bus tours available that take the visitor through the high points of San Francisco. Most of them begin at Union Square (or your hotel) and give a running commentary of what you're seeing. The commercial guided tour is the easiest way to get a wide view of the city.

For those with more time, I recommend the Muni bus (streetcar, cable-car) system. It's cheap, convenient, lets you off where you want to explore, and frees you from having to find a parking space. Using Union Square as a base (it's in the center of the downtown shopping district at Geary and

Powell), I've listed below the major points of interest and how to reach them by Muni.

THE No. 30 STOCKTON. To board, walk up Stockton to Sutter. It's a very handy bus that takes you to:

Chinatown. After you go through the tunnel, get off at Clay or Washington streets and walk down a block.

North Beach. Get off at Broadway. You can't miss it because of the topless joints. You're a block from Chinatown at the beginning of the Italian district and Upper Grant bohemia.

Coit Tower. Ask for a transfer when you get on (it's free) and ask the driver to let you off at Union Street. You'll see Washington Square. Board the *39 Coit Tower* bus on the corner for a painless trip to the top.

Ghirardelli Square–Aquatic Park–Maritime Museums–Fisherman's Wharf. Ghirardelli Square is at Larkin and North Point; Aquatic Park is at North Point and Van Ness.

Palace of Fine Arts–Exploratorium. Get off at Beach and Broderick streets. You'll see it to your left.

Marina Yacht Harbor. Get off at Broderick and Jefferson and walk to the Bay.

THE No. 2 CLEMENT. To board, walk up to Stockton and Sutter.

Clement Street. One of the finest walking streets in town. Get off at Arguello and enjoy 12 fine blocks.

Cliff House–Pt. Lobos. At the end of the line.

THE No. 38 GEARY. Board at the corner of Geary and Powell.

Polk Street. An interesting walking street.

St. Mary's Cathedral. Get off at Gough Street (variously pronounced "Go," "Gow," and "Goff"—"Goff" is correct).

Nihon Machi–Japan Town. Get off at Webster.

Cathedral of the Virgin Mary. 25th and Geary. The No. 38 ends at Ocean Beach.

THE No. 5 McALLISTER. Take either of the cable cars, or walk down to Market Street. On the Woolworth side of Market, the buses go west. On the Emporium side, they go east. First we will go west.

Civic Center. Get off at McAllister and Polk.

Golden Gate Park. This bus travels along the whole northern edge of the Park.

The Conservatory. Get off at Arguello.

Music Concourse, De Young Museum, Japanese Tea Garden, Aquarium, etcetera, are at 10th Avenue.

Spreckels Lake, buffalo paddock, polo field are at 33rd. The No. 5 ends at Ocean Beach.

Next we will go east. Board on the Emporium side of Market. This bus takes you through the center of downtown.

Financial district. Exit at Montgomery Street and go to your left.

Vaillancourt Fountain. The terminus of the bus is near the Embarcadero Park, the fountain, and the *Ferry Building.* The Ferry Building is the home of the World Trade Center and the Geology Museum.

Sausalito Ferry is to the left of the Ferry Building.

These are the most convenient public transportation lines to the major points of interest. If you have more time, the Muni system is a fine way to get into the heart of the city.

Jitney

THE MISSION STREET JITNEY. The jitney is a now unique form of supplemental transport that used to be common in American cities large and small. Halfway between a bus and a taxi, it's for people who will pay a little extra to make an express trip, but not as much as it costs to take a taxi. Jitney used to be a slang term for a nickel. That was the fare and the term attached to the type of conveyance that did the business.

The Mission Street jitneys now cost 35 cents from First and Mission to the County line (a dime over bus fare). Most vehicles used now are panel vans fitted with windows and 10 seats. They stop at every street corner along Mission Street—wave them down—and have the advantage over Muni buses in that they are faster and will let you off at the street you call—perhaps one where the Muni has no stop. The jitney is privately owned and so is dependent on the initiative of the driver to "make the nut" (pay for the cost of operation and a decent return). You're guaranteed a lightning trip from First Street to Daly City, though they travel only on Mission Street. It is an idea that should be permitted to expand through the city and begun in other cities with poor public transport.

San Francisco Ferry Boats

With the building of the bridges, the once-mighty ferry fleet of San Francisco Bay was abandoned. The bridges were a necessity because San Francisco was cut off from the North and East Bay entirely except for the passenger, auto, and railroad ferries. As the Bay Area grew, the ferry system couldn't handle the load of traffic. Autos were backed up three blocks on Market Street most hours on any given day in the slow movement to get aboard the ferry boats. The Golden Gate and Bay Bridges were the grand answer to the problem and the ferries, obviously redundant, were phased out. Unfortunately, after about fifteen years, the bridges so developed the suburbs that the commuter traffic into San Francisco became a serious problem—where to house the huge numbers of autos during working hours. Except for through traffic, the bridges caused as many problems as they solved.

There had always been a number of ferry-boat fans, even when the bridges were abuilding, who pointed out that ferries were not only practical, they were the best possible way to commute. They pressed, the ecology people agitated (one ferry boat automatically eliminates two hundred smog-producers every trip), and the result was a supplemental ferry system, quasicommercial, governmentally subsidized to some degree, that operates three ferry boat runs now. In 1972 (four years after its inception) the one-millionth passenger was counted. The Golden Gate Bridge Authority has commissioned three additional, larger, ferries to be built that should be in operation by 1975.

SAUSALITO FERRY. Ticket office is the little building to the left of the Ferry Building as you're facing it. Sausalito is a delightful town and the trip by ferry is very enjoyable, the best buy in exciting transportation next to the cable cars. At this writing, the one-way price is 75 cents for adults, 25 cents for children (6–12). The weekday schedule runs roughly once an hour (it's a 30-minute trip) starting from San Francisco at 7:50 AM, with ten trips between then and the last departure at 8:10 PM. The last ferry to San Francisco leaves Sausalito at 8:50 PM (keep that in mind if you don't want to come back by bus or taxi). The Saturday, Sunday, and holiday schedule is shorter. There are only seven runs, beginning at 10:25 AM, the last at 6:50 PM (last ferry from Sausalito is 7:30 PM).

One of the great things about the Sausalito ferry (over and above the ferry ride itself) is that it lands you in Sausalito. Sausalito is a delightful place, full of artists, writers, fine shops, good bars and restaurants. It's an adjunct to San Francisco, not really a suburb, as is Mill Valley, for example. As in San Francisco, you'll find some unsuburban goings-on. After many years of campaigning, for example, one of San Francisco's leading madams of the '20s and '30s was elected to the Sausalito city council. If you're lucky enough to be in town when the art fair is in progress, you mustn't miss it—it's finer than such fairs I've seen in Boston, Philadelphia, and San Francisco for that matter. On your way across Golden Gate Bridge to Muir Woods, stop in Sausalito; better yet, stop there to relax on your way back.

TIBURON FERRY. Pier 43½ Fisherman's Wharf. Prices and schedules are subject to change, so I'll list what the going rate is at this time. For current schedules and prices, look under ferries in the Yellow Pages.

The Tiburon Ferry has five departures from San Francisco between 10 AM and 5:20 PM—about every two hours. Right now the last boat leaves Tiburon at 5:55 PM (these are the Saturday, Sunday, and holiday schedules). Adult fare is $1.50 round trip. Tiburon-Belvedere is an island-peninsula, a very wealthy one. The downtown area, where the ferry boats tie up, is a miniature Sausalito, fine shops, great bars and intriguing corners. There are also places to take the kids. The main attraction, though, is the bar-restaurants along the marina. Sam's is the most famous, and representative of them all. It looks like any entrance to any rather seedy bar from the street, and through the front door, the impression is enhanced by the pinball machines and loafers· at the bar, but press on. The door straight ahead leads to the deck above the water. There you'll find perhaps forty tables full of people of all ages and nationalities enjoying the water-level view of the city, the comings and goings of the yacht club to the right, Sam's famous hamburgers—incredibly cheap for what you get, a meal in itself—and Sam's Ramos Fizzes (a delicious mixture of gin, cream, lime or lemon, and whatever makes them fizz—all frothed together). The kids, of course, drink Coke or milk. Sailboats tie up to Sam's floating dock and it's interesting to watch the maneuvers, especially when they're doing all the work and the sun is shining and the company is congenial and the setting is wonderful and you have just ordered another Ramos Fizz and the last ferry to San Francisco doesn't leave for three hours.

ANGEL ISLAND STATE PARK FERRY. Pier 43½ (same as Tiburon Ferry). This ferry runs only on Saturdays, Sundays, and holidays with four departures, from 10 AM to 3:45 PM (every two hours on the hour, or near it). The last ferry from the Island leaves at 6:50 PM. Round trip for adults is $1.75.

Angel Island is one of the most curious islands in the Bay. In the grand days of Oriental immigration, it was used as a quarantine station—the Ellis Island of the West Coast. Coast Guard station, troop-staging area, German prisoner-of-war Internment Camp, vegetable garden for the prisoners of Alcatraz (at least that's what the guide said when he pointed to the overgrown garden plots), missile site, and State Park, this island must have had the most varied tenants of any island in the world, considering it was discovered less than a hundred years ago. Now a state park (soon to be part of a national-park complex that will include 37,000 acres of coastline on either side of the Golden Gate), it is mostly wild. Deer are abundant. An elephant train (the local generic term for any cheap, open-air sightseeing conveyance), drives through the highlights and will stop for photographs whenever you pull the buzzer. It's a lovely place. At this writing, you must bring all you want to eat or drink. Concessions are planned for the future to make it more convenient for tourists, but let us hope that they will provide only the barest essentials so litter doesn't become a problem.

BART (Bay Area Rapid Transit)

The BART system is an innovative complex of aboveground and subway trains that follow the most heavily traveled commuter routes up and down the East Bay, across to San Francisco, and down to San Mateo County on the peninsula —about 120 miles of track or more, it's growing all the time. A long time in building, and extremely costly (as much as six or seven months of the Vietnam war), it is the finest interurban mass transport system to be found in the world. I had a chance to ride a shake-down ride before it went into service. The run was from Oakland to Fremont, down the East Bay involving perhaps seven stops. We started at Union City, and nothing went very smoothly that first day. Two trains broke down, there were computer, human, and managerial errors. But when they started, what a trip! The BARTs (you can't call them trains) are magnificent. The cars are comfortable and quiet. We were in the first car and through the glass window into the cab, I watched a spacecraft kind of speedometer go from zero to 78 miles an hour and hold that speed for the six to seven miles between stations, without any real sense of acceleration or speed except in leaving the platform. The ideal is a constant 50 m.p.h., stops included.

One saw only the East Bay stations in that trial run, but that was impressive. No expense has been spared to provide the best . . . the McArthur station has Mark Adams mosaics! Each station is color coded so that in giving directions, one may say, "Get off at the blue brick station" or the red brick, or whatever. By the time this book comes out, more lines will be open. You must try it.

Railroad

THE SOUTHERN PACIFIC RAILROAD. 3rd and Townsend streets.

The final mode of transportation to be found in the city is a train ride. Passenger train service has deserted most towns in America (it is to be hoped that, with Amtrak, things will change), but in San Francisco, if you want to let your kids experience a train ride, you can.

These are diesel commuter trains, and fairly expensive for the noncommuter, but, as they say, it's the only train game in town and most towns have none. A particularly great ride is to San Jose and back. The local runs along the east side of the Peninsula and stops at every station along the way, giving you a good look at things. Another good ride is the round trip to San Mateo, which goes through two railroad tunnels, switching yards with lots of rolling stock and back yards to look at. The fare at this writing is $2.20 round trip and the journey lasts about 25 minutes each way. It leaves the 3rd and Townsend Station about every hour on weekdays, every two hours Saturday, Sunday, and holidays.

11
Little-known Points of Interest

University of California Hospital Animals

The sheep, goat, and dog pens behind UNIVERSITY OF CALIFORNIA HOSPITAL are of considerable interest. To reach them, follow the path around Moffitt Hospital, the main building, and walk up the road circling Mt. Sutro. The view from above the pens is excellent, but the pens themselves command most of your attention, for you can learn much from studying the animals. These animals are used in various kinds of research and provide several object lessons. The greatest of these lessons is the relativity of importance of goals. These animals have been specially selected to work with some of the greatest and most original medical minds in the country to help conquer some of the most horrible diseases to inflict mankind. But by the way they hug the fence—trying to get the farthest away from the research building—you have the feeling that they are not at all impressed with the honor.

The dogs are another thing. They yap a lot, but don't seem to mind participating in research. The quality of dogs seen in the pens, though, is surprising and makes one wonder where they pick them up. I've seen purebred Weimaraners, Silkie terriers, and an English sheepdog among them. These are expensive dogs and don't just wander loose in the streets. The possibility that this is a hotbed of dognapping enters the mind, and this breeds a certain amount of suspicion about the researching doctors as aiders and abetters of low-class thieves.

The sheep and goat pens (especially the goat pens) also tend to put medical researchers in bad odor. And this is what makes them interesting. On contemplating them, you realize that as far as the relative values of ultimate goals is concerned, the goals of the strongest or most clever override the goals of the weak and the dumb every time. An obvious lesson, but one not often seen with such starkness.*

* Since this was written, there have been some changes. It appears that the yapping of the dogs disturbed the hospital patients, so the kennels have been removed to the very top of Mt. Sutro (can be reached through the student housing complex off Clarendon Avenue). Here the dogs enjoy one of the most glorious views in the city. It is indicative of San Francisco's wealth of views that a view as fine as this could go to the dogs.

San Francisco Memorial Columbarium

Like the poor, death is always with us but hard to contemplate in San Francisco. This is because there are only four burial grounds within the city limits of San Francisco—the Golden Gate National Cemetery in the Presidio; a pet cemetery, also in the Presidio; the graveyard beside Mission Dolores; and the SAN FRANCISCO MEMORIAL COLUMBARIUM. All are fine places to ponder the mysteries of existence and nonexistence, but the finest by far is the Columbarium, located on Loraine Court, which is the cul-de-sac off Anza between Stanyan and Arguello.

The Mission Dolores Graveyard is too historic to elicit thoughts of the dead as *dead*. It is rather a place for history buffs to discover on the tombstones names that they've read about—a group, I've found, who are only one cut above movie-star autograph fans (better-read, perhaps, but tending to be just as prideful in their tombstone name-dropping). Death is far away in the Mission Dolores graveyard.

But in the subdued light of the San Francisco Memorial Columbarium, when viewing tier upon tier of urns containing ashes of the dead, one is compelled to say to himself, "This, ultimately, is what we're reduced to." The building itself, a rotunda, properly whited as a sepulcher should be, with a beautifully patinaed copper dome, inspires reflection. Perfectly proportioned, pierced by stained glass windows, grandly decorated, it is of a type that will never again be constructed —as our City Hall's equal will never again be built.

Within the building, the setting compels a close look at death and contemplation of ultimate realities. Unlike a graveyard where earth hides the dead, in the Columbarium the urns inscribed with the names of the ashes they contain are within touching distance. The nearness of the remains and the small size of the containers produces an impact akin to awe for the first little while you are there. When the initial impact wears off, a very fine sense of the rightness of the place floods you. The dead human eventually needs no more space than this, a small pot for his ashes. A name engraved on a silver urn is at least as dignified as the social-security-type plaques used in cemeteries today. Here, also, your ashes rest in comfort out of the weather and away from the indignities of dogs, bugs, and flower thieves. If some of the urns are a little foolish—it seems a bit much to put your loved one in a miniature treasure chest, then padlock it—it is certainly no more of an indignity than ambitious grievers often inflict with larger monuments. My heart bleeds, for example, for poor Professor Dr. Helmut Altefelder, who must rest forever in the Göttingen cemetery beneath a four-foot Cupid playing the violin. Again, if there are some urns which vaguely resemble book ends or paperweights, others are grand. The Braunschweiger family rests in a matched set of beautiful alabaster urns, which is a very fine way to rest indeed. All in all, the San Francisco Memorial Columbarium is a very fine place to visit and the best location in the city to contemplate death.

Churches

There are many beautiful churches and temples in San Francisco. For the visitor, they offer rare opportunities for attending religious services in a new and beautiful setting. What follows is a short list of the churches and temples—not only for attending religious services but for visiting as legitimate, if often neglected, tourist features of the city.

In keeping with the other anomalies of the city, our oldest and most famous church, the Mission Dolores, is a tourist attraction but no longer holds regular religious services. (*See* Chapter 6.)

Catholic

CATHEDRAL OF ST. MARY. Gough Street and Geary Boulevard. Near Japan Town.

A magnificent new addition to the city, this cathedral should be visited by everyone. It was built under a great deal of controversy, both from inside the Church and from art critics. The costs were some five millions and many Catholics charged that the money would be better spent on social welfare projects than on a new church. The exterior design drew such comments as, "It looks like the dasher of an old-fashioned washing machine." When you enter, though, you know you're in a grand place and both objections are without value. You see people touching, for pleasure, the huge piers that support the structure. The organ loft with its glorious ranks of pipes, the beautiful shimmering sculpture over the high altar are wonderful things. For most non-Catholics who might feel hesitant about entering a Catholic church during Mass (or, for that matter, when no Mass is being celebrated), don't be shy. Catholics certainly aren't. There are several levels of Catholic services. The pontifical and solemn or High Masses are formal affairs—as are sometimes the votive and Requiem Masses. The churches are crowded at these times and it's best to wait until the service is over. Low Masses are said for the parish people several times a day. You're not interrupting anything if you visit a church while one is said. The comings and goings of worshipers during Mass is a constant surprise to non-Catholics.

If it happened to a preacher, he would be crushed. In Catholic churches, you may wander at will.

St. Ignatius. Golden Gate and Parker.
Sts. Peter and Paul. 666 Filbert.

Although they are in different corners of town, I've included them together because both are beautiful examples of a kind of Spanish Romanesque found mostly on the West Coast, the Southwest, and Mexico. St. Ignatius is in the vicinity of Golden Gate Park and is the spiritual center of the University of San Francisco. To reach it from Union Square, drive out Geary to Masonic (the big Sears store marks the corner), turn left to Golden Gate Avenue, then right five blocks or so up the hill to the church.

Sts. Peter and Paul is an equally impressive Romanesque church on Washington Square in North Beach. Near Columbus Avenue and Union Street, the spires of Sts. Peter and Paul dominate the views from Russian and Telegraph Hills, as St. Ignatius dominates the views from Twin Peaks. Both are lavish in sculpture and paintings.

St. Vincent de Paul. Green and Steiner Streets in the Marina district, a block up from Union Street. A small, but rich church. You must see St. Vincent de Paul if only to be dazzled by the magnificent stained-glass windows.

St. Boniface. On Golden Gate near Jones.

The San Franciscan Fathers at St. Boniface operate the St. Anthony Dining Room around the corner on Jones (next to Harrington's bar). Every day at noon, the doors swing open and anyone who is hungry picks up a tray and is served a hot lunch, no questions, no preachings, no social uplift— simple charity. In many of the bars mentioned in this book, you'll see collection containers from St. Anthony's. Be sure to put something in. Unlike United Crusade, or whatever, the money goes directly from you to the lunch tray of the hungry —80 percent isn't shortstopped by administrative overhead. From my yogi friends, I learned that of all the churches in town, St. Boniface has the best vibrations—no better place to meditate.

Jewish

TEMPLE EMANU-EL. Arguello and Lake streets. Go out Geary and turn right onto Arguello. It's four long blocks beyond.

This is the magnificent dome seen beyond the spires of St. Ignatius from Twin Peaks. In the heart of Presidio Heights, it is a rich temple and the interior is resplendent in marble, gold, and fine carvings. The Ark housing the Torah is a masterpiece. The temple is open to the public. While the foyer of St. Ignatius has a rack of Catholic pamphlets for sale, the foyer of Emanu-El has religious handcrafted stuff from Israel, such as menorahs, for sale and antique pieces on display. The ladies in the office will explain anything you want to know about the temple. I have to confess that this is one of my favorite places of worship in town. The first time I went in (to tour the temple), I overheard an old guy saying to the girl behind the desk, "My check comes in Monday, could I borrow ten dollars till them?" With no narrowing of the eyes and no hesitating, she led him to the bookkeeper in one of the most gracious acts of direct charity I've ever seen. It was the same kind of pure charity found in St. Anthony's Dining Room. He didn't look Jewish.

There are many music and cultural events held there through the year—some great lectures at a reasonable price. But Temple Emanu-El is a gorgeous place, something that no one should miss.

Russian Orthodox

HOLY VIRGIN CATHEDRAL OF THE CHURCH IN EXILE. 6210 Geary Boulevard (Geary and 26th Avenue).

A relatively new landmark to San Francisco's skyline, the gold mosaic Byzantine domes of the Holy Virgin Cathedral flash in the early and late sun. The richness of the church bespeaks the number of émigré White Russians in San Francisco—two Russian daily newspapers are published here. The church was established way out in the Richmond district in the heart of the White Russian colony.

I learned a deal about the San Francisco White Russians when I attended the short Russian course at the Army Language School in Monterey. The people who taught the courses came from every walk of life and had undergone the most hair-raising experiences imaginable. They had two things in common; that they were to a man (and woman) violently anti-Communist and that they were deeply and nostalgically Russian, also wise and cynical. Here was Mrs. N., a schoolteacher who was forced at gunpoint to dig anti-tank trenches outside Stalingrad, and Mr. L., a famous ballet dancer who described the dive-bombing of Leningrad. And there was one of the wisest and most cynical men I have ever met, Dr. C. He had been a professor at the University of St. Petersburg and fled the Reds across Asia to be a professor at the University of Shanghai. There Mao's Chinese Reds again forced him to flee to America, where he became a professor at the University of California. In the early '50s, Joseph McCarthy's anti-Red campaign made all Russians suspect, and he was forced out of his job there, to become a teacher of Russian at the Army Language School!

A lot of the Russian nobility who fled east still reside in San Francisco, just as, in Paris, a lot of the nobility who fled west established a colony. When you visit the cathedral, the person next to you may be a count, baron, or whatever, and on hot days on Clement and Geary streets, it's not unusual to see concentration-camp tattoos along the forearms of the older shoppers.

The interior of the Cathedral is unusual to the person used to Western churches, Catholic or Protestant. There are no ranks of seats. The Russian Orthodox stand during their services. The priests are resplendent in their robes and incense, the interior is awe-inspiring, and you are expected to offer a donation for your visit.

Protestant

GRACE CATHEDRAL. 1051 Taylor Street. On Nob Hill at Taylor and California streets, near the Fairmont and Mark Hopkins hotels.

This immense church is a must for visitors—a Gothic-type design, modified to employ reinforced concrete for earthquake safety. The exterior might seem unfinished because of lack of stone facing, but the interior is magnificent. There are three items of special interest. The gilded bronze doors are direct casts from molds taken from Lorenzo Ghiberti's famous "Doors of Paradise" at the Baptistry of Florence and are magnificent. John De Rosen's wax tempera and gold leaf murals on the blind arcades on either side of the nave are good. High above, though, in the clerestory, are a series of stained glass windows depicting *human endeavor* as represented by twentieth-century Americans. The choices are interesting; natural science, Albert Einstein; agriculture, Luther Burbank; government, Franklin Delano Roosevelt; labor, John L. Lewis; industry, Henry Ford; law, Thurgood Marshall; social work, Jane Addams; medicine, William Welch; education, John Dewey; the arts, Frank Lloyd Wright; letters, Robert Frost; and exploration—John Glenn. Can you imagine the infighting that went on in the selection of these particular twentieth-century Americans! Most are obvious, but the choices for law, medicine, the arts, and letters must have caused furious debates. There are tours of the Cathedral after every Sunday service and often through the week when guides are available. Check the bulletin board or the gift shop.

GLIDE MEMORIAL UNITED METHODIST. 330 Ellis Street (Ellis and Taylor in the Tenderloin section).

Next to Bill Graham's old Fillmore West ballroom, Glide Memorial Church is the second most famous underground tourist attraction in San Francisco. Run by the controversial Dr. Cecil Williams, this is one of the most unusual urban churches in America. It is unusual, in that it is an old, established Methodist church in the heart of the racy Tenderloin section and has an approach to religion that is wildly out of the mainstream. It is *most* unusual in that, while other churches in the downtown areas are starving to death, Glide Memorial has had to expand its Sunday services from one to three (all with turn-away crowds). Its popularity lies not only in the active proselyting of the junkies, thieves, and wasted male and female prostitutes in the Tenderloin, but in the preaching of an unconventional but relevant gospel in these times of social change. The congregation is the broadest spectrum of believers you've ever seen—rich, poor, young, old, sick, and sane. Of course, Cecil Williams, like the preachers of early America, is outspoken (or puts his oar in) on every facet of city life, so, in a way, it's old-time religion. The popularity of Dr. Williams' church shows what people want and, as other San Franciscan institutions have been leaders in the past, I wouldn't be surprised if Dr. Williams' Glide Memorial Church proves to be the beginning of a new, increasingly popular approach to Christianity.

Sigmund Stern Grove

The Midsummer Music Festivals at SIGMUND STERN GROVE have been a San Francisco tradition since 1938. Sigmund Stern Grove–Pine Lake Park combination is a two-block-wide, ten-block-long magnificent wild area at the outer edge of the Sunset district. Huge eucalyptus trees and a small lake form a beautiful park in the middle of two every-house-looks-the-same developments. Mrs. Stern gave the grove part to the city as a memorial to her husband (she was the head of the Recreation Commission for many years). Part of it is a natural amphitheater and the concerts grew from there. Part of the freeway revolt in San Francisco came about because the freeway builders, after ruining the Embarcadero, were headed for Golden Gate Park and Sigmund Stern Grove!

The performances, year after year, are of a quality that never ceases to amaze. It's a local San Francisco event, but one that draws music-lovers from all over the world and attracts the finest artists. The performances are given every Sunday afternoon in the summer, from early June to mid-August—vacation months when the audience level would appear to be thin. It's free, after all, with no great publicity push. But this year, the Midsummer Music Festival was so overly attended that there are thoughts of expanding it into two other locations to take care of the crowds.

A look at the 1972 schedule will give some indication why an expansion is thought necessary.

June 11 was the traditional opening, a carnival put on by the Recreation and Parks Department playground programs—thousands of performing kids with their families in attendance.

June 18, Isaac Stern directed the San Francisco Symphony Orchestra—to celebrate the sixtieth anniversary of the San Francisco Symphony.

June 25 was a new program, a college jazz mini-festival put on by award-winning college jazz combos from all over America.

July 2's program was *Fiesta Mexicano*, featuring the Ballet Folklorico Mexicano, the foremost touring cultural dance group from Mexico.

July 9 was a repeat performance by the Preservation Hall Jazz Band, the finest New Orleans–style jazz band to be heard anywhere. If the number of tape recorders present is any index, by the time this book is published, there will be a record, *Preservation Hall Jazz Band at Sigmund Stern Grove*.

July 16 was the annual opera performance, where budding stars could sing to a live audience—San Francisco has more budding opera stars than any other city in America, per population, and more opera fans.

July 23, Arthur Fiedler held a pops concert with the San Francisco Symphony Orchestra.

July 30 was the *Opera Concert*, where Kurt Herbert Adler presided over a presentation of the winners and finalists of the 1972 opera auditions.

August 6 presented *Fiddler on the Roof*.

August 13, Frankie Laine gave a concert.

August 20, *Die Fledermaus*, Act 2, was presented in celebration of the fiftieth anniversary of the San Francisco Opera, with the largest collection of high-priced operatic performers ever to perform at a free concert in the history of opera.

The 1972 free concerts at Sigmund Stern Grove took on a new dimension, because in addition to celebrating the fiftieth year of our opera, we marked the sixtieth year of the San Francisco Symphony Orchestra. It was a special year. But every year is a special year at Sigmund Stern Grove. Every Sunday during the summer, one may go to the Grove, spread his blanket, open his bottle of wine, and enjoy an extraordinary afternoon. The kids listen when they want to, and play with the other kids when they don't. It's crowded, but congenial; the only people who come there are fellow enjoyers; and here, the best things in life are free.

The Embarcadero

Although the word *to embark* or an *embarcation point* in English means to leave, or a place to start a journey, in Spanish, the opposite is true. *Embarcadero* designates a landing place, a place to tie up ships. In any Californian port where the Spanish had any influence, you'll find an Embarcadero. In San Francisco, the word is used in the Spanish sense, so, though Embarcadero, a street along the piers, runs only from Jefferson Street to Berry Street at Pier 46, the whole of the working waterfront from North Beach around to Pier 96 beyond Islais Creek is commonly referred to as THE EMBARCADERO.

Unless you've been born close to a port, it's a rare experience indeed to see close-up the working of ships. San Francisco's Embarcadero is an especially favorable place to look at the strange cargo, the bustle and excitement of a working port because the piers are spread out along about five miles of the northeast Bay waterfront.

The best way to see the ships is to begin at the extreme southeastern edge of the port at Pier 96 at Third Street and Arthur. If you begin there and travel back toward town, the ships are always to your right hand and you can pull out of the traffic of a heavily traveled street. If you try it in the other direction, to pull into a pier you'll have to cross train, truck, and auto traffic so fierce that it's another name for suicide.

To get there from downtown (Union Square), drive down (in this book the directions are literal, uphill-downhill) Stockton and cross Market Street into Fourth Street—it's one way going the way you want to go. You'll run into the Southern Pacific railroad track at Townsend and turn left. Turn right on Third and keep on Third. Just beyond the railroad station, at Third and Berry-China Basin, you'll cross one of San Francisco's two ships' drawbridges. This one is a cantilever bridge where the whole span tilts up to permit ships to pass beneath. Proceed out Third through the industrial, warehousing district until you cross the second ships' bridge. The ISLAIS CREEK BRIDGE separates in the middle of the span and the two sections lift. If you're lucky, you'll see one or both of the bridges in operation. As you cross this last bridge, look to your right to see if any freighters are tied up a couple of blocks up the channel. If there are, they're unloading copra at Pier 84 and we'll visit the pier on the way back. Immediately across the bridge turn to your left onto Arthur Avenue, which leads to Piers 96 and 92. You'll see a sign pointing to *PFE New LASH Terminal.*

Before we look at the ships, let us look at deep-sea freight handling. A freighter, whether tramp steamer or company ship, is a floating warehouse of goods gathered at various ports to be delivered to others. When you look at a ship, it seems neat and trim on the outside and uncomplicated. Inside, it's complicated, a three-dimensional jigsaw puzzle of loading and unloading. The labor cost of cargo handling is the biggest expense of the sea freight business. The average freighter is a short block long and three to four stories deep. All the hold space is utilized, and everything has to be loaded so that, when a shipment of Philippine mahogany to Seattle is put in, it doesn't have to be shifted to unload a consignment of Ceylon tea bound for San Francisco. The cargo also has to be expedited so that the ship is not tied up in port.

PFE NEW LASH TERMINAL. The new LASH terminal at Pier 96 presents the newest concept of ocean freight handling in the world. LASH stands for Lighter Aboard Ship. A lighter is a flat-bottomed barge used in loading and unloading ships, usually found in ports without deep-water docking. The LASH ships carry several lighters, already loaded, right on the ship. If it has cargoes for San Francisco, Oakland, Stockton, and Sacramento, the ship merely drops off the lighter at

one port and moves on to the next. The lighters are unloaded
and loaded and the ship picks them up on the way back. This
is an extremely efficient use of a ship, because the ship spends
hardly any time in port at all, except for victuals, water, and
fuel. The terminal has just gone into operation at this writing.
Unfortunately, one can't see more of it from the road than
the two huge ship's cranes. It is hoped that Pacific Far East
Lines will provide some public access so you will have a
chance to watch this fascinating operation.

PIER 92. The unloading operations of Pier 92 are easier
to watch. If a ship is docked and working, park at the gate
and go and watch. This is the main unloading pier for
Japanese cars—you'll see acres of Datsuns and Toyotas. At
the rate they get the cars out of the hold and onto the dock,
it's amazing that they aren't all smashed to pieces.

COPRA DOCK. If, on the way out, you saw a freighter tied
up in the Islais Creek Channel, on the way back, keep in the
left-hand lane of 3rd Street, make a U-turn at 26th, and go
back to Army Street. Turn to your left on Indiana and it will
take you to the copra dock. Park and walk across the wooden
bridge, and you can watch the automatic unloading operation.
The factory to which the copra is delivered processes the
coconut meats into a myriad of products—oil for margarine,
cosmetics, soap, etc. The residue is high-protein cattle food.

Coming back toward town on 3rd Street, turn to your right
on 22nd Street and left on Illinois. Here are the BETHLEHEM
STEEL SHIPYARDS. Bear right off 18th Street onto China Basin.
At 817 China Basin is MISSION ROCK, a restaurant, bar, and
sports fisherman's marina. Here on an outside deck on the
Bay you can watch the workings of the Bethlehem shipyards
and the Triple A Machine Shop over coffee or a beer, while
they repair and refit ships. The bar is full of lying fishermen,
who are also interesting.

Farther along is PIER 54, the Southern Pacific train ferry
dock. Although I've watched the operation, I still don't understand how they can match up the rails of the train barges

to the rails of the loading dock without derailing the freight cars—the barge is moving with the waves all the time.

PIERS 50 and 48 are good places to watch the ships. They come close to the street here.

Follow China Basin and turn right over the cantilever bridge, again a right at Berry Street.

PIER 46 is a newsprint-receiving pier, and from here to the Ferry Building keep on the lookout for ships to watch. Across from Pier 42 is MANJO'S PIER HEAD. It's a bar-restaurant that caters to longshoremen and serves breakfast and lunches till 2 PM weekdays. The waterfront has excellent breakfast-luncheon eating places, generous servings of good, hearty food at reasonable prices. Don't let the façades of the places deter you. The EAGLE CAFÉ, at the end of the Embarcadero, is one of the least inviting places on the outside you can imagine. But while the Fisherman's Wharf places a block away sell a mediocre hamburger for a buck and a quarter, the Eagle serves a baked half-chicken, potatoes, and vegetable for the same price. Manjo's is famous for its soups—the best on the waterfront; Thursdays and Fridays it's minestrone—a meal in itself for fifty cents, at this writing.

As you approach the FERRY BUILDING, you'll have a good look at the underpinning of the Bay Bridge, and a short way past the Ferry Building, at PIER 7, you'll have a chance to experience the immensity of these piers. It's a parking garage with a fishing deck on the face of it, open to the public. If you find a parking space on the Embarcadero, you will start to walk out the pier and continue to walk and walk and walk. The piers are about 1500 feet long, almost 200 feet wide, three or four stories high. As you walk, you can appreciate the cargo-handling facilities of the piers you've passed, and the bulk of goods that pass in and out. The deck on the face of Pier 7 gives a glorious water-level view of the Bay and the shipping traffic. Look down into the water and you'll usually see huge schools of flashing anchovies and smaller pulsating cotton puffs of jellyfish that use the piers for protection. The wooden piers are crowded with mussels and barnacles. Occasionally, you'll see a harbor seal. San Francisco Bay was dangerously polluted five years ago, but with the new controls, it has become much cleaner. The water is clear for at least ten feet down, and full of life, which speaks for itself.

Freighters work the piers down to Pier 35, but Pier 35 is a passenger pier for ocean liners. Now, these are truly the aristocrats of the sea. Without exception they are elegant, and some of them (the *Oriana* or the *Canberra*) are too elegant to be believed. The *Canberra* is like a 1930s movie set of a ship. She is still as she was in the old days. Her docking is a serene thing, her departure is a holiday with bands playing and streamers floating over the side of the ship. If you're lucky, you'll be in town on the departure day of an ocean liner. If you are, don't miss it.

From here to *Fisherman's Wharf,* the piers are seldom used for cargo handling, being too unsafe for the heavy traffic. Piers 37, 39, and 41, though, are often used for ceremonial visits by foreign naval ships—and the ships are open to the public. In the first six months of 1972, Japanese, French, English, and American ships of the line were docked on these piers, and open to visitors. These visits are well publicized, so check the newspapers—they're usually connected with a trade fair or the city-wide honoring of another nation, as in Great Britain week.

Muir Woods

The MUIR WOODS NATIONAL MONUMENT is outside San Francisco, but is such a part of the itinerary of visitors to the city that it must be included in any guidebook. Only twenty minutes from the city limits is a grove of magnificent redwoods, one of the few patches left of the Coast Redwoods that stretched all along the fog belt of northern California. The trees are not only majestic, but awe-inspiring—7-plus feet thick; upwards of 200 feet tall (in some, the first limb leaves the trunk 75 feet above the ground); many over two thousand years old. A visit to the grove gives immediate understanding of why our ancestors worshiped trees as divine things.

To get there, go across Golden Gate Bridge and turn off at the bottom of Waldo Grade where the signs say Muir Woods. You will go through the little community of Tamalpais Valley and start to climb up. There are two roads you may take from the crossroads, where one sign reads Muir Woods, the other Stinson Beach. The road labeled Muir Woods goes up and over a shoulder of Mt. Tamalpais. This is a spectacular road with terrific views of the ocean. The word is well chosen because the narrow, winding road clinging to the side of the mountain—unprotected dropoffs to the valley 400 to 500 feet below—terrifies many. The road labeled Stinson Beach is the low road through the valley. It approaches Muir Woods from a different direction, a little longer, but more or less level driving. Choose this road if you are nervous of heights.

Fleishhacker Zoo

At the end of Sloat Boulevard at the ocean, you can get there by taking the L Taraval (Zoo) streetcar on Market Street or drive out Geary Boulevard to the ocean, turn left and enter Sloat from that direction (you'll pass the Cliff House, Golden Gate Park, and a stretch of the houses of the Sunset district on your left. Take the first turn-off to the left after you've passed these).

The Zoo is open 365 days a year, and gained some publicity in President Nixon's first visit to China. Musk oxen from here were exchanged for the panda that went to the National Zoo in Washington. As a zoo, it does not rival the ones in San Diego or St. Louis, but it has its own very fine exhibits. The new habitats for the great apes—gorillas, orangutans, and chimpanzees; the new acquisitions—a pair of pigmy hippos, white rhinoceros—make the visit worthwhile.

There are playgrounds and small rides for children (merry-go-round, circle cars, rocket ride, steam train and pony rides). The playground has a cable car and old Southern Pacific engine to climb on. The Children's Zoo is a nice feature. For a small admission, the kids can look at, climb on, and slide down child-sized representations from Mother Goose rhymes and fairy tales (get into the oven where the witch would cook Hansel, for example). Tame animals that can be petted and fed roam loose; the new zoo babies are on display.

At this writing, the charge is 50 cents for adults, kids free, with one free Saturday every month.

Aquatic Park

At the foot of Van Ness Avenue (below the Maritime Museum and Ghirardelli Square) is AQUATIC PARK, a year round favorite resort of San Franciscans. It is a place of many attractions. As you walk down Van Ness toward the Municipal Pier, you'll come to the *bocce* courts on your right. *Bocce* is a very fine sport and would probably be very popular in America if more people knew about it. It's related to lawn bowling in that two opposing players (or teams) roll balls about the size of duck-pin bowling balls to see who can get closest to a smaller target ball. Lawn bowling uses close-cut grass as a court; *bocce* uses hard-packed sand. There are elements of billiards involved because the balls can be caromed off the wooden sides of a court to attack the jack from various angles. A strategic game, like shuffleboard and horseshoes, it involves a high degree of skill. It's fun to watch and the old Italian men who are playing it enjoy themselves immensely.

Farther down is an enclosed sunbathing area (you think they're crazy when the wind is biting, but out of the wind, it's warm). To the right is a series of wide steps on the other side of the Maritime Museum. On any given day musicians— congo drums and flutes—all try to emulate the Santana group that formed on the steps of Aquatic Park.

The glory of Aquatic Park, though, is the MUNICIPAL PIER. This is a broad cement pier that curves a quarter mile out into the Bay. It's a free fishing pier, no license required, no limits on size or bag of catch. It's a glorious place to watch the freighters come in and get a water-level view of the yacht races. But most of all, it is a haven for fish and fishermen. I have probably been there a hundred times and every time, something of interest happened—isolated things like catching a huge purple starfish in our crab net (it must have been a foot and a half across) that thrilled my little boy to pieces. Like seeing a wincing man with a two-foot sand shark at his feet, holding a bloody handkerchief around his fingers. He reluctantly said, "The hook was caught in his mouth, and when I tried to get it out HE BIT ME!" And all along there, the triumphant catchers of cod, flounder, sea bass, perch, etc. Once I saw a not-so-happy bait caster whose anchovie was grabbed by a seagull before it hit the water. He reeled in the seagull like an aerial fish and was faced with a flapping bird at rod's length. Another fisherman clipped the leader and the bird flew off in the direction of Alcatraz. He was concerned about the bird, but was consoled by fellow-fishermen who told war stories of the toughness of seagulls.

Even if you're not a fisherman, a walk on the Municipal Pier in Aquatic Park will be a high point of your visit to San Francisco.

12
The New San Francisco

If San Francisco, as a major city, is unique in no other way, it must be counted as unusual in its recent development of major tourist attractions. In the last sixteen years, while other major cities were crying the blues about the death of the inner city, the flight to the suburbs, the decay of tourist attractions, San Francisco has added at least three major features, another abuilding, two more in the end of the planning stages. San Francisco, like other major cities, has lost population to the suburbs, but unlike the others, has increased in tourist popularity—and without massive tax monies invested, as in Seattle's World's Fair. It is no wonder that this city is envied. The earthquake couldn't kill it, unfeeling plastic modern times haven't killed it; there is a surprising survival quotient in San Francisco—it's changing, but changing for the better.

Japan Town

The most surprising new development in town is the JAP-ANESE CULTURAL CENTER in Nihon Machi—JAPAN TOWN (called J-Town by San Franciscans). It is amazing that the most impressive Japanese cultural center in American should be erected in the city that did the most to destroy Japanese-Americans in World War II. It was in the federal courts here that the first ruling was upheld to move American citizens of Japanese descent to concentration camps in the wilderness beyond the Sierra. Of course, there was ferocious propaganda after Pearl Harbor. *Life* magazine at that time showed an impressive arsenal of bombs, radio transmitters, and guns collected by the FBI from the Black Dragon Society and infiltrated Japanese spies. Feelings ran high. Local Chinese wore buttons with the crossed American and Kuomintang flags, stating "I Am Chinese," to avoid the curses of the jittery citizens. There was great fear that San Francisco was next on the list of bombing targets. Distance hadn't protected the heavily fortified Pearl Harbor.

But the Japanese Exclusion Act was a racist act, pure and simple, and the citizens knew it in their hearts. The Japanese-Americans were hard workers, and had pulled themselves up by their bootstraps, especially in the truck-farming and food-processing industries. The Japanese-Americans were more assimilated into "American culture," than many of the other nationality groups, including the Chinese and the Italians— but they had no political clout. Although the German Consul had been caught red-handed in espionage, and the German-American Bund maintained a camp in rural Sonoma County where swastika-armbanded local Nazis trained in guerrilla warfare, the Germans were not touched. The Americans of Japanese descent were given a couple of weeks to dispose of their property, collect what belongings they could carry with them, and in armed caravans *forced to drive themselves in their own cars to the concentration camps*. The average San Franciscan who knew better—had a schoolmate who was Japanese, worked with a Japanese, traded with Japanese— watched them be herded away without a word of protest. Many, many San Franciscans profited by their internment— cheap property, businesses absorbed, less competition. It was a sorry time for this city and America.

As if to mitigate this sorry episode, San Francisco after the war became a good friend to Japan and the Japanese-Americans living here. Osaka, another hilly seaport, was adopted as our "sister city," an ongoing and sincere effort at cultural exchanges. The returning Japanese-Americans were aided in the re-establishment of their old neighborhood, and finally the Japanese Cultural and Trade Center was erected with the help of local and Japanese capital.

Japan Town runs roughly from Fillmore to Octavia, from Geary to Sutter and Bush. Post Street is the main street. In J-Town, the street signs are in Japanese and English (Chinatown street signs are Chinese and English). The Cultural and Trade Center at Buchanan and Post is the focus of this neighborhood, and a grand place it is indeed.

The large wood open structure at Post and Buchanan is a drum platform—drums as big as olive tuns are pounded by Japanese-American youths as an accent to the several festivals and parades held in J-Town during the year. Between the East and West buildings that make up the complex is the Peace Pagoda, with an eternal flame of peace that has been burning since the completion in 1968. There is a fine moss garden to the left of the plaza. On festival days, a stage is set up on the Geary Boulevard side of the plaza.

The center flows down Geary Street as follows: At Laguna stands the Japanese Consulate, next, the Miyako Hotel. Nine-tenths of this hotel is merely fine hotel, the other one-tenth is pure Japanese. Each expensive Japanese unit is what you'd find in an inn in Japan; down mattresses are rolled out on tatami mats, a landscaped garden is outside your sitting-bedroom window, a sunken Japanese tub is your bath, and there are enough kimonoed maids to make you feel truly pampered. As I say, it's expensive, but worth every nickel.

The East Building is full of retail outlets for Japanese clothing, souvenirs, and handicraft. On the second floor a coffee shop specializes in *Chinese* food! If you want to buy Japanese clothing for your kids or yourself, this is the place to go.

West Building is the Trade Center. Here are the showrooms that exhibit, and sell, autos, electronics, cultural items, books, and so forth. There is a cultured-pearl outlet where you can buy your own oyster with a pearl inside (guaranteed), and an elegant restaurant, a shop selling Japanese prints and fine art. Of especial interest are the shops that teach flower arranging, and the Japanese cooking school sponsored by one of the leading importers of soy sauce and other Japanese foodstuffs. Displayed in cases in the cooking school are models of the slices of beef used in *sukiyaki*, fish, and other cooked Japanese foods presented as they appear on a Japanese dinner table or picnic basket, with the lacquerware or china appropriate to each (with short notes telling how these came to be traditional meals). Downstairs is a replica of a Japanese palace and more businesses.

A walk through the short business section of J-Town is interesting for its shops, restaurants, and theater. The ladies will go crazy over the magnificent fabrics in the clothing stores. Don't miss the hardware store and the groceries. The hardware store sells nuts and bolts, of course, but also Japanese cooking utensils, exotic saws, chisels and other woodworking tools used in fine Japanese cabinetmaking; shears, pruners, etcetera, used in Japanese gardening, especially the growing of the dwarf bonsai trees. The business section is not large, but well worth a walk through.

On the waterfront, we find two other aspects of the new San Francisco. These are Ghirardelli Square and the Cannery.

Fisherman's Wharf

In the old days (say, ten or fifteen years ago) there was no sorrier tourist attraction than FISHERMAN'S WHARF. It was nothing but souvenir joints selling striped Alcatraz prison hats (and postcards of Alcatraz saying "Wish you were here"), abalone-shell ash trays and the same kind of tourist schlok you find everywhere. The restaurants gave it some reason for being (as did the crab boats, which were interesting to inlanders who didn't usually see boats). COST PLUS IMPORTS was the first mercantile establishment to rise above the mediocre on Fisherman's Wharf. It sold (and sells) small and large craft items from all over the world at a very reasonable price—Mexican pottery and glassware, Indian brass and wood inlay, Spanish hand-carved tables and chairs, Greek weaving—things from all over. It was exotic stuff not usually available and the store prospered.

With buying tourists flocking to Fisherman's Wharf (it's a natural shopping center anyway, the terminus of two cable-car lines), local entrepreneurs came up with a second look at that area. Being San Franciscan, they had wild ideas and spectacular results. The GHIRARDELLI (say Gear-Ar-Delli!) CHOCOLATE FACTORY was an old-time spice and chocolate house that dominated the West Coast. Signs advertising their goods were painted on every barn and fence throughout northern and central California.

The old brick buildings became outmoded for chocolate and spice processing, and the plant moved elsewhere. The buildings were perfectly lovely, though, solid, and too good to tear down. The brick was sandblasted, the interiors refinished, a central courtyard developed, and the GHIRARDELLI SQUARE complex is the result—62 shops, 2 theaters, 13 restaurants, art galleries, offices, and a radio station, at last count. There are at least 3 outdoor cafés, great views of the Bay from the others, and so many nice touches, you have to see it to believe it. These are smart people and while the mammas are off browsing the shops (here, you can see what an $800 dress looks like), the kids can be entertained at a puppet show or the perpetual Glue-In—an unlimited supply of oddly shaped wood scraps from furniture factories that build into castles, rocket ships, or whatever that the kids can take home (the 50 cent admission price is too low for the enjoyment felt all around). Dominating the courtyard is the most charming fountain in San Francisco, *Andrea,* by Asawa Lee. There are two mermaids, one holding a merchild, turtles, gleeful frogs, and other aquatic accouterments. It was put up in 1968, just five years ago and there was criticism at the time that the braless mermaids were too bare.

THE CANNERY is housed in the old Del Monte fruit canning complex. It is not an imitation of Ghirardelli Square, but it has developed along the same lines. Great old brick buildings made clean again, the tall rooms and interesting concourses between the various levels of the buildings a perfect setting for shops, restaurants, cinemas. They are of a piece, but completely different.

They have affected the Fisherman's Wharf area to the extent that opposite the Cannery, the headquarters of Christian Brothers' Winery, is a building which boasts a wine museum and tasting room on the boards outside. The North Point Shopping Center and Apartment Complex has already built a block from Cost Plus. The Shopping Center houses AKRON, a discount foreign import house, specialty shops, and fine delicatessens and food shops. Across from it, in the block between the Longshoremen's Hall and the Muni bus parking lot, we may see great things from the Southern Pacific which has just purchased the whole block and is on its way to development of yet another Fisherman's Wharf feature, the exact nature not disclosed.

Vaillancourt Fountain

And then, before the Ferry Building at the foot of Market, is the VAILLANCOURT FOUNTAIN. This is New San Francisco in its most perfect state. François Vaillancourt, a French-Canadian sculptor, won from the Arts Commission permission to build a fountain on the newly developed park land along the Embarcadero. The empty space for the park and fountain resulted from the Embarcadero Freeway tearing out most of the ratty hotels, bars, and merchant seamen's shops; the clearing of the old produce market section, which touched this area, and the tearing down of other buildings in the building of BART.

On paper, the Vaillancourt Fountain didn't look like much, except to the members of the Arts Commission. When it was in the process of being built, it was jeered at in the newspapers for looking like the *end* result of an earthquake hitting the Embarcadero Freeway—and indeed it did, it didn't look like anything new. When it was put together, it still looked like a wreck—absurd eyesore. Worse yet, the fountain didn't work at first; we learned that the expense of just manning the pumps for the thing would amount to $30,000 a year; and the first thing the sculptor did, when the fountain was dedicated, was to leap from the speaker's platform, wade through the pool, and deface the fountain with the spray-painted slogan "Free Quebec!" The papers shouted the sculptor out of town, and he left with much bad-mouthing of the city, and we were left with the fountain.

Well, the city did the same with Golden Gate Park, did the same with the Civic Center, and the criticism goes on about the Vaillancourt Fountain—but it's grand. Water has flowed over the outside of the deliberate archaic reliefs on the outer surfaces long enough to grow moss and algae—in these couple of years, it's beginning to look antique. The fountain spouts from a myriad of square apertures, and stepping blocks let you walk within and beneath the fountain, stairways let you walk over the fountain. Kids love it, and you can't help becoming involved in it yourself.

Street Merchants and Street Musicians

The EMBARCADERO PARK before the Ferry Building, where the fountain is, has been set aside for "street sellers," and this is another aspect of the new San Francisco. Itinerant street sellers and street musicians have been a part of every large city since cities were created. In the early days, it was a trade, more or less honorable—even if it shaded into mendicancy. Some of the larger European and South American cities have kept the trade honorable (London with its pavement artists and strongmen, Amsterdam with its two-man street organs, the roving mariachi bands of Mexico City and points south). It was also a way of living in American cities before the war. I remember streetcorner German *oompah* bands, organ grinders with their monkeys, a few good blind banjo players. Music, or vending on the street, though, became just a cover for begging.

Even three years ago, it was like that, but now, in San Francisco, there are free concerts on downtown streetcorners provided by singers, dancers, mimes, and musicians. They have made this delightful city even more delightful. These performers so charmed visiting Mexican government officials that in the summer of 1972 they put the members of the symphonic orchestra on the streets of Mexico City for the delight of their own citizens.

The street musicians make about union scale on their own and have no great trouble with the merchants or the authorities. The street vendors were another matter—the artists and handicrafters selling their own small wares. The merchants immediately complained, the state got into the act about the problem of sales tax, and so the authorities had to act. They did so not by banning street sellers, but by setting up special places where they could sell their goods. Embarcadero Park is one of these.

In the works are two new major tourist attractions. One is the new convention center south of Market Street in what used to be the Skid Row area. The facilities look great on paper and it should be ready in a couple of years. The second project is the planned National Regional Park that will include some 37,000 acres of land along the Golden Gate Headlands (San Francisco and Marin counties) and two Bay islands. This will guarantee the preservation of these lands for the public.

These are grand, governmental things, but it's exciting to watch what will happen next on the private level. The Cannery, Ghirardelli Square, and the street entertainers—vendors were privately conceived and have been important additions to the city. No one knows where the next element of the new San Francisco will emerge. Probably it will have something to do with BART. What is known is that there will always be unique and delightful additions. San Francisco seems to be made that way.

13
San Francisco through the Year

When you tour a major city, the primary object is usually to see the place—all that is timeless and enduring. But it can be a disappointment, when you go home and find that something special was going on that would have been interesting, had you known about it. To avoid missing all the special events that give color to the city, there are several sources you can consult. If your trip is planned ahead, write beforehand to the San Francisco Convention and Visitors Bureau, Fox Plaza, San Francisco, California 94102. They publish a quarterly brochure in March, June, September, and December, listing all the coming sporting and cultural events. The Oakland Chamber of Commerce Convention and Tourism Bureau at 1320 Webster Street, Oakland, California 94162 also puts out a similar calendar.

If, however, your visit to San Francisco is a spur-of-the-moment fling, an invaluable number to know is that of the San Francisco Convention and Visitors Bureau—391-2000. An extremely detailed, prerecorded message gives an almost day-by-day account of what is going on in the city. Another complete listing, from restaurants to art exhibits to yacht races, can be found in the pink section of the San Francisco Sunday *Examiner-Chronicle*. Hotels are regularly supplied with an index of the current theater and movie attractions, weekly goings-on, restaurants, and special events. If your hotel or motel doesn't have the current information, or if you're sleeping in a camper, you can still pick up one of these free brochures at hotel cigar stands and in parking garages.

One piece of advice should be kept in mind. San Francisco is the natural habitat of the "layered look." The coldest months of the year fall in July and August, and you will freeze here, morning and evening, unless you have brought clothes that can be gradually removed as the warm hours of noon approach. The reason for the atypical weather pattern is that, although the latitude of San Francisco, Sacramento, and the San Joaquin Valley is about the same as that of southern Greece (with consequent high temperatures), the Japanese Current that flows along the northern California coastline is cold, with summer temperatures averaging 55 degrees. The Golden Gate is the only sea-level opening through the Coastal Range for a hundred miles on either side of the Bay, and during the summer, the hot air in the interior valleys rises, drawing cold, wet air in from the ocean, across and through San Francisco like a horizontal chimney. You can be sweating to death in shorts at 105 degrees in Sacramento, drive to San Francisco, and wish you were wearing a fur coat. Refreshing fog air-conditions the city morning and evening, and the foghorns are lovely to go to sleep by, but it's "March in July," and fall clothing is a must on a summer visit. The following is an almanac of the most popular annual events in San Francisco and Oakland—the two major cities in the Bay Area.

Events

January

San Francisco *Examiner* Games. Indoor track and field meet. Cow Palace, mid-January.
British Motors Annual Pro Tennis Championships. Civic Center, mid-January.

February

Chinese New Year Celebration. Parade and festivities. Consult papers for actual date.

Spring Opera. Curran Theater. Month of February.

March
St. Patrick's Day Celebration. Parade and festivities.
Bay Area Science Fair. Academy of Arts and Science. Mid-March.
Macy's Flower Show. End of March, early April.
Spring at Maiden Lane. End of March, early April.
Golden Gloves Boxing. Cow Palace, early March.
Irish Football and Hurling. Balboa Park Stadium, late March, early April.
Hearst Regatta. San Francisco Bay, late March, early April.
Civic Light Opera. Curran Theater. Spring.
San Francisco Ballet. Palace of Fine Arts Theater, early March through April.

April
Junior Grand National Livestock Expo and Horse Show. Cow Palace, mid April.
Cherry trees in bloom. Japanese Tea Garden, early April.
Easter Sunrise Services. Mt. Davidson.
Nihon Machi Cherry Blossom Festival. Japan Town and Japanese Center, mid-April.
San Francisco Giants season begins. Candlestick Park.
Opening Day Yachting Parade. End of April.
Oakland Athletics season begins. Oakland Coliseum.

May
Rhododendrons in bloom. Golden Gate Park, Union Square, Civic Center, April-May.
Latin America Festival. Early May.
Master Mariners Regatta. San Francisco. mid-May.
Bay-to-Breakers Cross City Race. Mid-May.
Western Opera Theater. "Dollar Opera." Palace of Fine Arts Theater, May.

June

Street Fair. Upper Grant Avenue. Mid-June.
Concerts begin, Sigmund Stern Grove.

July

Fourth of July Celebration. Candlestick Park.
Soap Box Derby. Mid-July, Sunset Boulevard and Ulloa.
Municipal Pops Concerts. San Francisco Symphony–Arthur
Fiedler, during July.

August

San Francisco Flower Show. Mid-August Hall of Flowers.

September

San Francisco Municipal Outdoor Art Festival. Civic Center
Plaza. Mid-Sept.
San Francisco Opera Season. Mid-September–end of Novem-
ber.

October

Blessing of the Fleet (Church of Sts. Peter and Paul, Fisher-
man's Wharf). First Sunday in October.
Columbus Day Celebration. Parade and festivities in North
Beach.
Grand National Livestock Expo. End of October–November.
Cow Palace.
San Francisco Music Series. Opera House and Masonic Audi-
torium, October–May.
Chamber Music Society. Fireman's Fund Theater. October–
May.
American Conservatory Theater. Geary Theater. October–
May.
San Francisco '49ers football. Candlestick Park.
Oakland Raiders. Oakland Coliseum.
Golden State Warriors basketball. Oakland Coliseum.
California Golden Seals hockey. Oakland Coliseum.

November

Gray whales begin migration south from Arctic to Baja

California. Watch for spouting from Sutro Heights. November–February.

San Francisco Symphony Season. Opera House. November–December. May.

December
Cable Car Classic—invitational intercollegiate basketball tournament. Early December. San Francisco Civic Auditorium or Oakland Coliseum.

Shriner East-West Football. Candlestick Park, last of month.

Index

About the Author

FRANZ T. HANSELL was born and raised in Springfield, Ohio, and attended Ohio State University, where he studied accounting. This stood him in good stead when he quit school (because he couldn't stand accounting) to become a vault teller in a Las Vegas Bank for six months before he joined the Army. While studying Russian at the Army Language School in Monterey, he visited San Francisco for the first time; an uncle lived there. The visits were brief, because while studying Russian, he was also baking copper enamel jewelry in the post's Special Services shop and selling them in several Monterey stores under the name Franz of Monterey—the proceeds going towards the rent for a studio on Fisherman's Wharf.

The brief visits were enough to draw him back to San Francisco after the Army, but the only job available was as traveling bank examiner for Crocker-Anglo National Bank ("In my first year here, I was in the City only weekends. I saw lots and lots of bars, but I don't think I made it to Coit Tower.") The glories of the city began to unfold when he was working at Tro Harper's book store while getting his degree in Creative Writing at San Francisco State, but the first seed for this book was planted when he became a meter reader for the San Francisco Water Department. "Meter readers go everywhere, and I saw so many things that the tourist— and native for that matter—doesn't, and would like to." He lives with his wife and son in the Sunset District two blocks from the ocean. Although now involved in a novel, his fascination with the city continues even after having written a book about it . . . "Do you know this place out on Geneva? It sells frozen banana leaves, poi, and strictly Philippine ice cream imported from Manila—isn't that the damndest thing!"

THE COMSTOCK BACKPACKING GUIDE TO CALIFORNIA

Thomas Winnett

THE COMSTOCK BACKPACKING GUIDE TO THE PACIFIC NORTHWEST

THE COMSTOCK BACKPACKING GUIDES are comprehensive how-to and where-to books for all backpackers from the tenderfoot to the seasoned outdoorsman.

AUTHOR TOM WINNETT has lived and backpacked in California and the Pacific Northwest since he was four years old. In these books, he describes in detail numerous beautiful, historical and unusual trails in the country he knows so well.

Wilderness Press/Comstock Editions

To order by mail, send $1.50 per book, plus 10¢ for handling to Dept. CS, Ballantine Books, 36 West 20th Street, New York, N.Y. 10003.

SAN DIEGO
and the Back Country

Edited by Davis Dutton

A Westways/Comstock guide through four hundred years of California's oldest city—the city of gold, blue and green. Written by three generations of men and women who helped shape this jewel of Southern California. It's a fascinating original collection of people, facts, legends, true tales and anecdotes.

$1.50

A COMSTOCK EDITION

To order by mail, send price of book, plus 10¢ for handling to Dept. CS, Ballantine Books, 36 West 20th Street, New York, N.Y. 10003.

The Pacific Northwest

Moontrap
Don Berry $1.25

A Majority of Scoundrels
Don Berry $1.25

Skid Road
Murray Morgan $1.25

The Timber Beast
Archie Binns $1.25

You Rolling River
Archie Binns $1.25

Scarlet Petticoat
Nard Jones $1.25

Holy Old Mackinaw
Stewart Holbrook $1.25

The Laurels Are Cut Down
Archie Binns $1.25

Tales Out of Oregon
Ralph Friedman $1.25

Song of the Axe
N. C. McDonald $1.25

Westward the Women
Nancy Wilson Ross $1.25

Joe Hill
Wallace Stegner $1.50

Green Timber
Thomas Ripley $1.25

The Land Is Bright
Archie Binns $1.25

Trask
Don Berry $1.25

Spokane Saga $1.25
Zola Ross

Rocky Mountains

Rocky Mountain Tales
Levette J. Davidson & Forester Blake, eds. $1.25

A Lady's Life in the Rocky Mountains
Isabella Bird $1.25

A Curious Life for a Lady Pat Barr	$1.25
Mountain Charley Mrs. E. J. Guerin	$1.25
The Sound of Mountain Water Wallace Stegner	$1.25
Money Mountain Marshall Sprague	$1.25
Massacre Marshall Sprague	$1.50
The Pikes Peak People John Fetler	$1.50
Here They Dug the Gold George F. Willison	$1.50
Holladay Street Max Miller & Fred Mazulla	$1.25

The West—General

Great Short Stories of the West **(Volumes I and II)** J. Golden Taylor, ed.	each $1.25
The Watchful Gods Walter Van Tilburg Clark	$1.25
An Overland Journey Horace Greeley	$1.25
Lost Legends of the West Brad Williams & Choral Pepper	$1.25
The Mysterious West Brad Williams & Choral Pepper	$1.50
Notorious Ladies of the Frontier **(Volumes I and II)** Harry Sinclair Drago	each $1.50

To order by mail, send price of book, plus 10¢
for handling to Dept. CS, Ballantine Books,
36 West 20th Street, New York, N.Y. 10003.